NDY INFANTE · ALLEN TRAMMELL · BILL CARR · LARRY SMITH ·
S · LEE MCGRIFF · BURTON LAWLESS · NAT MOORE · DON GAFF
S · BRAD CULPEPPER · SHANE MATTHEWS · TERRY DEAN · SHAYN
S BATES · DANNY WUERFFEL · TERRY JACKSON · TRA MCGRI
N · LARRY LIBERTORE · BRUCE CULPEPPER
CARLOS ALVAREZ · JOHN REAVES · JOHN E MCGRIFF ·
BELL · KIRK KIRKPATRICK · TRACE ARMSTRONG · BRAD LPEPP
D DAVIS · JASON ODOM · BEN HANKS · JAMES BATES · DANNY W
TIM TEBOW · DOUG DICKEY · JIMMY DUNN · LARRY LIBERTORE
Y SMITH · GUY DENNIS · T DELNOUR · CARLOS ALVAREZ ·
RE · DON GAFFNEY · NEAL ANDERSON · KERWIN BELL · KIRK KIR
RRY DEAN · SHAYNE EDGE · CHRIS DOERING · JUDD DAVIS · JAS
TRAVIS MCGRIFF · JEFF CHANDLER · JARVIS MOSS · TIM TEBOW
DY INFANTE · ALLEN TRAMMELL · BILL CARR · LARRY SMITH ·
S · LEE MCGRIFF · BURTON LAWLESS · NAT MOORE · DON GAFF
· BRAD CULPEPPER · SHANE MATTHEWS · TERRY DEAN · SHAYN
S BATES · DANNY WUERFFEL · TERRY JACKSON · TRAVIS MCGRIF
N · LARRY LIBERTORE · BRUCE CULPEPPER · LINDY INFANTE · A
CARLOS ALVAREZ · JOHN REAVES · JOHN JAMES · LEE MCGRIFF

WHAT IT MEANS
TO BE A GATOR

URBAN MEYER
AND FLORIDA'S GREATEST PLAYERS

MARK SCHLABACH

TRIUMPH
BOOKS

Triumph Books and colophon are registered trademarks of Random House, Inc.

Library of Congress Cataloging-in-Publication Data
Schlabach, Mark, 1972–
  What it means to be a Gator / Mark Schlabach; foreword by Urban Meyer.
     p. cm.
  ISBN-13: 978-1-60078-116-2
  ISBN-10: 1-60078-116-0
  1. Florida Gators (Football team)—History. 2. University of Florida—Football—History. 3. Football players—United States—Anecdotes. I. Title.
  GV958.U523S34 2008
  796.332'630975979—dc22
                                        2008029064

This book is available in quantity at special discounts for your group or organization. For further information, contact:

Triumph Books
542 South Dearborn Street
Suite 750
Chicago, Illinois 60605
(312) 939-3330 • Fax (312) 663-3557

Printed in U.S.A.
ISBN: 978-1-60078-116-2
Design by Nick Panos
Editorial production and layout by Prologue Publishing Services, LLC
Photos courtesy of University of Florida unless otherwise indicated.

CONTENTS

FOREWORD

What It Means to Be a Gator

WE HAD JUST FINISHED UNDEFEATED AT UTAH during the 2004 season, and I felt I was ready to make a change. I had a tremendous opportunity to either coach at Notre Dame or Florida, and it was the most difficult decision I'd ever faced. I didn't make a big deal about it, but I loved Notre Dame. I loved what Notre Dame stood for, and I still do and always will. I'm Irish and I'm Catholic, and I believe in the purest sense of college football, there's no place better.

I also wanted to win a national championship but wanted to be able to recruit and not spend time in San Diego and Seattle and Detroit and Philadelphia. You can't do that at Notre Dame. I'm an active recruiter. A lot of coaches don't go out too much, but I go out all the time. The big reason I chose Florida, and I've never said this until now because I didn't want to offend anybody, was that I'm a football coach but I'm also a father. I love college football, and I love the pageantry. But I'm also a father. I have three kids, and they're at the age where I want to be around them all the time.

To recruit players to Florida, I have to recruit regionally. To recruit players to Notre Dame, I have to recruit nationally. I have a school plane that I can use all the time, so I'm at home with my family a lot. At Notre Dame, you're recruiting San Diego and you're recruiting New York. You're away from home all the time. When I looked at Florida, I saw the finest location of any place in the country. Most of the finest high school players in the country are five or six hours from your doorstep.

I became a fan of Florida football during the 1990s when I watched Steve Spurrier's teams play, watching their swagger and the way they moved the football. I was sold when I came down to Florida to recruit for Notre Dame.

I came down to Gainesville on a January day. I had just left South Bend, Indiana, where there was 40-degree weather and everybody had that pink-skin look on their faces. I came to Florida, and everybody was tan and was walking around smiling. I walked right into the Swamp and knew that was where I wanted to be. I wanted to one day become the coach at the University of Florida.

We inherited a pretty good team from Ron Zook before the 2005 season, but I think the injection of the 2006 recruiting class was what really helped us win the 2006 national championship more than anything else. If you take Reggie Nelson, Ryan Smith, Tim Tebow, Percy Harvin, and Brandon James out of there—kids who were developed or recruited—I'm not sure how good we really were. It was a great mix of older and younger kids. That was just such a great mix on that team.

I wasn't sure we'd have a chance to win the SEC championship or even a national championship in 2006 until we touched down in the Gainesville airport and were SEC East champions, after LSU beat Tennessee late in the season. It wasn't one of those things where I thought, *Boy, do we have a great team!* The SEC is too hard. At Utah, I felt if we took care of the football and played hard, we'd win every game. This is too hard of a conference. You can't feel that way here because there are too many great teams in this league.

After we beat Arkansas 38–28 in the SEC Championship Game in Atlanta, I thought we deserved the chance to play Ohio State for the national championship. I was very convinced we deserved to go after playing the SEC Championship Game. Before that game, I felt we had to take care of business. But when I saw who lost that day, with USC losing to UCLA, I thought we deserved to go.

What I remember most about the 2006 team is how it came together that one night in Arizona. On that day, that team could have beaten anybody. They were talented players, but their preparation and attention to detail was outstanding. I had Sonny Lubick, one of my good friends, come out to practice in Arizona, and he said he'd never seen anything like it. He had never seen that much focus and energy from a team.

Not a lot of people were giving us a chance to beat Ohio State, but Bob Davie and Lou Holtz, two former coaches, gave us a chance to win. When I first saw Ohio State on film, I didn't think we had a chance to win. But once you really evaluated it and studied it, you realized we were battle-tested and ready. The schedule prepared us for a game like that.

Urban Meyer became Florida's head coach in 2005. The next year the Gators won the national championship by beating Ohio State 41–14 in the BCS Championship Game.

I don't want to say winning a national title legitimized everything we do, but in this world of doubt it kind of had that effect. I was raised that if you don't have something nice to say, then don't say it. But it seems like the public—whether it's the media or just people talking—they always have ways of finding faults in programs. When something happens like winning a national championship—and you see how many lives were turned around and see a group of kids who bought into something and went as hard as they could—I don't want to say it legitimizes it, but it does.

The pressures of being the coach at Florida or Notre Dame and those kind of places, with the scrutiny that you're under with every step you take, winning that national championship kind of validated everything about our program. We do a lot of unique things, from Champions Club to Leadership Council to mat drills to spread offense, and everything is questioned and challenged. Beating Ohio State kind of validated everything we do. Not that it had to be validated, but it was with that victory.

I've said this before: I want Florida to be the place that everybody emulates. I want to have the highest graduation rate in the SEC, which we do. I want to win SEC championships and national championships, which we did. I want our kids to play in the NFL. Those are the three goals of our program: I want kids to graduate, win championships, and be blessed enough to play professional football. When people think about the Florida Gators, that's what I want them to see.

The biggest negative for Florida, if there is one, is the competition is unlike any place in America. I sit in those SEC meetings and see the coaches sitting around the table. I look at them and say, "Wow!" There are a bunch of coaches who have won national championships and coaches who have won SEC titles. They're some of the best Xs and Os coaches in America. Every Sunday when you wake up and get ready to play your next game, you better bring your best effort, or you're going to lose. You better stay on task—and staying on task for us is recruiting like crazy every day.

What does it mean to be a Gator? You come here with a purpose, and it's not just getting to the NFL. Your goal is to graduate with a degree, to play on championship teams, and, if you can, to go on and play in the NFL. I think because of those goals, Florida is different than a lot of places.

—Urban Meyer

INTRODUCTION

Alabama football coach Paul "Bear" Bryant might have been the first college football legend to refer to the University of Florida as a "sleeping giant." For too long, the Gators seemed to hibernate between August and November. Before prodigal son Steve Spurrier returned to Florida as its football coach in 1990, the Gators had never even won a Southeastern Conference title. There had been three first-place finishes in the program's long history, but each had been wiped out and erased from the record books by NCAA rules violations. Alas, the "Year of the Gator" never seemed to come.

Spurrier finally awoke the "sleeping giant," as his Florida teams won six SEC titles and the 1996 national championship during his ultra successful tenure at his alma mater. Along the way, Spurrier completely changed the way college football is played in the Deep South. Instead of the traditional "three yards and a cloud of dust" that made SEC programs such as Alabama, Auburn, and Georgia famous, Spurrier threw the football all over the place with his "Fun 'n' Gun" offense. Who knew the "Year of the Gator" would last a decade?

Only four years after Spurrier bolted for the NFL, Urban Meyer led Florida to the 2006 national championship with his spread offense. Florida's second football crown came just nine months after Billy Donovan led the Gators to their first national championship in men's basketball (a second basketball national title would follow less than four months later), giving Florida the unique distinction of becoming the first school to hold both coveted trophies at the same time. Indeed, it was *great* to be a Florida Gator!

What It Means to Be a Gator offers readers a rare opportunity to be educated by those who know Florida football best: the players who poured their blood, sweat, and tears into a program during its mostly lean seasons to those who are reaping the benefits of that hard work within the championship program it is today. In the last two decades Florida has become the program to emulate in college football. The school has produced more than 100 players who have earned All-America recognition since 1980, nearly 40 first-round selections in the NFL Draft, and three Heisman Trophy winners, most recently quarterback Tim Tebow, who became the first sophomore to win the award in 2007.

Among the amazing and truly improbable stories you'll read in this book:

• Carlos Alvarez, a native Cuban who grew up in Miami, became a record-setting flanker at Florida from 1968 to 1971. In his first season on Florida's varsity football team in 1969, Alvarez was named a consensus All-American following a record-breaking season, in which he caught 88 passes for 1,329 yards and 12 touchdowns. His extraordinary athletic skills earned him the moniker "Cuban Comet" from fans and teammates alike. Alvarez's football career was ultimately undone by injuries, but he became a renowned scholar and still practices law today.

• Kerwin Bell, from tiny Mayo, Florida, walked on Florida's football team in 1983 as an unheralded quarterback from Lafayette High School. Bell started his college career as the Gators' eighth-string quarterback. By the beginning of his freshman season in 1984, Bell was named Florida's starting quarterback and never relinquished the job during the rest of his college career. He led Florida to its first SEC championship in 1984 with a 9–1–1 record, although the SEC stripped the Gators of the title the following year.

• Don Gaffney, a native of Jacksonville, Florida, took a heroic step in becoming the first African American to play quarterback at the University of Florida. Gaffney arrived at Florida in 1972 and immediately worked his way onto the field. Gaffney became the Gators' starting quarterback midway through his sophomore season in 1973 and started as a junior and senior. He led Florida to three bowl games during his career: the 1973 Tangerine Bowl, 1974 Sugar Bowl, and 1975 Gator Bowl. Even after receiving death threats, Gaffney persevered and graduated with a degree from Florida. Three of his brothers, Derrick, Johnny, and Warren, and a nephew, Jabar, also played football for the Gators, creating a family legacy that is unmatched in Florida history.

• Ben Hanks, who grew up on the rough streets of Miami, was one of the greatest success stories in Florida football history. Hanks struggled to become academically qualified at Miami Senior High School and was accepted to the

University of Florida only after Spurrier asked university officials to give Hanks the opportunity to attend college. Hanks redshirted in 1991 to focus on his academics, then started at linebacker for four straight seasons, from 1992 to 1995. Spurrier even took his No. 11 jersey out of retirement and allowed Hanks to wear it. Hanks was a two-time All-SEC choice as a junior and senior and, more importantly, became the first member of his family to graduate with a college degree.

    • Terry Jackson, a native of Gainesville, Florida, was a second-generation Gator, following his father, Willie Jackson Sr., and older brother, Willie Jackson Jr., to the University of Florida. Jackson was the last person offered a scholarship in his recruiting class, but he became an invaluable member of the Gators' 1996 national championship team. He played running back, fullback, outside linebacker, safety, and all special teams for the Gators in parts of four seasons, from 1995 to 1998. Jackson helped the Gators win the school's first national championship, running for 118 yards and two touchdowns in a 52–20 victory over Florida State in the Sugar Bowl. During his time at Florida, Jackson served as student body vice president and was cocaptain of the football team. He is now a member of Urban Meyer's coaching staff at his alma mater.

    These are only a few of the remarkable stories in this book, which make Florida one of the most unique football programs in the country. It is a program steeped in tradition, from playing in the Swamp to Mr. Two-Bits to the Gator Chomp. Never before have Gator fans so proudly proclaimed: "Two Bits, Four Bits, Six Bits, a Dollar—All for the Gators, Stand Up and Holler!"

The
FIFTIES

DOUG DICKEY

QUARTERBACK

1950–1953

I WAS BORN IN SOUTH DAKOTA, AND MY FATHER was a speech professor. We moved to Baton Rouge, Louisiana, when I was three years old and stayed there for 10 years. Then we moved to Gainesville when my father took a position at the University of Florida. I attended P.K. Yonge High School in Gainesville.

I was working on the grounds department at Florida for summer money and had done that for a couple of years while I was going to high school. I remember one day in the summer of 1950, I saw Dave Fuller, one of the Florida assistant coaches, and waved at him. He waved back to me, and the next day I got a phone call from him. He asked me to come out as a walk-on for the football team. He said he knew I was going to school there, so I might as well play football. I walked on and played football, basketball, and baseball during my freshman and sophomore years at Florida. I got a scholarship after my first year there.

I had a chance to go to the University of Ohio, which had shown some interest in me through a friend of my father. I had an option to go there, but I decided to just stay at the University of Florida. I played on the freshman team in 1950, when freshmen were still ineligible to play on the varsity team. We had a fine freshman class. Rick Casares was in our freshman class, and J. Hall and Buford Long were a year older than us. Casares was a fine athlete. He played basketball and threw the javelin on the track team. He was a heavyweight boxer and could do just about anything. I think he was proba-bly the most terrific all-around athlete I've ever been around. He could do so many things as a big man. He was a 6′2″, 220-pound man. Rick wasn't that explosive because he was a big man, but Hall and Long were both track guys. They ran track in high school and in college, and J. Hall won the NCAA high jump one year and was also a sprinter on the track team. They were good players.

We went 5–5 in both 1950 and 1951. I thought everybody felt like we'd really be good in 1952. We had a great quarterback in Haywood Sullivan, who left after the end of the 1951 season. He signed to play baseball for the Boston Red Sox, so I got to play quarterback as a result of his leaving. If he had stayed, I don't know how good we would have been. We had a pretty good defense and were a good, solid football team. We beat Auburn [by a 31–21 score], Georgia [30–0], Miami [43–6], and some other folks. We won three really good games and lost some conference games.

We finished 8–3 in 1952 and went to the Gator Bowl, which was the first time Florida had been to a bowl game. It was a really big experience for us, and it was an exciting thing to do. We were proud of our team for accom-plishing more than Florida had accomplished in a very long time. We played a pretty good Tulsa football team and won the game 14–13. They had the greatest kicker in the country, and he missed a field goal and extra point, and we won the game. I couldn't play much because I pulled a hamstring muscle getting ready for the game. The team played well, and Freddie Robinson played quarterback most of the way for us. It was a good win.

My first recollection of coach Bob Woodruff was that he surrounded him-self with a lot of good people. He had a Tennessee-Army background, and between Tennessee and the United States Military Academy, he had crossed paths with a lot of good football coaches. He'd been at Georgia Tech, too, so he had an excellent coaching staff around him. Tonto Coleman was my fresh-man coach and went on to become commissioner of the Southeastern Con-ference. Johnny Rauch was my quarterbacks coach and became a head coach. Hank Foldberg and Dale Hall were head coaches. Frank Broyles was there my freshman year and was part of the coaching staff, and Johnny Sauer coached a long time at different places. We had a lot of good people around there. Coach Woodruff really knew how to hire good people. They helped put the team together really well, and Bob was a very bright man. He was not a very good speaker, but he was an extremely bright man about insights

Doug Dickey became the Gators' starting quarterback in 1952 and led them to an 8–3 record and a victory in the 1952 Gator Bowl. Dickey went on to coach the Tennessee Volunteers, where he compiled a 46–15–4 record and won SEC championships in 1967 and 1969. Dickey was named Florida's coach before the 1970 season and had a 58–43–2 record in nine seasons.

into things. He knew what it took to solve problems because he was an engineer by schooling, so he always had an answer for something.

When I left Florida after the 1953 season, I didn't know what I was going to do because I had to go into the Army. I really didn't know what was going to happen to me. I was trying to get a master's degree and coached for one year at St. Petersburg High School. Rather than be a graduate assistant at

Florida and stay there, somebody told me I should go coach in high school and I'd be better off. I did that and then I had to go into the Army. So I went back to Florida and got a couple of classes out of the way and then joined the military. I was in the Army for two and a half years, and Frank Broyles called me one day and asked if I thought I could come to Arkansas and coach. I told him I was in the Army and didn't think I could get out. I told him to let me call this one guy and see what he thinks. I'd coached the Army football team at Fort Carson, Colorado, and we won the All-Army championship. I had Willie Davis and Forrest Gregg and some other great players with me. After we won the championship, this general told me, "Hey, Lieutenant, if I can ever do anything for you, come see me." So I went to see him, and he and a couple of the Arkansas senators made a deal. They told me they'd let me out of the Army if I'd go join the Arkansas National Guard. I joined the National Guard and went to coach at the University of Arkansas. It was a nice break, and I spent six years in the Arkansas National Guard.

I was 31 years old when Coach Woodruff hired me as football coach at the University of Tennessee [in 1964]. It was a terrific break. Coach Woodruff was going to be the athletics director and he wanted someone he could work with. He didn't want some older guy telling him what to do, and he knew I'd listen to him and we could work together. He knew my background and knew my dad and my family. We were a good team and worked together well. He was a good athletics director and had already been the athletics director at Florida for 10 years, so he knew the Southeastern Conference pretty well. It was a huge help to me to have his knowledge of the league.

5

We won two SEC titles in six years at Tennessee, and it was a tough decision to leave [in 1970]. It was a very difficult decision. It was pretty much a personal decision for me. My family and my wife's father were in Florida. Our children were growing up, and we were both from Florida. It was one of those things we felt would be good to us for a long time. We hoped we'd have as much success at Florida as we had at Tennessee and wanted to see if we could make it work. It didn't quite work out that well, but we had some bright moments. It was a tough decision, but one that was the right decision at the time. I still think it was the right decision for us.

We were close to winning the SEC at Florida a few times. I remember the players more than anything. We had a lot of great relationships with the players and coaches. We had it going pretty good until about 1976. We had the program going up all the time, and that was what counted anywhere you were. You have to keep it up there at a high level and be competing for championships or you've got to be winning them. We were working at it and missed it by one game a few times. We were one or two plays away in one game in 1975 and 1976. I thought we had it going, but didn't get the quarterback we needed. We had one guy get a Rhodes Scholarship offer and he left, so it just didn't quite work out.

We had some great players at Florida. I'd say Wes Chandler was probably the most dynamic player I coached at the University of Florida. He was a receiver and running back. We had some other good linemen and linebackers. Burton Lawless was a really good player. Glenn Cameron played a long time in the pros and so did Sammy Green. Jack Youngblood was probably the best down lineman we had, but we only had him for one year.

Of course, everyone remembers the "Florida Flop" against Miami in 1971. It was an interesting thing, and we still laugh about it. We were not a very good football team and neither was Miami that year. I think we were about a 14-point underdog going into the game. I told our coaches we weren't doing anything good defensively going into that game. We were having a terrible time and had an open date before the Miami game. I told the coaches, "Why don't we just totally change the defense?" We went to an eight-man front, an old Tennessee wide-tackle-six look. Miami was pitching the ball to Chuck Foreman a lot, and I figured at least he wouldn't run around us playing that defense. I thought we could get a little more pursuit on him, at the very least. Well, in the process, Miami completely changed its offense and went to the wishbone. They moved Chuck Foreman out to wide receiver. So we got ready to line up and we didn't know what we were doing and they didn't know what they were doing.

The game was kind of a stalemate offensively, but we got ahead by a 38–9 score. We stopped Miami, and they punted. We needed to get the ball back for John Reaves to break the national passing record. So Miami punted, and Harvin Clark ran it back for a touchdown. We still didn't have the ball! I told Harvin Clark, "Dang, Harvin, you're causing me more pain than any man I've ever known. You run the punt back for a touchdown. If you just fall down somewhere, we get the ball and John breaks the record! There won't ever be anything said again." But then Miami got the ball back on the kickoff, and they put Chuck Foreman back at tailback and started driving. They started pitching him the sweep, and we couldn't get the ball away from him. They got it down to about our 20-yard line with about a minute to go.

Miami called timeout to stop the clock, and I told our guys, "Hey, guys, just let them score. Go full speed, but let them get into the end zone." One of our guys ran out there and told everybody to just lay down. They snapped the ball, and all of our guys laid down, and they ran into the end zone. Of course, that wasn't what I had in mind, but that's what the kids did. We let them score and got the ball back, and John broke the record on the next series. We received all sorts of criticism for it, but we accomplished our mission. Nobody liked the way we did it, but that's the way it happened. If Harvin Clark wouldn't have run the punt back for a touchdown, it never would have happened that way. Fran Curci, the Miami coach, was mad about it at the time, but we've laughed about it over the years.

Near the end of my Florida tenure, I hired Steve Spurrier as our quarterbacks coach. We hired Steve to come in and see if he could get us transitioned over to a better passing game. We needed a couple of years to do it, but we only got one year and didn't do it. Steve was a good, competitive guy, though. He didn't have any problems competing. I always enjoyed the way he went about it and always had a good strategy. He was just really competitive about getting it done. He's been able to recruit really good receivers wherever he's been, which has been a winning edge for him.

7

Having coached at Tennessee and worked as the athletics director there, I consider myself a part of both schools. I've got history and friends at both places, and I don't have any problem being comfortable at both schools. I don't have any problem in the competition and watching the teams play. I enjoy watching both schools play, and I'm very proud of both of them for what they've accomplished. When I look at my check every month, though, most of it comes from Tennessee.

It was exciting for me to play at Florida. I grew up there as a high school student and enjoyed watching the Gators, even though they weren't very good. I was a freshman when Coach Woodruff got there, and I knew things were going to get better. We had some terrific athletes around there. There were 100 players in my freshman class and they were from everywhere and were just terrific athletes. Probably 25 of us made it to our senior year, so it was a pretty tight-knit group. We had an exciting group of athletes that they built teams around. It was a very exciting time for me, and going back as Florida's coach was very exciting. I thought Florida was going to be one of those places that would have the opportunity to do great things, and we just didn't quite get it done, and some other people have.

Doug Dickey, who attended P.K. Yonge High School in Gainesville, was invited to walk on Florida's football team in 1950. Dickey, whose father was a speech professor at the school, received a scholarship the following year and played on the Gators baseball, basketball, and football teams. He became the Gators' starting quarterback in 1952 and led them to an 8–3 record. Dickey guided Florida to its first bowl game as a junior, beating Tulsa 14–13 in the 1952 Gator Bowl. After coaching high school football and joining the Army, Dickey was hired as an assistant coach at Arkansas. He was named Tennessee's head football coach six years later in 1964. Dickey had a 46–15–4 record with the Volunteers and won SEC championships in 1967 and 1969. While coaching there, Dickey was credited with adding the "T" to players' helmets and introducing the tradition of having the Volunteers run through the "T" before home games at Neyland Stadium. Dickey was named Florida's coach before the 1970 season and had a 58–43–2 record in nine seasons. He led the Gators to four bowl games: the 1973 Tangerine Bowl, 1974 Sugar Bowl, 1975 Gator Bowl, and 1977 Sun Bowl. Dickey worked as Tennessee's athletics director from 1986 to 2002 and was inducted into the College Football Hall of Fame in 2003. He is retired and lives in Jacksonville, Florida.

JIMMY DUNN

QUARTERBACK/CORNERBACK

1955–1958

I GREW UP IN TAMPA AND PLAYED IN THE HIGH SCHOOL all-star football game in Gainesville in the early part of August 1955. Before then, I was scheduled to walk on at Florida State, and the coaches there had promised me a one-year scholarship after my first season if I played well. But after that all-star game, Dick Jones, one of the Florida assistants, offered me a four-year scholarship. I guess I played pretty well in the all-star game because they offered me a scholarship and saw I could play against other guys who were going off to play college football. So I had the choice of a one-year scholarship at Florida State or four years at Florida, and I chose four years with the Gators.

I was a small guy. At the end of my senior season, I got up to 142 pounds. They tried everything to try to get me to add weight. They gave me these special milkshakes that were filled with molasses and eggs. I didn't gain a pound, so they quit trying. You are what you are. I was a freshman in 1955 and played on the freshman team. When I got there, I was 13th on the quarterback depth chart.

But after we went through spring practice before my sophomore season in 1956, we had some guys who were injured, ruled academically ineligible, or just quit. All of the sudden, I was the third-team quarterback. We played the 1956 opener at Mississippi State in Starkville, Mississippi. Joe Brodsky had a big game for us and intercepted some passes, and we went ahead early in the

10

Jimmy Dunn became Florida's starting quarterback by the fourth game of his sophomore season in 1956. As a two-way player, Dunn helped lead the Gators to three consecutive winning seasons, from 1956 to 1958. After graduation, Dunn became an assistant coach at Florida and Tennessee.

game. They put me in the game in the fourth quarter. I didn't do anything really bad. I caught a punt and punted a couple of times. I didn't drop the ball and didn't throw an interception. I felt pretty good about it.

We started the 1956 season with a 1–1–1 record [Florida beat Mississippi State 26–0, tied Clemson 20–20, and lost to Kentucky 17–8]. I played a little bit in each of those games, and in the fourth game against Rice, they started me at quarterback. Rice had a couple of NFL quarterbacks in Frank Ryan and King Hill and a great wide receiver, Buddy Dial. They had a really good football team and were throwing the football really well.

Back in those days, you had to play both offense and defense. Everybody had to play both ways. The quarterback had to play safety on defense, and you had to play in the kicking game, too. It was like small high school rules. You just went in and played. They had rules that you could only substitute into the game once in a quarter. If you started, you could only go back into the game once during that quarter. Fortunately, I didn't make many mistakes against Rice, and we won the game 7–0. I started the next week against Vanderbilt, and we won 21–7. We were off and running. [The Gators won five consecutive games, also beating LSU 21–6, Auburn 20–0, and Georgia 28–0, to improve their record to 6–1–1.]

At the end of the 1956 season, we lost to Georgia Tech 28–0 in Jacksonville. For some reason, I did not start that game. Harry Spears started that game at quarterback. I heard from the coaches that Harry had been around for a while and deserved to start, and he had served in the military and was older than me. It was a big game. We were playing for the SEC championship, and they started him in the game. We finished the season losing to Miami 20–7 in Gainesville. Miami had a really good team and had recruited a bunch of big, strong guys from the Northeast. We finished the season with a 6–3–1 record and felt pretty good about the team coming back.

Before the 1957 season, a bunch of us came down with the Asian flu, and we were forced to cancel the opener against UCLA. We only played nine games that season. We were also on NCAA probation for illegally recruiting a baseball player, of all things. I was fortunate that I didn't get the flu at the beginning of the season, so I was one of about 30 guys who were still out practicing while everyone else was sick. We beat Wake Forest 27–0 in the first game we played, then I came down with the flu the following week. I spent the entire week in the infirmary or at home, and they picked me up on the way to the airport to fly to Kentucky for the game. I had been laid up the whole week, so I had pretty fresh legs. I started the game and played pretty well, and we won 14–7.

One of the highlights during my junior season in 1957 was beating LSU in Gainesville. The Tigers were ranked No. 10 in the country, and they had Billy Cannon and Jimmy Taylor, who were great players. We played really well and won the game 22–14. We came back and lost at Auburn 13–0. Auburn was ranked No. 4 in the country, so it was a tough stretch against some really good teams. We beat Georgia 22–0 in Jacksonville, and our defense just played really, really well and had a couple of times when we turned Georgia away close to our goal line. We tied Georgia Tech 0–0 in

11

Atlanta. It was a great defensive game in the rain. We scored a touchdown on a halfback pass by Jimmy Rountree in that game, but it was nullified by a penalty because we had players downfield, and the game ended in a tie. We should have beaten Georgia Tech. We were better than them that season. We ended the season by beating Miami 14–0 in the Orange Bowl after losing to them the year before.

We had a really good team coming back for my senior season in 1958. We had a great player named Bernie Parrish, who was a great halfback and great defensive cornerback. In the spring, he signed a bonus contract with the Boston Red Sox and didn't play his senior season. We were left with a bunch of little guys and didn't have any off-tackle strength. We all looked like little defensive backs and couldn't run the football. Since you had to play both ways, our running backs were 5'9" and weighed 175 pounds. Bernie was bigger than that and was a really good running back. We really missed him.

We still had a good football team. To me, the late 1950s was the period of time in Florida football history when we got out of being invited to be the homecoming guests of all our opponents. People started realizing we could play. We were no longer sought after to be a homecoming opponent. We went to LSU, and Billy Cannon had a big run for them. They kicked a field goal late to beat us 10–7. They had a three-team system they called the "Chinese Bandits." They had one team that played strictly offense, one team that played both ways, and one team that played nothing but defense. They ended up winning the national championship that season. We played Auburn the next week and lost 6–5. Auburn was ranked No. 4 in the country and they had won the national championship the year before in 1957. We played both those teams right to the wire. We had the ball inside the 10-yard line at the end of the game and missed a field goal that would have won the game. We were a pretty good football team but didn't have the players that could make big plays. We had a bunch of good players and played extremely well. But we couldn't win nine games.

We beat Georgia 7–6 in Jacksonville after losing two close games. They killed us for three quarters. Fran Tarkenton ran all over us, and they had a big, strong fullback named Theron Sapp. But our defense played really, really hard. I had a 75-yard run in that game. I got some great blocks downfield and just cut across the grain. We played Arkansas State and won 51–7. I didn't even dress out for that game.

My senior season was the first time we played Florida State. We played them in Gainesville. It was the first time we'd ever played Florida State, so it was a really big win for us. I played well in that game and scored a couple of touchdowns and intercepted a pass. We won the game 21–7. On the opening kickoff, they ran a deep reverse and fooled us, no doubt about it. I was the safety man and went to midfield and stopped, which was what I was supposed to do. I was supposed to get to the ball if they got through our guys. They got through, and I just kept back-pedaling. They were running down the sideline, and all of a sudden the ball carrier decided to run to the middle of the field. I guess I was a couple of steps faster than him and stopped him. They still scored a touchdown and went ahead 7–0, but we were able to come back and win the game.

We beat Miami 12–9 in Jacksonville. We gave up a safety at the end of the game and kicked it back to them and held on. That's kind of how all those games went. With the rules they had in place, that's kind of the way you had to play. Everybody had to play offense, defense, and special teams. There wasn't enough time to practice offense. Today, guys go out and practice nothing but offense for two hours. We were limited in what we could do.

We played Ole Miss in the Gator Bowl at the end of the 1958 season, which was my first bowl game. It was two evenly matched SEC teams and was really a defensive struggle. We had a couple of chances. I ran back the opening kickoff 50 yards and put us in position to score. We settled for a field goal. We had a couple of other chances in the game but couldn't capitalize on them. I don't think many people will remember much about that game, other than it was played in Jacksonville. We finished the season with a 6–4–1 record.

I played for coach Bob Woodruff, and he was a quiet guy. He was very, very smart and had a dry sense of humor. It was difficult for players to talk to him because he was so much smarter than us. He really left the coaching up to his assistants, and we were closer to them. Coach Woodruff was kind of an introvert. He cared about us and would do anything in the world for us, but we related more with our assistants.

I thought we did pretty well with what we had at Florida. I didn't know it at the time. Once I got out of school and was older and got into coaching, I thought we did extremely well. I think it was the beginning of establishing Florida as a very good football program. Ray Graves came in as coach, and we started winning eight or nine games, instead of five or six every season.

Jimmy Dunn, a native of Tampa, Florida, was one of the last players to be recruited by the Gators in 1955. He began his career buried on the team's depth chart but was Florida's starting quarterback by the fourth game of his sophomore season in 1956. As a two-way player, Dunn helped lead the Gators to three consecutive winning seasons, from 1956 to 1958. During his junior season in 1957, Dunn led the Gators to a 22–14 upset of LSU in Gainesville. As a senior, he helped Florida beat Florida State 21–7 in the first game played between the schools. The Gators played in the Gator Bowl during his senior season, only the school's second trip to a postseason game. After graduation, Dunn became an assistant coach at Florida and Tennessee. He returned to Florida as an assistant under coach Doug Dickey in 1970. Dunn later worked as an assistant coach under Steve Spurrier with the USFL's Tampa Bay Bandits and was a long-time head coach in arena football leagues. Dunn lives in Tampa.

The
SIXTIES

LARRY LIBERTORE

QUARTERBACK

1959–1962

I CAME TO FLORIDA IN 1958 AS A FRESHMAN, and you couldn't play on the varsity team. Miami, Florida State, and Tennessee also recruited me, but I was really interested at that point in going to Notre Dame or Ohio State because I grew up in Canton, Ohio. As I grew up, those were the schools I cheered for, along with Army and Navy.

My family moved to Miami in 1955, when I started junior high school. I had a rude awakening because if you were from Canton, Ohio, you started playing football when you were, like, in the fourth grade. I was a quarterback there at a Catholic school. When I moved to Miami's Edison High School, they were running a single-wing offense. It was a large school, and I could tell I wasn't what you'd want in a single-wing quarterback. Quarterbacks didn't run the ball, and the tailbacks did most of the running. I wasn't big enough to be a tailback.

I was considering transferring to Curley High in Miami, but the coach at Edison decided he would switch to the T formation. I had already been running that offense for years, and there wasn't another guy on the team who had a clue as to how to play quarterback in that offense. They tried all the guys who were big, but none of them could do it. So I played quarterback there for two years and then went on to Florida.

My high school coach at Edison High School talked me out of even discussing going to those schools up North. He talked me out of it and stressed how important it was to go to a college in Florida. It was good advice. After meeting with the other three schools who were recruiting me, I decided Florida was the best situation for me.

I went to Florida in 1958, and we played three freshman games. I redshirted in 1959 because most everybody redshirted back then. I think we had 65 incoming freshmen, which was a huge class. By the end of your redshirt year, the coaches pretty much knew what you could do. You'd played on the freshman team and then worked against the varsity offense and defense as a redshirt. It was much more difficult than playing any games. They could determine over those two years what your position was going to be and whether or not you could help the team.

Jimmy Dunn was the quarterback on the varsity team in 1958, and then Ricky Allen succeeded him the following season in 1959. Allen was a 26-year-old guy who had come back from military service. There were about seven quarterbacks on the varsity team before the 1960 season, and I'm not sure where I actually ranked. I was probably sixth or seventh, to be honest. They were all bigger than me. But you go through that process, and sometimes things work out. I think things just happen for whatever reason. I think I had the quickness, dedication, and will to play. But because of my size, I think they were going to see if they could get that same effort out of someone bigger than me. I just think through the process of spring practice and what they saw from me as a redshirt, I moved up to fifth then fourth and then second. It just happened.

I played quarterback throughout the 1960 season. It was the first season I was eligible to play on the varsity team. I returned all the punts, played quarterback, and played safety about half the time on defense. That was a time when you could only substitute so many players. I was probably about 135 pounds. That was the best season Florida had while I was there.

We opened the 1960 season against George Washington in Jacksonville. It was a night game, and it was a terrible, sloppy game for us. We had a mixture of guys that were left over from the Bob Woodruff era, and then Ray Graves came as coach, and there were some of us new guys mixed in. We kind of had to get everybody together, and it took a little while to do it. So that first game was sloppy, but we did beat George Washington 30–7. It let you know that you're in the big time. I think all of us learned a lot from that game, and we moved forward from there.

Bob Woodruff was a defensive-minded coach. He would quick kick on third down, and the games always ended with scores of 7–6 or 10–7. They were very cautious in what they did on offense. I think he was asked to leave because they went to Vanderbilt in 1959 and punted three or four times on third down. They just weren't aggressive. When Coach Graves came to Florida, he had Pepper Rodgers with him, and they were really aggressive on offense. At the time, no teams were really throwing the football a lot. We ran the option some and ran a spread offense. We were more aggressive and took some chances under Graves.

Running the option play was always a very natural thing for me. I don't really believe you can teach a quarterback to run the option. Having done it in high school, it was just something that was easy for me. Being able to do the foot work and hand work were just natural, so it was easy for me to fit into that type of system.

I split some playing time with Bobby Dodd Jr., who wasn't an option quarterback at all. He was slow and methodical, but he was very smart and was a pretty good drop-back quarterback. There was a huge difference in our abilities. In that day and time, I don't think defenses were as sophisticated as they are today. So it's hard to say if playing two kinds of quarterbacks gave us an advantage or not. When Bobby went into the game, they knew for sure that it wasn't going to be an option play and that he was probably going to pass. When I went into the game, we would probably be in an option formation or in the spread. I used to run the quarterback draw a lot, so I suspect the defenses had a lot different preparation for me.

18

We played Florida State in the second game of the 1960 season. We won the game 3–0 when Billy Cash kicked a late field goal. Florida State and Miami weren't in the SEC, so no matter how you look at it, those games were much bigger games to FSU and Miami. I won't say we weren't prepared to play those teams, but it just seemed the attitude of the team wasn't the same as when we were getting ready to go play Georgia Tech or Auburn. Schools like Florida State and Miami were sky-high because they were going to go beat the mighty Gators. You went into those games and they just always seemed to play way over their heads. We'd play mediocre, and you know what happens when teams do that. It always became a real battle.

After beating FSU, we played Georgia Tech in Gainesville and were behind with about two or three minutes to play. We were on our 30-yard line and we had never practiced a two-minute offense. I can't remember ever calling a timeout and going to the sideline to talk to the coaches about what to do. Somehow, we went the length of the field against Georgia Tech and scored a touchdown on an option play. It was fourth down, and I pitched it out to Lindy Infante, who later became the head coach of the Green Bay Packers. Lindy scored a touchdown, but we were still down 17–16. Instead of going for the extra-point kick to tie the score, we had already determined what two-point play we were going to run. I had come out of the game earlier in the series, when Bobby Dodd had come into the game. The coaches were putting up their fingers signaling for two points, and it was an option pass. Instead of running the option, where I would fake to the fullback and pitch it to the halfback, there was no halfback. I was either going to run it or throw it to the fullback, who I had just faked a handoff to. I really started to run with the ball, but I would not have made it. The fullback, Jon MacBeth, just kind of slipped behind everybody at the last second, so it was really easy to just pop a pass to him. We won the game 18–17.

I kind of like to think that was the beginning of what turned out to be a Gators football tradition. Florida had never really won a big game up until then. They were always a good defensive team but had never come from behind to beat a good team like that. After we beat Georgia Tech, we lost to Rice 10–0 in Miami. Everything was great against Georgia Tech, but Rice was just ready for us. They were in our backfield, and the option didn't work. It was a rude awakening. But I think we became a better football team by losing to Rice than we did by beating Georgia Tech. We came back and beat Vanderbilt 12–0 and LSU 13–10 in Baton Rouge.

Then we played Auburn, and they were ranked pretty high. The Auburn game was a tough battle and went right down to the wire. I can remember we were down around the 20-yard line, and I threw a pass on third down. I thought it was fourth down. I don't know why I thought it was fourth down, but I shouldn't have thrown it, and the pass was intercepted. If I'd thrown it away, we might have gotten a field goal to tie the score. But those are things after the fact. Auburn was extremely big and extremely fast, and we lost the game 10–7.

I think we were a little too cautious on offense and a little too predictable, in my opinion. If you were an 18- or 19-year-old kid playing football back then, you didn't say anything. You did what they told you to do. But I can remember telling my dad, who was an avid football fan and came to every game, about our game plan. He said, "Well, that's not going to work. They know you're going to do that!" But that's what they told me we were going to do, and I did it.

We came back and beat Georgia 22–14 in Jacksonville. The Bulldogs had Fran Tarkenton, who could really, really run. If the game had another quarter, Georgia probably would have won the game. When Tarkenton got going, it was really hard to stop him. But we had a really good defense and kept the ball away from him. We beat Tulane 21–6 in Gainesville and then went to Miami.

It always meant more to me to beat Miami. We played all our high school games in the Orange Bowl, so it was kind of comfortable for me. Most of the guys who went down to the Orange Bowl, even as freshmen, were throwing up in the locker room, knowing that we would be playing in the Orange Bowl. But I was used to it, having played in that stadium for two years in high school. It was a special game, though, because Miami had recruited me. Most of the guys from Edison High School went to Miami on scholarship. I considered Miami, but they had a quarterback who was going to be there for a while. I didn't want to wait. I wanted to play as soon as possible.

We finished the regular season with an 8–2 record and went to play Baylor in the Gator Bowl, which was a big game for us. We didn't know much about Baylor, but it was an honor for us to be in that game. They had two or three guys who went on to play in the NFL. Their tailback, Ronnie Bull, was a great player. I was honored to be named MVP of that game. We were a little bit more aggressive on offense, and we threw a long pass on the first play and caught them off-guard. We were a little bit innovative, but not a lot. We finished 9–2 in Coach Graves's first season, which was a good start for him. If we had beaten Auburn, we would have been SEC champs, which I didn't know at the time. I just don't think we were as aware as players are today about what meaning the games really have. We didn't really pay attention to where we were in the standings and things like that.

During my junior year in 1961, we opened the season against Clemson. It was probably the best game I had at Florida. It was just an excellent win, and we beat Clemson 21–17. After that game, though, things just seemed to turn, and I'm not sure what happened. We lost a lot of seniors from the year before, and I think that season was a learning process for a lot of players. We tied Florida State 3–3 after they blocked a punt early in the game. That was a real letdown. We had squeaked by them the year before. It's tough to lose to a team in the state that's not supposed to be as good as you. But they fought hard and played hard. We lost to Rice 19–10 in Houston and then beat Vanderbilt 7–0. But we lost four out of our last five games. We'd beaten a lot of those teams the year before, and those coaches aren't going to let you beat them twice in a row. It was just a tough year, and we finished with a 4–5–1 record.

We opened the 1962 season, my senior year, and beat Mississippi State 19–9 in Jackson, Mississippi. We lost to Georgia Tech 17–0, but that Yellow Jackets team was ranked really high. We went to Jacksonville and lost to Duke 28–21. That was a bad loss. I'd injured my knee the week before and didn't play at all against Duke. Tommy Shannon came in at quarterback, and Duke was ahead 21–0 early in the game. We almost came back and won. After that, I didn't play quarterback anymore the rest of the year. I started on defense, and Shannon was having an excellent year at quarterback. He was from Miami and was a good friend of mine. He was a left-handed quarterback and was a good passer.

My knee injury lasted about 10 days, and we were still running the option. I think teams were beginning to zero in on our option offense, and we were too predictable. We had to make some kind of change, and a lot of times it's the quarterback who is changed. I did finish the rest of the season starting on defense, and we had a really good defense. Florida always had a good defensive team. All of the teams back then, except for Georgia, were not passing teams. We finished 7–4 and beat Penn State 17–7 in the Gator Bowl. It was a great way to go out. Penn State had a really good team, and we didn't know much about them. We worked so hard for that game and were prepared like we were going to play the Green Bay Packers. I'll never forget it. I think Penn State was just shocked when we got on the field. They probably thought they were going to run away with the game, but we were playing at our top level. It was a great way to go out.

I think we all felt pretty good about things making a turn at Florida. You could just feel it. Things were a little bit more wide open. Coach Graves had been a defensive coach at Georgia Tech, and there was a transition he needed to make. Coach Graves was a very good father figure and was extremely forthright and honest. You felt like you were being led by the right person. He had a stature about him, and you could tell he meant business. When he took over, they made some changes to let everybody know we were going to head in the right direction. When we left, we felt like things were heading in the right direction at Florida.

Larry Libertore, a native of Miami, started at quarterback and safety at Florida for three seasons, from 1959 to 1961. An undersized quarterback with good speed and mobility, Libertore held the Florida record for rushing yards by a quarterback until Tim Tebow broke his mark in 2007. Libertore was an All-SEC selection in 1960 after leading the Gators in total offense and punt returns. He helped lead the Gators to a 9–2 record in 1960, including a 13–12 victory over Baylor in the Gator Bowl. Libertore was named MVP of that bowl game. He was inducted into the Florida Athletics Hall of Fame and Gator Bowl Hall of Fame in 2004. After graduation, Libertore was elected to the Florida state legislature in 1970 and 1972. He currently lives in Lakeland, Florida, and operates a real estate firm.

BRUCE CULPEPPER
CENTER/LINEBACKER
1959–1962

W<small>E GREW UP IN</small> T<small>ALLAHASSEE, AND</small> F<small>LORIDA</small> S<small>TATE</small> was just in the infancy of having a football program. Back then, if the University of Florida offered you a scholarship, that's where you went to school. Florida State was just beginning to evolve in football and really wasn't an option at that point.

My father was on the Board of Regents at Florida and later became the first chancellor of the University System in Florida. So there probably wasn't much doubt as to where I was going to attend college. I looked at some of the other Southeastern Conference schools, but with a brother playing at Florida and my father having graduated from there, it seemed like the perfect fit. It was the perfect distance from Tallahassee and was a great school. I was pretty sure where I was going to school.

We grew up going to Gators football games. My brother, Blair, played at Florida for a couple of seasons and was a fabulous athlete. Then he got hurt during his sophomore season and, when they cut on your knee back then, you were never really the same. He played most of his sophomore season, and I have vivid memories of him playing against Kentucky and [Wildcats All-American defensive tackle] Lou Michaels just mashing him. I enjoyed watching him very much, and they included me in some of those activities.

I went to Gainesville in 1959 and played on the freshman team. We were recruited by Coach Bob Woodruff's staff, and John Eibner was actually the assistant who recruited me. We had a great freshman group and, of course, we couldn't play on the varsity team. So we scrimmaged against the varsity and had three or four freshman team games of our own. I think we played Auburn, Miami, and Georgia and just blew them away. We had a great freshman team, and I joined the varsity the next year.

Our backfield was Bob Hoover, Richard Skelly, and Lindy Infante, and Bobby Dodd Jr. was one of our quarterbacks. We had a number of guys who contributed on the line, including Bruce Starling, who was my roommate. Sam Holland played on the line for four years, and Sam Lasky contributed a lot during our careers. Gerald Odom was on the team, and his son, Jason, later played on the same team as my son, Brad. Jimmy Morgan was an all-state center who played for us. It was a really good group.

They changed coaches after the 1959 season and hired Ray Graves. I don't think it affected us much at all, to be honest. We didn't have a lot of interaction with Coach Woodruff. He came over and talked to us for walk-throughs before our freshman games, but beyond that I don't ever recall being in a meeting with him. We were excited about having a new coach and knew a lot about Georgia Tech, which is where Coach Graves came from. We were excited about that and all the new things that were taking place. It was all new to us, and we were new to the varsity team as sophomores.

Coach Graves came in and made a terrific impression on us. We were all excited about it and just got to it. I remember our first meeting with him, and it was very simple. He said, "I want ya'll to go to church, go to class, and show up for meetings on time." That was it. We thought that was pretty good. Coach Graves truly inspired us, and all of us would run into brick walls for him. It was really because of our commitment to him. He was more of a father figure for us. Any of us could have gone to him if we were in trouble or needed advice or help. He was just a friend as well as a leader for us.

Coach Graves brought in some fantastic assistant coaches. I worked mostly with Jack Green, who worked with the defense. I was crazy about Jack Green. He did a great deal at Florida and went on to become head coach at Vanderbilt. He had been a tiny little All-American guard at West Point during the war. He was very cerebral and thought there should be a defense for every offensive set there was. I worked with him for three years, and we had hundreds of variations of defense, and that was back when the center linebacker would call the defenses. All we did was work on defenses. They didn't call them from the sideline. Not until the Duke game during my senior year did we start calling plays from the sideline. He and I worked together all the time, and I can still call out all the various defensive sets and alignments in my sleep.

I played center and linebacker on the varsity team in 1960. We had two other centers who were seniors. Bob Hood was the team captain and got hurt midway through the season and didn't play as much. He clearly was the first-team center. Bob Wehking was the other center and played there. Bob and I switched off back and forth, and I'd go in and play sometimes with the first team. You had to play both ways back then, and if you came out of the game, you could not go back in during that same quarter. The Blue team would start and play both ways for about seven minutes, and then the second team would come in and play the rest of the quarter. Sometimes I'd get stuck in there with the first team, which was wonderful. We had great seniors that year and Coach Graves inherited a good team.

The Georgia Tech game stands out during the 1960 season. They started the last drive with the second team because it was toward the end of the game. Bobby Dodd was playing quarterback and threw a pass to keep the drive alive. Coach Graves was desperately trying to get the first team back on the field. He was throwing in the guards, tackles, ends, and halfbacks as we drove down the field. I ended up staying out there during the whole drive, which was fun. When Lindy Infante scored a touchdown to pull us within 17–16, I didn't see him score. I had a red-headed, freckle-faced guy playing over me, who was a very good guard. All I remember is trying to hang on to him, so I didn't see Lindy go across the goal line. As a lineman, I remember blocking down and trying to hold the block. Lindy made it, and everybody cheered. I remember being out there with all the first-team players. We were hugging each other, and I felt like one of the boys for the first time. Of course, I don't think there was any question about going for two points to win the game. It was a no-brainer for Coach Graves, and we scored and won the game 18–17.

We went to LSU and won 13–10, which was really big because we hadn't won games like that before. We were Florida, and everybody kind of looked at us like they look at Vanderbilt today. We'd put up a good fight, but usually lose the game. So to beat LSU in Baton Rouge was a big deal. Larry Libertore had a great run in that game to help us win. After beating LSU as sophomores, we didn't do much against them the next two years [the Tigers won the next two games against Florida, each by a 23–0 score]. It was kind of like beating Georgia Tech. I don't think we scored against Georgia Tech the rest of our careers after beating them as sophomores.

We won nine games in 1960, which was the first time Florida had won nine games in a season. I don't think we knew the history or consequences of doing that. Nowadays, if you don't win the SEC, it's a disappointment. Our history didn't promote that. We hadn't been involved in the SEC race much up until that point and had never won an SEC title. During my sophomore season, we were unaware of it and didn't know we were leading the SEC. We just went game to game and played. I do know if we'd beaten Auburn in 1960, we would have won the SEC. We lost that game on a partially blocked field goal. Pat Patchen partially blocked the kick, and it wobbled over the goal post. Auburn beat us by a field goal, 10–7.

We weren't disappointed and didn't really think about it until after the season. That wasn't the motivation back then. They certainly have that motivation now and start thinking about national championships at the beginning of the season. We just enjoyed showing up and playing. We were college kids who liked to play football. We went to class and joined fraternities and had normal student lives. We lived in dorms with other players but were still integrated with all the other students. We had typical college lives.

We went 4–5–1 during my junior season in 1961. We didn't have a very good team. A lot of the freshmen were playing as sophomores a year later, and we just didn't have a very good senior class. The sophomores were still developing, so we didn't have a good team. We didn't have a lot of depth, and I played 58 minutes in one game. You can't be effective doing that. But we had to do it because we just didn't have much depth. We tied Florida State 3–3, and that was an embarrassment. They wanted it more than we did—and they always did. They had a pretty good team because they were picking up players from around the country. Bill Peterson was the FSU coach and brought the LSU attitude there. He had SEC expectations, and they were becoming a pretty good team. Truth be known, they were probably a better team than us that season. They were all celebrating like it was a win, I can tell you that.

Lindy Infante and I were cocaptains during our senior season in 1962. It was a really special honor, and I appreciate it to this day. It was a distinction that I will always cherish. There were some great players on that team, and just to be able to go out on the field and represent them was wonderful. I loved it. Unfortunately, both Lindy and I got hurt fairly early during that season. If it had happened today, I could have been a medical hardship and come back for another year. I was injured during the first part of the third game

Bruce Culpepper helped guide the Gators to a 9–2 record as a sophomore in 1960, the first time a Florida team had won nine games in a season. As a senior, Culpepper helped lead Florida to a 7–4 record, including a 17–7 victory over Penn State in the Gator Bowl.

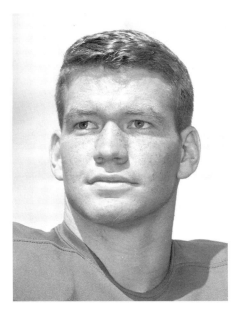

against Duke in Jacksonville. That's when we started signaling plays from the sideline. We had all these signals, and they had a lonesome end look that was kind of unusual. We had special defenses for them, and I got hurt in the game. We had a great linebacker named Roger Pettee playing behind me. He had a super sophomore season but hadn't worked enough with Jack Green to know all the defenses. We were over-shifted into the end zone half of the time, while they were over-shifted into the wide side of the field. We went up 21–0 in the game, and then our defense just collapsed. So for the rest of the season, they started calling signals from the sideline.

I wanted to come back and play because it was my senior season. Back then, they put casts on your knee, and I didn't have any surgery. I got into the shower and knocked the cast off with a hammer. I went out and tried to run around and missed about five games. I came back for the Florida State game, which was big, and played against Miami. Roger Pettee was doing a great job, so I slowly worked back into the lineup. It was disappointing to not be able to come back all the way, and Lindy ended up missing most of the season.

We finished the 1962 regular season with a 6–4 record and were invited to play Penn State in the Gator Bowl. Dave Robinson played for Penn State and went on to have a great career with the Green Bay Packers. He was a terrific All-American defensive end and played both ways. I believe he was the first African American player we ever played against. Initially, Duke was asked to go to the Gator Bowl and decided not to go because they had final exams. We were the second choice and had a team meeting to decide whether or not to go. Typically, Coach Graves said, "You guys decide if we're going." We had a closed-door meeting with just players and wanted to go. It was sort of hyped as a North-South game. Penn State was considered the monsters of the North and won all the trophies up there. We were second choice and had a solid team. We even put Confederate flags on our helmets. I walked out to practice one day with a Confederate flag on my helmet, which I had picked up from the bookstore. We wouldn't do that today, but back then it was just a symbol of the South. We thought we'd just go out there and beat the Yankees. The equipment manager liked it so much he put Confederate flags on all of our helmets.

We won the Gator Bowl 17–7, which was wonderful. We knew it was the end of our football careers. Some of us knew we would never play football again. Some of us would go on and play pro football, but most of us wouldn't. I got some letters from pro teams, but it really wasn't an option for me. I wanted to go on and attend law school. Most of the guys were moving on and beginning their careers. We were big underdogs, and it was on national television and it was a fun event. My final memory of that game was having the ball on offense and being over it playing center. I waited for time to run out and grabbed the last game ball. I tucked it under my arm, and my son has it to this day.

If anybody asks me about the highlight of my life from playing at Florida Field, I would start describing some plays that my son, Brad, made there and not mine. Having Brad play at Florida [Brad Culpepper was an All-American defensive tackle for the Gators from 1988 to 1991] meant a great deal. I loved every minute of it when Brad played for Florida. It was a wonderful experience. Watching Brad be a part of the first official SEC championship team in 1991 was great. Of course, we were at the game in Kentucky when Florida won the SEC title, and it was just a neat thing to see. Brad came over and gave me the SEC championship hat they gave the team, which meant a lot to me.

Florida has brought me a lifetime of friends and an identity with friends and an institution that has made us proud. I met my wife there, and each of my children went to school there. My best friend, Bruce Starling, was my roommate at Florida for four years, and we continue to see each other and care for one other today. We know the territory and the customs and traditions and what it all stands for. They call it the Gator Nation now, but I kind of still think of it as the Gator Family.

Bruce Culpepper, a native of Tallahassee, Florida, started at center and linebacker at Florida from 1960 to 1962. He was cocaptain of the 1962 team, along with halfback Lindy Infante. Culpepper helped guide the Gators to a 9–2 record as a sophomore in 1960, the first time a Florida team had won nine games in a season. As a senior, Culpepper helped lead Florida to a 7–4 record, including a 17–7 victory over Penn State in the Gator Bowl. Culpepper's older brother, Blair, preceded him to Florida, playing on the 1957 and 1958 football squads. Culpepper's son, Brad, was a standout defensive lineman at Florida from 1988 to 1991 and was named All-American in 1991. Culpepper lives in Tallahassee and practices law.

LINDY INFANTE
RUNNING BACK
1959–1962

Ⅰ GREW UP IN MIAMI AND DIDN'T START PLAYING FOOTBALL until junior high school. It was at a Boy's Club in Miami, and that kind of got the whole thing started. I attended Miami Senior High School. Dade County only had about five high schools at the time, so you had a lot of students in the schools. We had about 4,500 students at Miami Senior and graduated about 900 seniors each year. It was a pretty big school. We had more than 100 guys come out for football every year.

I got really lucky in high school. Back then, you had to be a senior to really get a chance to play on the varsity team. But I got lucky and started as a junior on defense. I moved to running back my senior year. The head coach at Miami Senior High came to me after my junior season was over and mentioned that if I could get my act together and get my grades up to where they needed to be, I might have a chance to get a college scholarship. Some people had already showed interest in me, although you couldn't recruit someone until his senior season. Luckily for me, it became a motivating factor because I had never even thought about college—I knew I couldn't afford it. I never even gave it much consideration until my senior season.

I had a good senior year, even though I got hurt and missed three or four games. I was able to come back and prove I was healthy and played in the last few games of my senior season. Florida State recruited me, but it had been an all-girls school for a long time and was only in the embryonic stages of its football program. Miami was home for me and was a fun place to live and grow up, but I wanted to move out of town. I wanted to get away for my college years and then come back if I chose to.

I had a few good friends who had gone to Georgia, and I had a good visit when I went up there. But there was a big difference between Georgia and Florida for me. If I was going to live in Florida for the rest of my life, which is what I thought I was going to do at the time, then going to the University of Florida as opposed to an out-of-state school made a lot more sense to me. I had a handful of friends who were going to go to Florida, and of course you knew and read a lot about Florida at the time. It was the major state school at that particular time. I didn't have any deep loyalties to Florida because I hadn't even thought about it until then, but certainly that grew with time.

I went to Gainesville in 1959 and played on the freshman team. Back then, you played a four-game freshman schedule. We usually played Florida State, Georgia, Miami, and Auburn. We would go out on practice days and be cannon fodder for the varsity guys. They'd beat us up pretty good and send us to the locker room all bruised up. Then we'd go off and practice on our own every now and again so we'd be ready to play our freshman games. You kind of did a lot of on-the-job training during your freshman season and moved on from there.

Bob Woodruff was Florida's coach in 1959. He was let go after my freshman season, so I never really played for Bob. Freshmen were kind of a nonentity because you weren't eligible for the varsity squad. We had a few occasions where we were in a meeting with Bob, or he talked to us in the locker room after practice, but that was about the extent of our association with each other. The coaching change really didn't affect us much because we hadn't played for Bob. We were on his football team, but we had our own coaches and went out on the practice field and did whatever we were told to do, showing the other team's offense or defense to get the varsity ready to play in its games.

When Ray Graves came in as coach before the 1960 season, it was kind of a new start for everybody. Obviously, with the changing of the head-coaching position, assistant coaches changed, too. A lot of guys stayed on with Ray, but there were some new faces, too. It was kind of like the beginning of a new era, and everybody was anxious to see what we could do. Luckily, we had a pretty good recruiting class when I was a freshman.

Coach Graves was just a fine man and put together a really good coaching staff. They were guys you enjoyed playing for, including him. He was just a very quality man and was well-versed in football. But he had the good common sense to delegate authority and hired coaches who were good people and leaders. They were good people to be around.

We opened up the 1960 season and beat George Washington 37–0, and then we beat Florida State 3–0. We were getting ready to play Georgia Tech, which was really a big game back then. Ray Graves had come from Georgia Tech, so we were playing against the school he had come from. They thought well of him, and he thought well of them. Bobby Dodd Jr. was one of the quarterbacks on our team, and he was playing against his father, so that added to the mystique. We were playing in Gainesville, but I don't think we were given much of a chance to win the game.

We fell behind 17–10 in the fourth quarter, and it was a memorable finish. We were behind a touchdown, and there wasn't a lot of time left. We got the football at our 15-yard line and drove down the field with a 17-play drive. Larry Libertore was our quarterback, and we ran a version of the old wing-T offense. There were some option plays in there, and Larry was a little guy but a fine runner. Usually, if he had the ball on any kind of an option play, he was going to keep it and run with it. We had an option play called on fourth and goal at Georgia Tech's 4-yard line. We called an option play to the right, and I was the back that was the intended pitch man if Larry didn't keep it. I remember taking off to the right and thinking in the back of my mind, *Well, Larry is going to take it in and score.* I didn't think he was going to pitch it. Actually, when he pitched the ball to me, he caught me a little bit off-balance. I wasn't quite expecting the ball. I was lucky enough to get hold of the ball, and at that point the sideline was creeping in on me. I made a dive to the pylon at the corner of the goal line and just barely got it in.

We ended up scoring a touchdown with 33 seconds left on the clock. Everybody in the stands was yelling, "Go for two! Go for two!" I don't know if Ray got swept up in the moment or if he was planning to go that way all along, but he held his hand up and said we were going for two. We ended up going for two and scoring and won the game 18–17. It was really memorable.

We lost to Rice 10–0 the next week and then won six of our last seven games to finish the season with a 9–2 record. We went out and played LSU during my sophomore season. I got hit in the middle of my back on a short little run and had trouble breathing. I couldn't play, and they sent me to the

As a sophomore, Lindy Infante helped Ray Graves's first team finish with a 9–2 record in 1960, the best finish by a Gators team to that point. Infante is perhaps best remembered by Florida fans for scoring a touchdown with 33 seconds left in an 18–17 upset of Georgia Tech in Gainesville on October 1, 1960.

hospital to take X-rays. They said nothing was broken and everything was fine. But I had trouble breathing through the night, so they sent me for some more X-rays and tests when we got back to Gainesville. Everything came back fine, so I actually went back on the practice field and was trying to practice. I couldn't do much of anything and was still having problems breathing.

After that practice, they picked me up in an ambulance and took me to the medical center. The doctors told me I had a defect in my lungs and that one of my lungs had popped. They told me I'd never play football again. They said if I was lucky, I'd be able to get up and move around in a wheelchair in six months. They told me if I was lucky, I'd be able to walk again in a year. They ended up shipping me down to Miami on a train because they thought the altitude on an airplane might pop the other lung. They took me to my sister's house, where they sat me up in a hospital bed. A couple of days later, I was feeling a little bit better and decided I wanted to get another opinion. I went to see my doctor in downtown Miami, and he gave me a completely different diagnosis. He said when I got hit from behind, my lung had expanded so quickly that it popped like an inner tube. There was a hole in my left lung, but it had already started repairing itself. Two weeks later, I was back on the football field playing again.

I'm not sure any of us knew all the history of being the first Florida team to win nine games. I don't think anybody got caught up in all of that. It just happened. We had a good young team and had a good season. We had a good recruiting class that came in and jelled well with the senior class that was there. We ended up winning nine games, and that was the most Florida had won in a season until that point. Once we got there, we said, "Hey, we're pretty special. We did something people hadn't done before us."

We opened the 1961 season with a 21–17 win over Clemson and tied Florida State 3–3. We finished 4–5–1. I really don't know exactly what happened. Schedules change, and you play teams that are on hot streaks when you're not. We still had the nucleus of a pretty solid team. I wouldn't say we were a bunch of dogs out there. It was a lot of the same guys who had played as sophomores. We had a few injuries and had players graduate at certain spots. The chemistry of a team changes each year in college because of graduation. Obviously, we weren't even close record-wise to the team that had played the season before.

We finished 7–4 during my senior season in 1962. We played Penn State in the Gator Bowl and won the game 17–7. Unfortunately, I spent that game wearing a cast on the sideline. I had gotten hurt earlier in the year and missed the last half of the season. I was hurt against LSU again. I had a dislocated ankle and a broken leg. I have a lot of memories of that LSU squad because I'd injured my lung as a sophomore and broken my leg and dislocated my ankle as a senior. They were historically one of the best teams in the country, and they'd knock the heck out of you. I can still remember how tough they were to this day.

It was still a special year for me because I had been voted cocaptain of the team, along with Bruce Culpepper. Then it turned out by the time the season was over, both of us had gotten hurt and were done for the year. I had ankle surgery and a broken leg. I remember the Gator Bowl because I was standing on the sideline with my crutches, and it was a tough way to have to end your career. It was still a memorable game for a lot of reasons. Having a 6–4 record during the regular season, not a lot of bowl games were talking to us. We weren't hot on a lot of bowl lists. We kind of backed into the Gator Bowl, but we won the game. It was a fun way to finish the season. It put a nice little cap on what was a fun tenure at Florida.

After I finished playing, I was drafted by the Buffalo Bills of the AFL and the Cleveland Browns of the NFL. I signed with the Bills and broke my toe during training camp. It never really healed, so they let me go. Buffalo sent me up to Hamilton in the Canadian Football League. I played two or three games, and they let a handful of guys go when a bunch of guys came back from military service. Hamilton wanted me to come back, but my real goal was to go back to school and become an architect. I hadn't quite finished up a quarter of my education degree from Florida. All I needed to do was intern to get my degree.

35

I went down to Edison High School in Miami to complete my internship, and the football coach there asked me to come out and coach a little bit while I was there. It sounded like fun and got me around the game from a different perspective. When that season was finished, I'd acquired my degree from Florida, and my coach from Miami Senior High called and asked me to become a full-time assistant coach. I was the backfield coach, and we ended up going 12–0 and winning a state championship and national championship. I remember thinking, *Hey, this is pretty easy.* It was a lot of fun and I hadn't even tasted defeat as a coach. I thought it was a pretty easy thing to do.

I was going to just stay at Miami Senior High, but Florida called me and wanted me to become a graduate assistant. I thought it was a way to go back to school and kill two birds with one stone. I could go back and get some more coaching experience and continue my education. I had the good fortune to go back as a young assistant at Florida for seven years, and five of those seasons were under Coach Graves. From that point forward, it just seemed that things happened. I was a grad assistant making virtually nothing the first year, but then a coach left and created a vacancy on the staff. I was hired full-time to coach the freshman team. After a few years, I was elevated to the varsity team and then started bouncing around the eastern half of the country coaching football.

Coaching in the NFL was the furthest thing from my mind at the time. My wife and I were married in 1965, and I remember telling her, "You know what you're getting with a guy like me, don't you? You're getting a guy that's probably not ever going to ever make a whole bunch of money." I planned on coaching for a long time and enjoying it. I enjoyed coaching more than I worried about the money that was coming from it. She agreed and used to work a job herself until we had a few children. I thought it would be nice to become an offensive coordinator or a position coach for the rest of my life. I just enjoyed coaching and being around the game. I never thought it would lead to becoming coach of the Green Bay Packers or Indianapolis Colts. In fact, I never even thought I wanted to coach in the NFL.

Playing and coaching at Florida pretty much meant everything to me professionally. Had I not started off there and gotten a good background and worked under some good people, I'm not sure where I would have gone. I was lucky enough to be at a good place at a good time. Without getting a scholarship to Florida, which I'm eternally grateful for, I don't think I would have had the limited success I had during my coaching career. I owe Florida a lot. It kind of catapulted me to bigger things as time went on, and it's something you can't ever repay them for. To this day, you make so many friends, especially in football, because you're part of a unit and part of a team. You're part of an effort, and that's to win and have success. It helps build a lot of character. I owe a great deal to Florida for getting me started.

Lindy Infante, a native of Miami, Florida, started three seasons in Florida's offensive backfield from 1960 to 1962. As a sophomore, Infante helped Ray Graves's first team finish with a 9–2 record in 1960, the best finish by a Gators team to that point. Infante is perhaps best remembered by Florida fans for scoring a touchdown with 33 seconds left in an 18–17 upset of Georgia Tech in Gainesville on October 1, 1960. After graduation, Infante returned to his alma mater as an assistant coach from 1968 to 1971. He later became head coach of the USFL's Jacksonville Bulls and the NFL's Green Bay Packers and Indianapolis Colts. Infante is retired and lives in Crescent Beach, Florida.

ALLEN TRAMMELL

DEFENSIVE BACK

1961–1965

I GREW UP IN EUFAULA, ALABAMA, AND WENT TO FLORIDA via Chattanooga, Tennessee, where I went to Baylor Military School and played football. Coach Ray Graves came and spoke at our football banquet during my senior season at Baylor Military, and our head coach and Coach Graves were good friends at Georgia Tech. My coach recommended to Coach Graves that Florida take me. He thought I could help them, and Coach Graves asked me to come visit. I did and fell in love with the campus, the weather, and the pretty girls. That's where I knew I wanted to go once I visited.

I was going to walk on at Auburn or walk on at Alabama before I visited Florida. I looked at going to Duke because they were interested in me. I don't know if I would have ever made it there academically, to be honest. Really, Auburn is where I thought I was going to go because my family was full of Auburn fans. They still are to this day—I'm the only Gator in the group.

I went to Florida in 1961, and that was back when freshmen couldn't play. Actually, I had a scholarship from Florida, but it was not one that was known because they were down on numbers. Coach Graves was able to get me into school, but to this day no one knows I was on scholarship, so we've always said I was a walk-on. We probably had 100 freshmen come in that year.

We had our freshman schedule with four games against Auburn, Georgia, Florida State, and Miami. It was a fun year because I knew a lot of those guys and had been on recruiting visits with a few of them. I knew a lot of those guys we played against from high school. It was fun to play against those guys as freshmen and get a pulse and a feel for what it was about. It was kind of a fun year, although we did work our tails off in terms of practicing against the varsity. It was kind of hard and demanding, but it was gainful in that we learned a lot.

They put me at tailback and cornerback as a freshman. We just played a three-deep zone defense all the time. I sprained my ankle in the fall of 1962. It was a really bad sprain, and I was out for a couple of weeks. Fortunately, that injury happened to me when I was redshirted, which really allowed me to grow.

During my sophomore season in 1963, we opened against Georgia Tech in Atlanta. It rained like hell. I'll never forget it. We had about three inches of rain during the game. I watched Georgia Tech's quarterback, Billy Lothridge, warm up throwing to Ted Davis and Billy Martin. Those two tight ends were the biggest animals I'd ever seen. I'd never seen anybody that big before. They were both 6'6" or taller and weighed about 250 pounds. I was 5'11" and weighed about 175 pounds. Those were two guys that stood out in college football at the time. When they ran out on the field, I said, "Oh, my God. Goodness, gracious, I've never played against anybody like this before." Actually, we played pretty well but lost the game 9–0. Lothridge played well and really threw the ball well, even in the rain. I sprained my ankle during the game. I stepped in a hole and will never forget it. I had ankle problems throughout college. I sprained my ankle against Georgia Tech and had to miss the next game against Mississippi State [a 9–9 tie].

I came back to play against Richmond, and we won the game 35–28 in the fourth quarter. Quite frankly, I do remember the focus that week wasn't on playing the Spiders. The focus was on playing Alabama in Tuscaloosa the following week. I'll remember that for the rest of my life. We were fortunate to beat Richmond, but once we got rid of them, we were chatting Alabama in the dressing room a week before playing them.

Playing Alabama was big for me because I was an Alabama boy. Just getting a chance to play against Alabama, which won the national championship the year before, and playing against a Bear Bryant–coached team was big. They had a bunch of great athletes and a bunch of guys who were my friends. I wanted to go and play well in Tuscaloosa. It was quite a day. I'll never forget the experience as long as I live. We beat Alabama 10–6, and it was the first time Bear Bryant lost a game in Tuscaloosa. You couldn't help but see Bear Bryant when you ran on the field. He was just such a dominating figure. He stood around the goal posts during warm-ups, smoking a cigarette by himself. You don't see things like that anymore. But he'd lean against that goal post, smoking a cigarette, and it kind of looked like God standing there.

I knew we were going to make history that day. I had a premonition about it. I had dreamed about it. I knew we were ready to play because we didn't speak to each other Friday night when we went to see a movie. We had some very physical outbursts by individuals before the game. One of the guys threw a helmet through the blackboard before the game, and we just about killed each other trying to get out on the field. We were ready to play. It was an incredible emotional experience. It was the most emotional experience I've ever had in my life.

We won at Vanderbilt 21–0 the following week and then lost to LSU 14–0 in our homecoming game in Gainesville. We lost at Auburn 19–0, which was really a big game for me, too. I really wanted to win at Auburn because I had a lot of friends going to school there. Tucker Frederickson and Jimmy Sidle had a little sweep play in that game. They rounded the corner, and I came up and was the only guy there. Tucker lifted his knee about five feet off the turf and hit me in the head. I was out for about five minutes. It's funny how you remember the little things about the games. The combination of Frederickson and Sidle was a great one-two punch for Auburn.

40

We came back and beat Georgia 21–14 in Jacksonville. I had a couple of interceptions in the game. I'll never forget that game. It was the first time I'd ever played Georgia. Knowing how big the rivalry was between the schools, it was a very big game for us. We beat Miami in the Orange Bowl 27–21 and then beat Florida State 7–0 to finish the season. We won our last three games to finish 6–3–1 in 1963. We had a lot of people coming back the following year, so it was good to get momentum.

We went into the 1964 season feeling pretty good and won our first four games. We beat SMU [24–8], Mississippi State [16–13], Ole Miss [30–14], and South Carolina [37–0]. We went back to Alabama and lost to the Crimson Tide 17–14. We were trailing by three points in the fourth quarter, and Steve Spurrier was our quarterback. He'll tell you to this day that he thought the football was at Alabama's 1-yard line, when it was really at the 6. He called a quarterback sneak before the field-goal try because he thought the ball was at the 1. Steve just misread the play, and the ball was at the 6. He did the right thing if the ball had been at the 1. We've talked about that play a lot of times through the years. After he ran the sneak, we had to run on the field because we didn't have any timeouts left. We tried to kick a tying field goal, and I was the holder on the play. To this day, Jimmy Hall, who is a dentist in Pensacola, Florida, tells me I never got the ball down. I always tell him, "No, I got the ball down. You missed the damn thing!" Obviously, over a few more beers that story gets a little more amplified. But he missed the kick wide right, and we lost the game. But I did get the snap down! Bill Carr snapped me the ball, I got it down, and he just missed the kick.

We played Auburn in Gainesville the following week and won the game 14–0. It was Tucker Frederickson's senior year, and we shut him down. We killed him the whole day. We went to Jacksonville ranked ninth in the country to play Georgia. We lost to Georgia 14–7. It was a tough game. I had two rib injuries, one on each side. I got hit at the same time by two guys running a punt back. We didn't wear rib pads during those days, and I was just miserable. It hurt so bad. Georgia kicked our tails that day and got us.

We lost to Florida State 16–7 in Tallahassee, which was the first time FSU had ever beaten us. Gene Ellenson, who was our defensive coordinator and master motivator and real leader, decided he was going to put a patch on our jerseys that said, "Go for seven." We had won six games in a row against FSU. On the back of the jerseys, he put, "Never, FSU, never." Those FSU guys saw that stuff on our jerseys, and you could just see the fire coming out of their noses and eyes. They were so mad. They had a big, emotional game, and Steve Tensi and Fred Biletnikoff had really big games for them. They were great athletes. They wound up beating us in Tallahassee.

We finished the season by beating Miami 12–10 in Gainesville and LSU 20–6 in Baton Rouge. We called that LSU game the "Hurricane Bowl" because that was our bowl game in 1964. We had been scheduled to play LSU in October, as we always do, but a hurricane forced the cancellation of the game, and they moved it to December 5. A big cold front moved through there, and it was about 15 degrees at kickoff. It was cold and the wind was blowing. But we were ready to play. We kind of saw it as our bowl game. LSU was always a big rivalry anyway—anytime you got a chance to play at Tiger Stadium was really special.

During my senior season in 1965, we started the season against North-western and won 24–14. We lost to Mississippi State [18–13]. Mississippi State had a great little running back named Marcus Rhoden, who was from Mac-clenny, Florida, which was right next to Gainesville. He really wanted to go to school at Florida. State's quarterback was Rocky Felton, who was from Montgomery, Alabama, and was a good friend of mine. Mississippi State always had great athletes and always played us really tough. We've always had a big rivalry with Mississippi State, which has been there through the years, but most people really don't know about it. We always got after each other big-time. We'd always win half the games and they'd win half, for whatever reason.

We came back and beat LSU 14–7. LSU was ranked No. 5 in the country at the time, so that was a really big win for us. We beat Ole Miss the follow-ing week 17–0. I ran a punt back for a touchdown and had an interception in that game. We beat NC State 28–6 in our homecoming game. We went back to Auburn and lost 28–17. We beat Georgia 14–10 in Jacksonville. That was huge. It was really big.

As seniors, we beat Georgia and had won two out of three games against them during my career. That was a great way to leave Florida. We beat Tulane 51–13 and lost to Miami 16–13 in the Orange Bowl. Miami always had great teams, and they were big and fast. Quite frankly, I could never get fired up about Miami. Some guys from South Florida were always fired up about playing them, but I never could. I'd get fired up about playing Florida State, but I didn't get all fired up about Miami.

We played Florida State in Gainesville and were down 17–16 late in the game. Steve drove us down the field and hit Charlie Casey in the end zone for a touchdown with 1:12 to go. We went ahead 23–17. On the next series, we deflected a pass. I ripped it out of T.K. Wetherell's hands and ran it back for a touchdown. We won the game 30–17. It was a great way to go out. It was our senior year and our last game at Florida Field. Having lost to Florida State the year before, it was really a way to go out.

At the end of the 1965 season, we played Missouri in the Sugar Bowl and lost 20–18. It was my first bowl game, so it was a neat experience. Steve Spurrier was named MVP of the bowl game, which was the first time a player from the losing team won the award. Steve played extremely well in that game, but I don't think we were ready to play. I think we had a little too much going on in New Orleans before the game. Missouri had some darn good athletes and they were a good Big 8 Conference team. They were big and strong. They had a great running back named Charlie Brown.

I played baseball during my junior and senior seasons and really enjoyed it. I didn't have a major league arm as an outfielder. Had I been an infielder, I might have had a chance to play in the majors. I wish that would have been the case, and I might not be limping around like I am today. My orthopedist told me I played football two years too many. I went to the Houston Oilers in 1966 and 1967 and got hurt my second year. I tore my ankle up, and that's what has bothered me to this day.

After two years in the pros, I decided to get involved in coaching at Florida. I started there in the late 1960s, and I coached under Ray Graves and then Doug Dickey. I was there for eight years and left before the coaching staff was fired. It was good timing, I guess. I just decided I didn't want to coach anymore. I had a young son and never saw him, so I decided it was time to move on to something else. I've been in the insurance business ever since.

I made a lot of friends at Florida. Coach Graves was just a loyal man and was really a father to all of us. I'll pick up the phone once every two weeks and have a 15-minute conversation with him. He talks like he's 50. He's 90 years old and still sharp as a tack. He's just a wonderful, wonderful friend to this day. We'll get to talking about old times, and he'll remember stuff that I don't remember. It's incredible how sharp he still is today. We get together once a year during our Silver Sixties reunions and we all go and have a great time seeing each other and seeing each other's kids grow up. None of us would miss it for anything. It's been a real family affair for all of us.

Allen Trammell, a native of Eufaula, Alabama, was a starting defensive back for the Gators from 1963 to 1965. Trammell was named second-team All-SEC by the Associated Press after leading the Gators in punt returns and interceptions as a junior in 1964. As a senior in 1965, Trammell helped lead the Gators to a 7–4 record and an appearance in the Sugar Bowl. Trammell is perhaps best remembered by Gators fans for intercepting a pass and returning it for a touchdown in the final seconds of a 30–17 win over rival Florida State on November 27, 1965. Trammell also played two seasons on Florida's baseball team, hitting an SEC-high .425 in 1965, the highest batting average by a Gators outfielder. After graduation, Trammell played two seasons for the AFL's Houston Oilers. Injuries cut short his professional playing career, and then he returned to Florida as an assistant football coach from 1972 to 1977. Trammell owns an insurance firm and lives in Orlando.

BILL CARR

CENTER

1963–1966

My father is a native Gainesvillian, and we consider Gainesville our family home. I was born in Gainesville, but I never attended school there until I went to the University of Florida. My dad was a minister, and we moved around. We lived in Fort Worth, Texas; Vero Beach; and Pensacola. Every summer we'd come back to Gainesville to see family.

I got into sports the usual ways, through youth leagues. I started playing football in seventh grade on the junior varsity. This was back when the earth was still cooling. When I think back to how long ago it was that I played it seems like I made it up. I played a lot of baseball, which was my favorite sport, and it kind of evolved into football. I always played center. I kind of selected myself for the job. We had a coach who was running our rear ends off in seventh grade, and he asked if anyone knew how to snap the ball. I stuck my hand up. I didn't want to do all of that running. Some people are made to run and others aren't. My body wasn't made for running.

I was fortunate in high school to have Jimmy Haynes as my coach at Pensacola High. He would later be a coach at Florida. And he brought Bob Wehking in to coach the line. Bob had been the center at Florida and came right out of college to coach us. I really benefited from my coaching in high school. Bob really passed on a lot of knowledge to me. I had a tremendous advantage to have someone who knew so much.

Once the recruiting got going—and it certainly wasn't a big deal then—I knew I wanted to go to Florida. I only took one other visit and that was to Vanderbilt. My dad was a Florida grad and a Gainesville High grad. He told me, "You don't have to go to Florida, but if you want a place to stay in the summer…"and he'd grin and just let his voice trail off. Really, though, to get an offer from Florida was a dream come true.

They actually signed three from my school—Don Knapp and Larry Sammons also signed. It was a special class that included Steve Spurrier, Graham McKeel, Jim Benson. We couldn't play as freshmen and we didn't scrimmage the varsity, so we had our own group. It was insulation mentally and physically, and I think it was conducive to further development. I made a list when I was at Graham McKeel's funeral and came up with the names of 27 freshmen but I think there were 30. And that was a small class back then. We played our freshmen team games, and I can still remember George Grandy, who was a running back, being taken off the field against Miami shaking his fist trying to get us going.

That was in 1963 and the next year I was fortunate enough to be there at the right time. The center had graduated, so I stepped in as the starter. The first game was against SMU, and this was during the transition year between one-platoon and two-platoon football. You could only substitute two players at a time, so I had to be in on all of the punts. I covered 13 punts in that game and I ran myself ragged. We played two quarterbacks in 1964, kind of the way Chris Leak and Tim Tebow did in 2006, with Tommy Shannon and Steve. Shannon was very competitive but wanted what was best for the team. Both of them did, and there was never any problems. Over time, Steve emerged.

We had a nice season, and in 1965 we lost some games we should have won. We went 7–3 and ended up in the Sugar Bowl. For that game against Missouri, we went to an unbalanced line and changed our blocking assignments. We finally adjusted late in the game and rallied from 20–0 down. But the coaches decided to go for two each time, and we lost 20–18. I just came across a picture of that team taken in the Blue Room of the Roosevelt Hotel.

The next year was special because we kept reeling off wins. Then we got to the Auburn game, and it was crazy. I remember I was blocking Gusty Yearout, who was their nose tackle, and all of a sudden he left me. He had seen the ball pop up in the air. He went and grabbed it and ran the length of the field for a touchdown. It was 27–27, and Steve led us down the field. He told Coach Ray Graves that he had to do it, and he had that square-toed shoe.

Bill Carr became Florida's starting center in 1964 and became a mainstay on the offensive line. As a senior, Carr was named first-team All-American and was cocaptain of the 1966 team that finished 9–2 and beat Georgia Tech 27–12 in the Orange Bowl.

He put it on, and I snapped it to Larry Rentz, and he kicked it to win 30–27. I said right then and there, "He just won the Heisman." The hype was not what it is now, but there was the reality that we hoped he would win it.

The next week was a disappointing loss to Georgia [by a 27–10 score], when we didn't adjust tactically. I felt like we were running uphill all day. We were running into the teeth of their defense. A defense has to give you something, but we never could find the sweet spot that day. It was still a great senior season capped with the [27–12] win in the Orange Bowl over Georgia Tech.

I was named All-American, which was an honor I never felt like I deserved. Steve won the Heisman, that's why I got it. Reporters didn't have the access electronically to be accountable. It was more mythical. I was smart enough to snap it to a guy who knew what to do with it. And during my career, I played next to five different guards who were named All-SEC. I was in some good company. I was a smart player and I played a very cerebral game with a lot of technique and some degree of quickness. At the end of the day, it doesn't matter whether you knock your guy down, only that the running back can get through the hole.

To play at Florida was a tremendous fulfillment for me. It meant a lot to my family. I had five sets of aunts and uncles living in Gainesville, so if I needed a home-cooked meal I'd go to Aunt Kate's and bring some teammates. I had a network of support that made my time at Florida special. And it meant so much to my dad for me to play for the Gators. That sweetened it for me. If I had a checklist of 10 things, they were all checked in bold. And then to have a chance to see my son out there as a walk-on is something I really cherish. The whole Gator experience has meant a lot to me.

48

Bill Carr was born in Gainesville, but moved around quite a bit as the son of a preacher. After settling in Pensacola, Florida, Carr became a standout football player and accepted a scholarship to play for the Gators. He became Florida's starting center in 1964 and became a mainstay on the offensive line. He helped lead the Gators to a 7–4 record and appearance in the Sugar Bowl as a junior in 1965. As a senior, Carr was named first-team All-American and helped quarterback Steve Spurrier win the Heisman Trophy. Carr was cocaptain of the 1966 team that finished 9–2 and beat Georgia Tech 27–12 in the Orange Bowl. After graduation, Carr was drafted by the expansion New Orleans Saints and spent a year on the taxi squad before enrolling in the Army. He returned to Saints training camp in 1970 before going back to his alma mater as a graduate assistant under Doug Dickey. Carr coached for four years and then turned his attention to the administrative side of things, working his way up the ladder to become Florida's athletics director in early 1979. He remained at the job for more than seven years and now has a business called Carr Sports Associates Inc., which works with colleges and conferences seeking to make hires. He still lives in Gainesville.

LARRY SMITH

RUNNING BACK

1965–1968

I GREW UP IN TAMPA, FLORIDA, AND ATTENDED Robinson High School. I was recruited by a lot of schools, just about most of the Southeastern Conference schools and some schools up in the Northeast. I visited Duke, Auburn, and Vanderbilt, but my father was a University of Florida graduate and I'd been going to Florida football games since I was a small kid. I'm not sure there was ever any thought of going someplace else.

There were a lot of Gators fans in Tampa, and I was one of them. Everybody would go to high school games on Friday nights, which were always the biggest games in town, and then to Gainesville to see the Gators play on Saturday. Sometimes we'd come home and go to Tampa University games on Saturday nights.

I went to Gainesville in 1965 and didn't play as a freshman. Freshmen weren't allowed to play on the varsity team, and we had our freshman team and played about four games that first season. We had a really good recruiting class with Guy Dennis, Jim Yarbrough, and Larry Rentz. We played four games and were essentially the scout team for the varsity. The practices weren't too bad. Some schools were still bringing in 100 freshmen, but our recruiting class only had 35 freshmen and was supplemented with maybe five or six walk-ons. I was playing running back on the freshman team. We didn't have enough backs as freshmen, so we played all positions during the freshman games. Sometimes, we played both ways in the games.

I moved into the starting backfield on the varsity squad as a sophomore in 1966. Steve Spurrier was our quarterback, obviously, and he won the Heisman Trophy. It was a lot of fun playing with him. He was a great player, and I thought he deserved to win the Heisman Trophy. He had a great season and was somebody who really loved to play football. Obviously, he had a lot of confidence.

We had a good chance to win the Southeastern Conference title during my sophomore season in 1966, but we lost to Georgia 27–10 in Jacksonville near the end of the season. It was pretty disappointing, but Georgia was just better than us that day. We came back and beat Tulane [31–10] and lost to Miami [21–16] in Gainesville.

We played Georgia Tech in the Orange Bowl at the end of the 1966 season. I made a long run in that game, a 94-yard touchdown that put us ahead 14–6. I really don't remember much about the run. It was kind of a fluke run, to be honest. Georgia Tech got in a short-yardage defense and everybody blocked their guy. I just popped through the line and took off running. It was just one of those fortuitous things, really. I was wearing these plastic hip pads that were riding up on me, so it looked like my pants were falling down. At least that's what it probably looked like on television. Bobby Downs intercepted a pass late in the game to help us win 27–12. Bobby was a really good cornerback.

We opened the 1967 season and won four of our first five games [Florida beat Illinois 14–0 and Mississippi State 24–7 before losing to LSU 37–6 in Gainesville. The Gators then beat Tulane 35–0 in New Orleans and Vanderbilt 27–22 in the Homecoming game in Gainesville. After losing to Auburn 26–21 on the road, Florida had a 4–2 record going into the annual contest against Georgia in Jacksonville]. We beat Georgia 17–16, and I think Richard Trapp made one of the finest catches and runs I've ever seen. We were down 17–6, and Trapp scored a touchdown to get us back in that ball game. That was a big win because Georgia was always the biggest rivalry that we had. There was always a lot of emotion involved in that game. [After beating Kentucky 28–12 the following week, the Gators lost to Florida State 21–16 and Miami 20–13 to finish the 1967 season with a 6–4 record.]

My senior season in 1968 was a very frustrating year. We won our first four games, but I popped my hamstring before the first game and never really felt healthy. In the Vanderbilt game [a 14–14 tie to drop Florida's record to 4–1–1], I sprained the arch in my foot. It was just one of those years where

In 1968 Larry Smith became only the fifth offensive back in SEC history to earn All-SEC honors three straight seasons. He left Florida in 1968 as the school's all-time leading rusher with 2,186 yards. He also set Florida records with 520 career carries, 26 touchdowns, and 156 points scored.

I never felt healthy. [After tying the Commodores, Florida lost to Auburn 24–13 and Georgia 51–0 in Jacksonville. The Gators rebounded to beat Kentucky 16–14 to move to 5–3–1 heading into the finale against Miami at Florida Field.]

Miami had a very good defense with Ted Hendricks playing on the end. We hadn't beaten Miami in my first three seasons, and it was my last game at Florida. All of the seniors had a lot of emotion going into that game. We fell behind 10–0, and our offense didn't do much in the first half. We scored in the third quarter [Charlie Walker scored on a one-yard run to make it 10–7], and our defense kept us in the game with a couple of stops. Late in the game, we drove to the 6-yard line, and I took a handoff and ran off tackle. There was great blocking, and I made it to the corner of the end zone for a touchdown. We won the game 14–10, and it was a great feeling. It just meant a lot to win the last game of my college career.

Coach Ray Graves was always a gentleman and he really cared about his players. I'm still very close to Guy Dennis, Jim Yarbrough, Eddie Foster, and a lot of the guys from the freshman team. The Silver Sixties group that played for Coach Graves gets together every summer with our families and has a nice reunion. You have people that you know a lifetime, and to maintain those relationships and contacts is really rewarding. Coach Graves is there every summer and he's still a gentleman and a great guy. I just think his honesty and integrity is something that you never forget. He was a man of his word.

I just really enjoyed my time playing at Florida. I think the biggest thrill anybody can have as a football player is when they come out of that tunnel onto the field and hear that crowd roar. That is chilling.

Larry Smith, a native of Tampa, Florida, was the Gators' starting fullback from 1966 to 1968. In 1968 Smith became only the fifth offensive back in SEC history to earn All-SEC honors three straight seasons. He left Florida in 1968 as the school's all-time leading rusher with 2,186 yards. He also set Florida records with 520 career carries, 26 touchdowns, and 156 points scored. As a sophomore, Smith set an Orange Bowl record by running for a 94-yard touchdown in Florida's 27–12 victory over Georgia Tech on January 1, 1967. After graduation, Smith was a first-round selection of the NFL's Los Angeles Rams. Smith played five seasons for the Rams before he was traded to the Washington Redskins. He broke his hand, foot, and leg during his one season with the Redskins and retired from pro football. At the age of 34, Smith graduated from Stetson University law school and still practices real estate law in his hometown of Tampa.

GUY DENNIS
GUARD
1965–1968

THE LITTLE TOWN I GREW UP IN WAS DAVISVILLE, which is in Florida, but is so close to the Alabama line we used to get our mail delivered from Atmore, Alabama. In fact, when Florida was recruiting me, they were concerned they'd have to pay out-of-state tuition. They had some second thoughts because of that until we worked it out.

As a kid, I used to hop on my bike and ride four miles to Atmore after school to play Little League baseball. Then I'd ride home and not get back until after dark. But back then, you never gave it another thought. It's just the way it was. I started playing baseball at 12 and went to elementary school in Davisville, where the school was within walking distance. But in seventh grade, I had to take a bus to Walnut Hill and went to Ernest Ward High.

I was a big kid, and the first day I was in the school a coach came up to me and told me to report to the gym after school and he'd give me a ride home. That's how my football career started. Because I was so big, I not only played junior varsity football, but a little on the varsity as well. I didn't know it was illegal to be playing two games a week. We barely had enough players to practice. There were only 22 kids on the varsity. I was just a kid who grew fast and by my senior year I was as big as I was at Florida.

I played defensive line and fullback until my junior year of high school, when they moved me to offensive tackle. There was an attorney in Pensacola named Herbert Latham, who heard about me and came to see me play. He

Guy Dennis helped lead Florida to a 9–2 record as a sophomore in 1966, beating Georgia Tech 27–12 in the Orange Bowl. As a senior in 1968, Dennis was named team captain and All-American. He played in the 1969 North-South all-star game and was selected in the fifth round of the AFL-NFL Draft by the Cincinnati Bengals.

got a writer from the *Pensacola News Journal* to come watch me, and they got the idea for a picture. So they took two of the smallest guys on the team and had me hold them by the shoulder pads. They jumped at the same time, and it looked like I was holding them up. That picture made the wires, and that's when a bunch of schools started recruiting me.

We had pretty good teams at Ernest Ward High. We won the Escambia River Conference during my sophomore and junior years and lost to our rival, Century High School, in the championship game my senior year. All three Mississippi schools were recruiting me, along with Florida State, Auburn, and Florida. Vanderbilt went after me really hard because I had a good grade-point average and ACT score. They were very aggressive—either that or their recruiter liked my mom's cooking.

Being from such a small town and being raised in that environment, I was very respectful of the people who were recruiting me. They were all very impressive, but Fred Pancoast, who was an assistant at Florida, was the most impressive. I visited Florida and saw Florida Field with the hedges and I just fell in love with it.

My high school coach, Jim Latham, was the biggest reason for my success. He told me very early that there would be more talented players, but that I could always work harder than them. The more talented guys might think they didn't have to work hard, but I worked hard at it. I had limited speed—the old joke applied that you had to line me up next to a light pole to see if I was moving—but I worked hard. I got a chance to play at Florida Field the summer before my freshman year in the North-South all-star game, and I'll tell you, I was so nervous I put my thigh pads in the wrong way.

At Florida, they moved me to guard because Jim Benson was graduating and they needed someone to step into his place, so I was very fortunate there. We played four games as freshmen—they called us the "Baby Gators"—but being at Florida was quite a shock. To come from a school with 48 in my class and go to lecture class with 200 or 400 people was a big change.

55

As a sophomore, I had the pleasure of blocking for Steve Spurrier. He was an amazing player. He'd call his own plays, and they would usually work. Of course, he won the Heisman Trophy in 1966, but we lost to Georgia to keep us from winning the SEC. We beat Georgia Tech 27–12 in the Orange Bowl, and Larry Smith had a 94-yard touchdown run right between Bill Carr, who was our center, and myself.

The next two years, we had some bad luck with injuries, but we had really good teams. It's funny because you tend to remember the bad games more than the good ones. The one I remember was my senior year, when Ray Graves switched the offensive and defensive coordinators and we lost to Georgia 51–0 in 1968. It was miserable being on the field that day.

Coach Graves was an amazing person to play for because he cared more about you getting your education and getting ready for life after football more than anything else. He wanted to win, sure, but he really cared about his players.

In my senior year in 1968, I was named All-American and I felt very humbled by that. I felt undeserving but I was very appreciative. For a guy from such a small town to receive such a great honor was amazing. Just to play with so many guys with so much talent was a humbling atmosphere for me. We finished on a high note during my senior season in 1968, beating Miami 14–10, with Larry running for the winning touchdown—that was a good way to go out.

Being at Florida was such a wonderful experience. Being a Gator is just phenomenal. Probably the thing I cherish the most is all of the friendships I made and continue to enjoy at the Silver Sixties reunions. I appreciate what Urban Meyer has done bringing back the players for a reunion every year.

The things I learned at Florida really allowed me to have a long career in the NFL. Ed Kensler was my line coach, and we passed more than most college teams. So I learned how to pass block really well, and when I went to the NFL, those bigger and stronger guys from Nebraska had to learn how to do it.

The bottom line is that I got more out of the University of Florida than I could ever give back. And when I was finished in the NFL, I moved back to Gainesville because I love the place. I love the whole college atmosphere. I really cherish everything about the University of Florida and Gainesville. It was and is very special to be a Gator.

Guy Dennis, a native of Davisville, Florida, was a starting guard at Florida from 1966 to 1968. As a sophomore, he helped block for Gators quarterback Steve Spurrier, who won the Heisman Trophy. Dennis helped lead Florida to a 9–2 record as a sophomore in 1966, beating Georgia Tech 27–12 in the Orange Bowl. As a senior in 1968, Dennis was named team captain and All-American. He played in the 1969 North-South all-star game and was selected in the fifth round of the AFL-NFL Draft by the Cincinnati Bengals. He moved right into Cincinnati's starting lineup. He stayed there for four years and played three more seasons for the Detroit Lions, starting at both guard and center. After being traded to the San Diego Chargers, Dennis retired to Gainesville to become a coach. "Then I found out what teachers were making," Dennis said. He found a job with a company that sold paper products before starting his own company—Hillman Supplies—out of his garage. He still owns the company, located in nearby Alachua, Florida.

TOM ABDELNOUR

LINEBACKER

1966–1969

I WAS A MIAMI BOY AND HAD A LITTLE BIT of an unusual recruiting process. I was originally recruited by Georgia Tech after my senior season at Miami Senior High School, and they told me to go to prep school. I went to Gordon Military Academy in Barnesville, Georgia, for one semester, then Georgia Tech reneged on its scholarship offer to me. The only school I could afford to go to was Florida, so I went there and tried out for the football team in the spring of 1966. I got a scholarship from Florida after trying out.

I was only 5′8″ and was pretty small, relatively speaking. I guess a lot of schools thought I was too small to play football. I tried out with all the other walk-ons at Florida. At first, I thought the Florida coaches were a little hesitant to give me a chance to try out for football, but I played in the North-South high school all-star game in Gainesville that summer, and I had to use that clip just to convince them to give me a uniform to try out for the team. It was a little tenuous at first, but fortunately it worked itself out.

After that 1965 high school all-star game, we all went out drinking in Gainesville. A guy named Bill Trout from Key West, Florida, and myself were in the car going back to the dorms. We were doing everything we weren't supposed to be doing and saw this alligator in the street. I got out of the car and put my belt around the alligator's neck to catch him. We put the alligator in the trunk of my car and drove back to the dorm where we were staying. Bill went into the trunk and pulled out the alligator. We walked into the dorm, and this kid was in the shower and had the shower curtain pulled. Bill threw the alligator into the shower and immediately the kid comes running out of the shower screaming and yelling. We scared the living crap out of him! A few minutes later, a cop showed up and said, "Whose alligator is this?" Bill picked it up and said, "I don't want it anymore." The cop made us take the alligator down to a lake and release him. The kid in the shower was Mac Steen, and he and I ended up becoming cocaptains together at Florida. Mac still hasn't gotten me back yet, but I'm sure he will. We're still good friends.

I was on the freshman team at Florida in 1966 and was a second-string linebacker. I was not eligible to play on the varsity team because I had been enrolled in college for only one semester. They required you to attend school for two semesters before you could play on the varsity squad, so I ended up going back to the freshman team. Steve Spurrier won the Heisman Trophy in 1966, and I watched most of that season from the sideline.

As a sophomore in 1967, my first game at Florida was against Illinois [a 14–0 victory at Florida Field]. Illinois got down to the goal line, and Coach Gene Ellenson called a blitz. For some reason, the Illinois kid never even touched me to tackle me. I drilled the guy for a big loss right at the goal line. That was a triumphant moment for me, for sure. For an 18-year-old kid, it was pretty remarkable. I never even thought I'd make it that far with having to try out and all that stuff. It was just a remarkable experience for me. I have nothing but the greatest memories from my experience at Florida. For a kid from Miami, to be able to do that after not being recruited, it was amazing.

We beat Georgia 17–16 in Jacksonville in 1967. They lined up to kick the football, and Paul Maliska ran in to try and block the extra point. He got hit and knocked up into the air, and his foot actually hit the football and saved the game. Richard Trapp had the run of the century in that game and dodged a ton of guys.

We lost to Florida State 21–16 in Gainesville that season, but it was a memorable experience for me. I blitzed and somehow nobody touched me. A guy touched me in the backfield, but I pushed him off me and grabbed Kim Hammond, the Florida State quarterback. I went with both my left arm and right arm. I grabbed his face mask by accident with my right arm.

At the same time, I grabbed the back of his shoulder pads right below his helmet with my left arm. I realized I had my hand on his face mask and immediately pulled it off. I pulled Hammond down and knocked him out. Everybody thought I was being a dirty player, but it was a clean hit that looked bad. I must have gotten 20 letters from people telling me I was the dirtiest player in the league and all that stuff. It always happens that way. There are plays like that in every game, where a guy makes a hard, clean hit. What are you going to do?

Gene Ellenson gave me the nickname the "Sheik." He tried a couple of different nicknames and none of them stuck and then he just landed on Sheik. Ellenson was very good to me. He was almost like a father to me. That name has stuck with me today. Those guys still call me Sheik. If you go up to those guys I played with, very few of them will call me Tommy. They always call me the Sheik.

We tried to put a lot of pressure on the quarterbacks then, and Ellenson was a very intelligent coach. I think people forget there were a lot of sophisticated pass patterns that were going on back in those days, so you had to put pressure on the quarterbacks. We had cornerbacks like Steve Tannen, who could play receivers one-on-one. We could do what we wanted to do to put pressure on the quarterback. Steve didn't need much help from the safety and could play man-to-man, which was a huge help to us. People don't realize the help you get from other players.

59

Gene Ellenson was a remarkable guy and he always wanted us to blitz. There was one game I recall where he was blitzing me, blitzing me, and blitzing me. I was going against this guy who was huge, and he was just drilling me every time. He was knocking the living crap out of me. We'd almost get to the quarterback, almost get to the quarterback, and almost get to the quarterback. But we're not getting there! Gene wouldn't give it up, and he sent in the signal for one more blitz. He sent the play from the sideline, and I shook my head to say no. Immediately, Gene sent in a replacement for me and pulled me off the field. He grabbed me by the jersey and said, "Sheik, I'm not the pitcher and you're not the catcher. Don't you ever call my signs off again!" He scared the living crap out of me. I'll never forget that.

Coach Graves was such a gentleman. He was a great coach, don't get me wrong. But just the manner in which he always held himself was remarkable. He was a coach and he'd get mad, but he never would go over the edge. He knew how to handle the pressure and made changes if he had to. I remember one game against Tulane, he got mad at Jack Youngblood and thought he was dogging it. He benched him the next game. How many people would bench Jack Youngblood? Coach Graves did because he knew what to do and how to motivate players. He could be as benevolent as possible. He was always really sweet to me, and we got along. We always knew where he stood and where we stood with him.

We moved to Michigan in 1974. I remember one of the first Michigan games I saw. Bo Schembechler went over the edge with some of the calls. Sometimes his players would have to grab him to keep him from running onto the field. We never saw anything like that from Coach Graves. Ray Graves knew how to handle himself. He was never like Woody Hayes. That's what I remember about Ray Graves—he always held himself as a gentleman and was a great coach.

I was named cocaptain of the 1969 team, which finished 9–1–1. I still look at the media guide from that season, and the difference between our junior year and senior year was remarkable. We threw two touchdown passes during my junior year in 1968. The next year, John Reaves threw 24 touchdown passes. The team always had the right energy to make a comeback. Gene Ellenson, my defensive coordinator, was a brilliant guy. Ellenson coached Steve Tannen, who returned a number of punts for touchdowns. In the Gator Bowl, it was Gene Ellenson's idea to block a Tennessee punt, which helped us win the game 14–13. Ellenson was the coach who came to us and said, "We can block a punt. I'm positive about it and this is how we're going to do it." It's the type of thing where the coaches put together the right kind of kids and mold them into a team. It was just a remarkable year.

For a kid like me, whose mother was an immigrant and whose father never went past the eighth grade, I just remember vividly that I thought I was on the top of the world playing at Florida. I was playing football, which I loved to do, and was getting an engineering degree. I just couldn't have been happier, and it couldn't have worked out better for me. My original goal was to play Division I football, and I didn't want to go to a small school. I knew there was a risk in going to Florida, but every kid has his dream. I got the chance to live that dream. All those guys I played with were real sweethearts and made me feel so welcome. We had 40 recruits on our freshman team, and just the fact I have all these friends is great. We all received a Florida education and were able to play football at Florida Field. It can't get better than that. It was just absolutely wonderful.

Tom Abdelnour, a native of Miami, was a lightly recruited player after a four-year career at Miami Senior High School. He was originally recruited to Georgia Tech, but after spending one season at Gordon Military Academy in Barnesville, Georgia, the Yellow Jackets reneged on their scholarship offer. So Abdelnour walked-on Florida's football team in 1966 and was awarded a scholarship. A 5'8" linebacker, Abdelnour earned the moniker "Sheik" from his coaches and teammates. As a cocaptain in 1969, Abdelnour helped guide the Gators to a 9–1–1 record. Florida beat Tennessee 14–13 in the 1969 Gator Bowl. Abdelnour lives in Ann Arbor, Michigan, and is a construction project manager for the University of Michigan.

The
SEVENTIES

CARLOS ALVAREZ

FLANKER

1968–1971

GROWING UP IN HAVANA, CUBA, WAS DIFFERENT. I lived there until I was 10 years old, playing a lot of baseball. I really didn't know about football until we moved to North Miami. My dad knew Fidel Castro well enough to know that when he took over, we had to leave. My mother didn't want to leave, but she finally was convinced.

So we took a ferry to Key West, Florida. We had our car on the ferry, and it was loaded up with everything we could cram into it. Our pockets were stuffed with silverware and things. We made it by about a month before Castro closed the door.

It was definitely a shock because none of us spoke English and nobody in North Miami spoke Spanish. It took me about a month, but I learned to speak English. I really only started playing football because all of the kids at the Boys Club who played baseball and basketball went out for football. I was fast but I didn't play wide receiver. I was a tailback in high school and, after my junior season, I committed to play football at Vanderbilt. I couldn't believe they were offering me a full scholarship.

In my senior year, a bunch of other schools started offering me scholarships. Florida started recruiting me with assistant coach Lindy Infante, who was from Miami as well. Both of my brothers were at Florida, and we all went up there on a visit and it seemed like the perfect match. Miami was after me, too, but in head coach Charlie Tate's office there was a stuffed alligator

Carlos Alvarez was a record-setting flanker at Florida from 1968 to 1971. After the 2007 season, Alvarez still held Florida records for career receiving yards (2,563) and single-game records for receiving yards (238 against Miami in 1969) and catches (15 against Miami in 1969).

hanging on his wall. That bothered me enough that I knew I was meant to be a Gator.

Florida's coaches recruited me as a defensive back and a running back, but I knew pretty early that running back was not for me. Larry Smith was in his senior season and, even with all of the injuries he had to deal with, he was a monster. He outweighed me by 25 pounds. Now, I was in good shape. I had worked hard in the off-season because I didn't want to look back at some point and say I should have been better prepared.

The coaches moved me to receiver, and we had a fun freshman season in 1968 before freshmen were eligible. We played a few games, won all but one of them, and when we scrimmaged against the varsity we did pretty well. A lot of the 1968 team's skill players graduated so it was going to be me and [quarterback] John Reaves hooking up in 1969. We didn't waste any time. During summer practices, we would put up incredible numbers against the freshmen and B-team players. We beat them 93–0 in our last scrimmage.

So we were ready to go against Houston in the 1969 season opener. The plan at the beginning of the game was to run the ball twice and then go deep. It couldn't have worked any better. My first college catch was a 70-yard touchdown pass [in a 59–34 victory over the Cougars]. And we were off, rolling through teams and putting up big offensive numbers. We had a blip against Auburn [a 38–12 loss] when they threw a defense at us we hadn't seen and a [13–13] tie against Georgia. But that was it.

My favorite game came when we went back to Miami. I had so many friends and family in the crowd—I got to spend time with them before the game—and went out and caught 15 passes in the game. My brother Arthur came down the field after the game, which we won 35–16, and that really made it special.

We still had a bowl game to play after the 1969, season and there were rumors swirling that Ray Graves was out as our coach and Doug Dickey would be the new coach. Dickey was Tennessee's coach, and we were playing the Vols in the Gator Bowl. It was a very confusing time. Our coach, whom we loved like a father, was being pushed out after a great season built around a bunch of sophomores. We won the bowl game [by a 14–13 score], and I caught the winning touchdown pass against the Vols.

Then the changes started. Dickey was in as our new coach. A lot of us had resentment—not aimed at Doug Dickey the man—but we felt betrayed by the school. At one point, I tried to organize an athlete's union because I felt we had no rights as players. But I had bigger problems. During the summer of 1970, I worked hard on the track trying to get faster. But I overdid it. I developed arthritis in my knees and was never the same player. We also had lost a great group of seniors after the 1969 season. And we were switching to a different offense.

I went from 88 catches as a sophomore to 44 as a junior, and we finished with a 7–4 record in 1970. We won five of our first six games, but then lost badly at Tennessee [38–7] and against Auburn at home [63–14]. We came back and beat Georgia [24–17] in Jacksonville and beat Kentucky [24–13] in Tampa. We closed the season by losing to Miami 14–13 in Gainesville.

It didn't get any better my senior year in 1971. A lot of guys weren't thrilled with the offense. They had John Reaves, who was a drop-back passer, running the veer. I only caught two touchdown passes as a senior, and we went 4–7, losing our first five games. It was miserable. We won four of our last six games, but lost at Auburn [40–7] and Georgia [49–7] in Jacksonville.

But there was one bright spot during that senior season. In our last game of the season, again down in Miami, John had a shot at the all-time passing record for a career. We went after it. He kept throwing to me, and I was finding ways to get open. He was closing in on the mark late in the game, and we were going to get the ball back. But Harvin Clark ran back a punt for a touchdown. Miami took over and tried to run out the clock and keep him from getting the record. That's when we pulled off the famous "Florida Flop," where all of the defenders [except safety John Clifford] fell to the ground and let Miami score.

We got the football back, and John hit me with a pass to break the record. After all we had been through, we celebrated wildly as if we had just won something important. We even went to the pool in the Orange Bowl that housed Flipper and jumped in, splashing around like crazy.

Even though there were some difficult times for me at Florida, I still get back as much as possible because being a Gator has simply meant great joy for me throughout the years. When I was at Florida, it was pure ecstasy when I ran on to Florida Field to the cry of "Heeeeeeeeeeere come the Gators!" and tens of thousands of fans shaking the stadium. It is adrenaline on steroids.

Since that time, it has meant wonderful friendships with teammates, coaches, and fans that have lasted the test of time. It has opened many doors that would have been much harder to open if I was not a Gator. And it has meant a continuous flow of memories, some old, some new, of Gator games, Gator friends, and the University of Florida that have enriched my life and my family's life immensely. The true test of it all is that I when I look back on all of it, I would not change a thing, except to have more of all those experiences and to have beaten Auburn in 1969.

Carlos Alvarez, a native Cuban who grew up in Miami, was a record-setting flanker at Florida from 1968 to 1971. In his first season on Florida's varsity football team in 1969, Alvarez was named a consensus All-American following a record-breaking season, in which he caught 88 passes for 1,329 yards and 12 touchdowns. His extraordinary athletic skills earned him the moniker "Cuban Comet" from fans and teammates alike. After the 2007 season, Alvarez still held Florida records for career receiving yards (2,563) and single-game records for receiving yards (238 against Miami in 1969) and catches (15 against Miami in 1969). He ranks second in career receptions with 172, a mark that was broken by Andre Caldwell during the 2007 season. A three-time academic All-American and member of the GTE Academic All-American Hall of Fame, Alvarez was awarded an NCAA postgraduate scholarship after graduating from Florida in 1971. He was drafted by the Dallas Cowboys after his senior season, but opted to attend law school at Duke University and graduated summa cum laude in 1975. He taught law for several years before beginning a law practice in Tallahassee.

JOHN REAVES

QUARTERBACK

1968–1971

ATTENDED ROBINSON HIGH SCHOOL IN TAMPA after I moved to Florida from Alabama. Larry Smith, a star running back at Florida during the 1960s, grew up on the street next to me and was four years older than me. He was like one of my boyhood idols. I grew up reading Tom McEwen's columns about the Gators and Steve Spurrier in the *Tampa Tribune* and became a Florida fan. I always wanted to go to school there. I was recruited by several schools in high school. Florida State, Tennessee, and Georgia Tech were the main schools that recruited me hard. Some other schools didn't even try because they knew I was going to go to Florida.

I was a freshman at Florida in 1968 and wasn't eligible to play on the varsity team. We had a freshman team that played four games against Auburn, Georgia, Florida State, and Miami. We had a lot of good skill people in our freshman class, but not that many great linemen, which ended up hurting us later on. We had a lot of brilliant skill players, like Carlos Alvarez, Tommy Durrance, and Mike Rich. Mike Rich was a tailback, but they moved him to fullback because his legs were like trunks. The first time I saw him I was like, "Gosh." He looked like Li'l Abner or something, and he could fly. They moved him to fullback, but he could have been a great tailback. During a Kentucky game one year, we were in a goal-line play, and I handed him the ball and he leaped over both lines. He had a great vertical leap and unusual spring and legs.

I knew Carlos Alvarez was going to be a great player because we played in a high school all-star game together. I threw the winning touchdown to him in that game, although he was playing running back. He was a running back in high school, so I had no idea at that point that he'd become a great receiver. We went to two-a-days as freshmen, and they moved him to wide receiver. They moved a lot of people to wide receiver. Some of them stayed there and some of them went to defensive back because they couldn't catch. I used to tease all the defensive guys and say, "The only reason you're playing defense is because you couldn't catch!" All the cornerbacks and safeties were wide receivers that couldn't catch, and the fullbacks were running backs that couldn't catch.

During the course of two-a-days in 1968, it became evident that Carlos was pretty special. We had our first big scrimmage in the Swamp after two or three weeks of practice, and our first series was the freshman offense against the second-team defense. We drove right down the field in four or five plays, and they couldn't cover Carlos. He was running precision routes and—boom!—we scored on them. The coaches were like, "What in the world is going on? Our defense is terrible!" If Carlos hadn't gotten hurt, there's no telling what he would have done. His records stood forever, and he only played in about 15 games. He was only healthy his sophomore year and he was about half the man as a junior and a quarter of the man as a senior. He was so hurt and hobbled during his career.

In the spring of 1969 they divided the teams, and it was mostly us freshman guys against the returning varsity players. We beat them, like, 48–0 in the first scrimmage. We had thrown two touchdown passes during the entire 1968 season, when we were freshmen. As a matter of fact, the most talent Florida ever had while I was there was during my freshman season. But they didn't have any receivers and the quarterbacks didn't work out. I think if freshmen would have been eligible, it really would have been the "Year of the Gator." They had some beasts like Larry Smith, Jim Yarbrough, and Guy Dennis. That was by far the most talented team. After the spring game in 1969, the coaches kind of hinted to me that they wanted me to stay around that summer and watch film and hang out.

We went into two-a-days before the 1969 season, and they still hadn't announced the starting quarterback. We had our first scrimmage and beat the B-team and the freshmen 93–0. We hung 93 points on them! I was sitting there scratching my head and thinking, *This is unusual.* It's hard to score 93 points. Sure enough, we played Houston two weeks later and scored 59 points against them. We had a heck of a passing game and a pretty good running game. We had a good defense with Jack Youngblood and Steve Tannen, two first-round NFL picks.

We opened the 1969 season against Houston—they were ranked No. 7 in the country. They ran the veer offense, and people were having problems stopping it. They had some great athletes. They were in the Southwest Conference and were recruiting a lot of great players from Texas. They'd beaten Tulsa 100–6 the year before. They lost two games in 1968, and one of them was against Florida State, 40–20. I watched that film about a dozen times and saw that Houston's defense lined up in man-free, cover one all day long. The cornerbacks lined up about five yards off the receivers and couldn't cover them. You can't cover anybody that way. I don't care if you're Mel Renfro. You can't line up five yards off a guy and cover him man-to-man. But that's the way they lined up because they played in a conference where everybody ran the ball and they had good run defense.

We went out for the first series against Houston, and they lined up in cover one. The cornerbacks were lined up eyeball-to-eyeball with the wide receivers, and the strong safety was eyeball-to-eyeball with the tight end. The linebackers had the running backs, and the free safety was eight yards behind them. We didn't think they could cover us. I told Coach Doug Dickey, "Let's throw a bomb on the first play of the game." He said, "Nah, we won't do it the first play." We ran for three yards off tackle and on third-and-seven, he sent in the bomb. Sure enough, I looked out there and there was Carlos all by his lonesome. I dropped five or seven steps and set my back foot, just like in practice, and let it fly. Carlos was about 15 yards behind the guy, and that place went wild. It was just like a bomb exploded. I think about 300,000 people went to that game—if you believe all the people who have told me they were there. I threw four touchdowns in the first half, and we won 59–34.

I don't know if there could have been a better start to my college career. We had a great season in 1969, and if we hadn't missed a field goal against Georgia, we would have been co-SEC champions. We had lost to Auburn 38–12 the week before we played Georgia in Jacksonville, and it was like we were still in shock. I know I was still in shock, after throwing nine interceptions against Auburn. Auburn had a great team and played cover two, which was the first time I'd ever seen that defense. Bill Oliver, Auburn's defensive coordinator, invented that defense and was a great defensive mind. He was almost like a cult hero in the coaching circles. They played cover two and got a heck of a rush out of their four linemen. They had a linebacker named Larry Strickland who caught three of my passes. I ran into him years later and he told me, "John, I want to thank you. Nobody had ever heard of me until we played you, and now I'm famous around here." Every time I threw it, somebody from Auburn would be there. We were still kind of in the game late, until I threw a couple of interceptions they returned for touchdowns. We threw the ball 66 times.

My confidence level was still down going into the Georgia game, and you don't want to go out there and take the chances that you normally would take out of fear of throwing another interception. Georgia had a good team, but I think if we would have been rolling, we would have won the game. We got down to the 6-yard line late in the game, but we missed a field goal and the game ended in a 13–13 tie. It wasn't a bad snap. It was about six inches off the ground, but they tried to blame it on the center. Heck, you've got to make the play. They can still blame it on me, though. I had nine interceptions the previous week at Auburn and we lost.

We came back and beat Kentucky 31–6 and Miami 35–16. We went to the Gator Bowl and beat Tennessee 14–13. Mike Kelley blocked a punt early in the game and ran it in for a touchdown. It was a heck of a play. We were losing 10–7 in the third quarter, and I threw a corner route to Carlos for a touchdown. I threw it right over the safety's head, and Carlos caught it for a touchdown to put us ahead, 14–13. We had a chance to score right at the end, but let the clock run out. We should have scored again because we played Tennessee the next year and they killed us, 38–7. Under the rules now, we would have been SEC champions by beating Tennessee in the Gator Bowl. They were the SEC regular-season champs and it would have been like the SEC Championship Game is today.

We finished 9–1–1 in 1969, which was the best record a Florida team had ever had. It stayed that way until 1991. We should have been better, but that was still the best record. Coach Graves retired after the 1969 season, and it was a huge shock. All of the rumors said he was leaving after the Gator Bowl, and they denied it. But as soon as the game was over, Florida announced Coach Graves was stepping down and Tennessee coach Doug Dickey was coming back to Florida. It really blew a lot of people's minds. The transition to Coach Dickey was not easy. We had not done a great job of recruiting

John Reaves was Florida's starting quarterback from 1969 to 1971. Following the infamous "Florida Flop" in his last college game against Miami on November 27, 1971, Reaves became the NCAA's all-time leading passer with 7,549 passing yards.

linemen, honestly, and in defense of Coach Dickey, he was not left with a full cupboard of players. We had some good linemen, but not a lot of them. From that point forward, it seemed like everybody got hurt. Carlos got hurt. Andy

Cheney got hurt. Jimmy Barr, one of our great safeties, got hurt. Tommy Durrance missed five games during our senior year. Everybody just got hurt from that Super Sophomore class. Of course, the one that really hurt was Carlos because he was just brilliant.

It was almost anticlimactic after that 1969 season, especially after Coach Graves left and Coach Dickey came in and installed the veer offense. In that veer offense, you took the snap and looked for the defensive end. You're supposed to read him. If he tackles the back, then you pull the ball out and go to the next level. If he goes for you, then you pitch it and cut up. Hell, I could never find that defensive end. My whole life I'd been on a passing team. Even in junior high and high school, it was always bombs away! You look at the secondary and the linebackers. All of the sudden, I've got to look for the defensive end? I was like, "Where is that guy?" It was real quick. I got to where I was decent running it, but never was great. I had a 33-yard run against Kentucky in one game, but it was called back for a clip. Thanks a lot, Fred Abbott! In the spring game during my senior year I had a 57-yard run off of it. But I was never a good option runner.

We finished 7–4 during my junior year in 1970. We beat Georgia 24–17, and it was a great game. I was on the sideline late in the game and was mad because I'd fumbled on the previous series. Georgia got the ball back and was leading 17–10. It was three yards and a cloud of dust. They drove right down the field and it looked like they'd score again. But then Jack Youngblood ran through three or four guys and ripped the ball from Ricky Lake at the goal line. It was like he picked him up with one hand and shook the ball loose. Jack recovered the ball and gave it back to us. We scored in two plays, both passes to Carlos. Then the second touchdown was the same play as the first touchdown. It was a skinny post between the safety and cornerback, and I fired it in there before they could get to him. We scored two touchdowns in the final five minutes and won 24–17. It was a great game and a big win for us.

We went 4–7 during my senior year in 1971. We lost our first five games and things looked bad. Everybody on the team was like a true sophomore starting on offense, except for me. We had a 212-pound center and a 208-pound guard and 228-pound tackles. Those sophomores were better than the veteran players we had there, but they weren't like the Super Sophomores. We were undersized and played a brutal schedule. We played six teams ranked in the top 25 and lost four or five close games. We should have been better. We lost to LSU 48–7 in Baton Rouge to fall to 0–5. We were playing Florida

State the next week, and the Seminoles were 5–0 and ranked No. 19 in the country. It was an inspirational game for us. I always thought you couldn't live in the state of Florida and lose to Florida State. We played our best game of the season by far and won 17–15. Something I remember is that we'd had a few problems with field goals in that game. We had a couple of shaky holds, so at the end of the game when we were leading 14–7, Coach Dickey told me, "John, you go in and hold." I'd never held on a field goal in my life. I got a good snap, and Richard Franco, who was a brilliant kicker for us, boomed it through from 42 yards. That kick was the game-winner, and that victory really turned it around for us.

We played pretty well the rest of the season. We beat Maryland and then lost to Auburn and Georgia. We beat Kentucky 35–24, and then played Miami in the Orange Bowl to finish the season. I was close to breaking the all-time NCAA passing record, and we were trying get the ball back late in the game. The culprit, as I like to call him, was Harvin Clark. He returned a punt for a touchdown when we were trying to get the ball back for the offense. I tease him and tell him that he was trying to steal the thunder by scoring on a punt return. After Harvin scored, we didn't get the ball back, and they started their wishbone attack again. They marched down the field, and it looked like the clock was going to run out. The fans were yelling, "Let them score! Let them score!" Harvin was our defensive captain and he was feeling bad about what had happened. He went up to Coach Dickey and said, "Coach, we've got to let them score!" I was standing over there listening and finally Coach Dickey said, "Well, okay." So Harvin ran out on the field and told everybody to flop down. Sure enough, our defense did it and Miami scored a touchdown. We got the ball back and threw a couple of balls. I threw one to Carlos, which broke the NCAA record.

Unfortunately, we weren't smart enough to know how controversial that ending would be. I don't think it had ever been done before. It ended up being a dubious mark. I heard from Howard Cosell, Joe Garagiola, and Jim Plunkett himself. I was Public Enemy Number One. It's a good thing they didn't have ESPN back then or I would have been tarred and feathered. It wasn't even my idea! But it was very nice of Harvin and the guys to feel good about me to do that. It's really a team record more than a quarterback's record. It was everybody's record.

It was a great honor to play at Florida. When you look back, it really seems like it never happened. It was really a blessing to have the opportunity to play there. It provided amazing benefits for me and my family. People still remember me from playing there to this day. They come up to me and start talking about it. It's been so helpful to me and my relationships with my teammates and everyone at Florida have been unbelievable. It was great to be a Florida Gator.

John Reaves, a native of Tampa, was Florida's starting quarterback from 1969 to 1971. In his first college start against Houston on September 20, 1969, Reaves threw a 70-yard touchdown to fellow sophomore Carlos Alvarez on the game's third play. In a 59–34 upset of the No. 7 Cougars, Reaves completed 18 of 30 passes for 342 yards and five touchdowns. Led by Reaves, the 1969 Gators were dubbed the "Super Sophs" and finished 9–1–1, the best-ever record by a Florida team to that date. Florida beat SEC champion Tennessee 14–13 in the Gator Bowl to end the 1969 season. Following the infamous "Florida Flop" in his last college game against Miami on November 27, 1971, Reaves became the NCAA's all-time leading passer with 7,549 passing yards. After the 2008 season, Reaves still ranked fourth in Florida history in career attempts (1,128), sixth in completions (603) and yards (7,549), and seventh in touchdowns (54). Reaves was a first-round draft choice of the Philadelphia Eagles in the 1972 NFL Draft and played 11 seasons for five NFL teams. He was also starting quarterback of the Tampa Bay Bandits in the United States Football League for three seasons. Reaves later returned to Florida as an assistant coach under Steve Spurrier during the 1990s and also coached at South Carolina. He lives in Tampa and owns a real estate company.

JOHN JAMES
PUNTER
1968–1971

I WAS BORN IN PANAMA CITY, FLORIDA, in the panhandle and was raised there as well. My dad, Wilbur, played for the Gators, so I grew up a big Gators fan.

I didn't play football in high school. Golf and basketball were my two sports. We had a really good golf team, district champs. But the reason I didn't play football in high school was because of something that happened in junior high. I was the third-team quarterback, and the coach told me to stand back there and not to evade anybody, not to throw the ball, don't even move. I was basically a tackling dummy. I was told to wait and get hit.

Well, I decided I had better things to do with my spring, so I went out for the golf team. Because my dad had played for the Gators, we made the trips from Panama City to Gainesville, which took us about eight hours, for all the games since I was four years old. We'd always stop in Tallahassee for breakfast or lunch, depending on what time the game was. It was a huge part of my growing up.

It was great for me because I got to spend all that time with my dad. He was a really good player in his day at Florida, All-Southern Conference as a guard and fullback. So there was never any question where I was going to school. I always wanted to be a Gator. Heck, I was a Gator. I never even considered another school. I loved the University of Florida from day one. But I was really just going to go to school there.

John James has been a Gator his entire life. He grew up watching the Gators play in Gainesville with his father, Wilbur, an All-SEC lineman at Florida. James averaged 37 yards per punt in 1970 and 40.3 yards in 1971. After a playing career with the Atlanta Falcons, Detroit Lions, and Houston Oilers, James became executive director of Gator Boosters, a position he still holds proudly today.

I wanted to play on the golf team, so I went out for the team as a freshman. They had these orange-and-blue qualifying matches at the University Golf Course, and the top so many would make the team. I played pretty well and shot two-over for eight rounds in qualifying. But there were guys who were 27-under par. They had Steve Melnyk, Bob Murphy, and John Darr. They won the national championship that year, in 1968. So much for my golf career.

In 1969 I went to the Gator Bowl game between Florida and Tennessee. Doug Dickey was the Tennessee coach, and Florida won 14–13. I decided after that game, sitting there with my sisters and parents, that I would go out for the team as a punter because Florida needed one. Little did I know that by the time I went out, Dickey would be the Florida coach.

I had stayed in shape playing in fraternity leagues, basketball, and other sports. I went to Coach Dickey and told him I was going to go out so I was actually his first player at Florida. I got ready for the tryouts by buying two footballs at Jimmy Hughes Sporting Goods and taking them over to J.J. Finley Elementary. I'd kick for hours. I put two towels 60 yards apart and kicked from one to the other. When I felt confident enough, I went out for the team.

I remember when I got out there, someone said, "Come on, we got a bunch of them." There must have been nine or 10 punters out at practice. The best thing that happened to me was that Bobby Joe Green, who was an excellent punter at Florida and was kicking in the NFL, came out for spring practice because it was his off-season. He saw I had a good leg and he really helped me. He said I had what he called a farm leg. I didn't know how to turn the ball over, though, and he taught me how to do that.

Our first game in 1970 was against Duke in Jacksonville, and I didn't punt. Hunter Bowen did the punting. I was really mad. The next game I followed Coach Dickey all over the place, just boring holes in him. He got the message and finally put me in there. I won the job and ended up averaging 37 yards a punt. It was like a dream for me to be putting on that uniform for the Gators and playing in the games. It really was. I remember we went up to play Tennessee and lost 38–7, but I had a really good game. I had a great day, and the coaches named me player of the week. I had one punt that went 50-something yards and pinned them back at the 1-yard line. The bad thing was that Tennessee drove 99 yards for a touchdown.

We went 7–4 in 1970, but the next year was better for me but not the Gators. We went 4–7, and I averaged 40 yards a punt. We started 0–5 and has Florida State coming up next. The players had a meeting—we locked the coaches out—and promised that if we lost that game, we'd all shave our heads. It must have worked because we upset Florida State 17–15. Every successful team has to do that, say, "It's just us."

And we went on to win four of our last six games. The one that sticks out for me was the last one in Miami. John Reaves broke the all-time NCAA passing record in that game, which became known as the "Florida Flop." Everyone wanted to let Miami score so John could get the record. Harvin Clark, who was a defensive back, kept asking him on the sideline. Finally, he agreed to let Miami score. But Harvin went into the huddle and told everybody to lay down. Miami scored, John got the record, and we celebrated in the pool where they used to house Flipper. I had a great game, averaged 52 yards a punt. It was a great way to end the season. Because we struggled so much that year on offense, I had a lot of opportunities to punt. I think that helped me get ready for the NFL.

The thing about being a Gator is that it helps define you. One of the greatest thrills I've had in life was running out of that tunnel, being a part of the Gators football team. I have a picture in my office of me and my dad on the field for what is now Senior Day but what used to be Dad's Day. I couldn't be any prouder.

The University of Florida means so much to me. My job today as executive director of the Gator Boosters is a passionate one. I believe in it so strongly. It's really special. I wouldn't do this at any other university. I couldn't go to another school and do what I'm doing now. It's a job of passion for me to see this university, not just athletics but the whole university, continue to improve. I loved being a Gator and I love being a Gator today.

John James, a native of Panama City, Florida, played two seasons on Florida's football team, after joining the Gators as a walk-on punter. James has been a Gator his entire life. He grew up watching the Gators play in Gainesville with his father, Wilbur, an All-SEC lineman at Florida. James averaged 37 yards per punt in 1970 and 40.3 yards in 1971. After graduation, James went undrafted by NFL teams. Undaunted, he wrote a letter to 12 pro teams asking for a try-out. Only one team replied to him, the Atlanta Falcons, who declined his offer. James asked Gators coach Doug Dickey for help, and Dickey secured James a tryout with the Falcons. James punted for the Falcons for 10 years. He also played for the Detroit Lions and Houston Oilers. After retiring from football, James became executive director of Gator Boosters, a position he still holds proudly today.

LEE McGRIFF

WIDE RECEIVER

1971–1974

As a kid, all of my heroes were Gators football players. My dad ran track at Florida and started the sports program at P.K. Yonge High School, so I was around sports and the Gators all the time. My parents split when I was nine, and I moved to Tampa. It's always difficult to pick up and leave everything behind, but there were so many Gators in Tampa it wasn't that hard for me.

I played all kinds of sports at the Anderson playground and started playing junior high football. But the next year, they put a weight restriction in, and I had to sit on the sidelines. It about tore me up. But I got bigger and started playing the next year. By the time I was a junior, I was leading the Western Conference in receiving. But it wasn't like guys were lining up to recruit me.

Miami sent a coach, Charlie Bailey, to see me, but he told me I was too small. Ray Graves had told me they had a spot for me at Florida, but then Doug Dickey took over. He came to our house during the Christmas holidays. He had played for my dad at P.K. Yonge. He told me I wasn't ready to play for the University of Florida. I thought my dad was going to kill him. I went to the Orange and Blue game in the spring of 1971, and Coach Graves was there. After the game was over, he told me I should walk-on at Florida because that was the place for me. So I decided to give Florida a try even though they were loaded at wide receiver.

I started for the freshman team in 1971 and had a big game against Miami. Coach Dickey walked into the shower after the game and told me I had a

Lee McGriff was the Gators' leading receiver, with 38 catches for 703 yards and five touchdowns, and was named second-team All-SEC as a junior in 1973. As a senior, McGriff led Florida with 36 receptions for 698 yards and seven touchdowns and was named first-team All-SEC. He now serves as the color commentator for the radio broadcasts of Florida football games.

scholarship. The 1972 season was up and down, but we had this guy named Nat Moore. Once the coaches figured out what to do with him, we were pretty good but we finished 5–5–1. It was hard for me because I had a hard time getting on the field. I got into fights this one day in practice, and Coach Dickey came down from the tower and pulled me off the field. I told him I will break everybody's legs if you sit me down again.

So I started from then on. The next year, in 1973, was supposed to be our year. I really felt like we were heading for something special. But Nat got hurt, and we were struggling mightily. Nat was special and if he had stayed healthy, I don't know how it goes. But we were 2–4, and Coach Dickey made the switch at quarterback, which broke my heart because David Bowden was a dear friend of mine. But he put in Don Gaffney, and we went to Auburn and beat them 12–8, which was the first time Florida had ever won there.

The next week against Georgia was the game I'll always remember. It was cold and windy and it seemed like Georgia was leading, 7–3, forever. We got the ball for one last drive, and I made a diving catch down the sideline. I just wanted to do whatever it took to make the play. We got down to the Georgia 20 and set up a perfect screen pass. Vince Kendrick, who had the best hands in the world, dropped it. On fourth down, they called for me to run a curl and I ran it a little deeper than normal. Don let it rip, and I went as high as I could to catch it in the end zone. I threw the ball in the air I was so happy, so we got a 15-yard penalty on the kickoff. First, we had to get the two points, and Don hit Hank Foldberg for the 11–10 win. It was a great feeling.

That whole November was great because we won five straight games, including FSU [by a 49–0 score] and Miami [14–7]. Every game during that stretch felt like a championship game. We were on a roll and it was pretty exciting. I was second-team All-SEC because Bear Bryant had gone to the wishbone and decided they needed three backs and one receiver on the first team.

We had a great team in 1974, beating Auburn [25–14] when we were both ranked in the top five in the country. We stumbled against Georgia [a 17–16 loss], losing by a point when Don was stopped on a two-point conversion. Still, we were invited to play in the Sugar Bowl, which was a pretty big deal. It's also the game that is hard to shake off. We were dominating Nebraska until some things happened that changed the game. Tony Green scored a touchdown , but they said he stepped out of bounds, which was very controversial. And then James Richards slipped on a fourth-and-goal play. At that point, we were still up 10–0. But we made a mistake. We picked off David Humm three times, and they switched quarterbacks to Terry Luck. They just started pounding the ball, smashing it down the field on us. They scored 13 points in the fourth quarter and won the game 13–10. That was heartbreaking.

When I look back at my career at Florida, there were plenty of highlights. But the biggest thing was running onto Florida Field for the first time. Really, it was bigger than life. It really mattered to me more than just running around playing football that I was playing for the Gators. It was a passion. For me, from the time I was a little boy, the Gators were my team. I always felt so connected to them. It's all I really wanted and I wanted it really, really bad.

I was born in Gainesville, and my first hero was Larry Libertore, who was a quarterback in the early 1960s. Being a Gator is what I am. I wanted to be there so bad and to be told I wasn't good enough was hard, but to fight back and prove that I was good enough is something that will always be a part of me. My son, Travis, played there, and I coached there, so it continues to stay a big part of me.

When I was in high school, a coach from Richmond came by the house and said he'd call back but he never did. To go from that feeling to being an

83

All-SEC wide receiver in such a great conference was really special for me. My time at Florida was great, and I made so many great friends. But really, my whole life has been surrounded by Gators. It's what I was meant to be.

Lee McGriff, who was born in Gainesville and moved to Tampa, walked on Florida's football team in 1971. It didn't take McGriff long to earn a scholarship. He was the Gators' leading receiver, with 38 catches for 703 yards and five touchdowns, and was named second-team All-SEC as a junior in 1973. As a senior, McGriff led Florida with 36 receptions for 698 yards and seven touchdowns and was named first-team All-SEC. After graduation, McGriff spent a training camp with the Dallas Cowboys and then played in the World Football League until it folded. He played with the expansion Tampa Bay Buccaneers for a year before turning to coaching at Florida State and Florida. He was a part of Charley Pell's staff before deciding to enter private business. He is now a part owner of McGriff-Williams Insurance in Gainesville and also serves as the color commentator for the radio broadcasts of Florida football games.

BURTON LAWLESS
GUARD
1971–1974

I WAS BORN IN DOTHAN, ALABAMA, and my family lived in Bessemer. But we moved to Punta Gorda, Florida, when I was nine months old. My mom and dad were both school teachers, and my dad ended up being the superintendent in Charlotte County.

My father was 6′3″ inches and I was big, too. But when I was a kid, I was just this little round guy, a fat little kid. We would play football all day in the yard, tackle football, even though we weren't supposed to be playing tackle. Three kids in my neighborhood went on to be all-state.

I started playing organized football in eighth grade. By the time I got to high school, I was tall and lean and played middle linebacker. In my senior year, they moved me to tight end and outside linebacker. By then I was 6′4″inches and 210 pounds.

The main schools which recruited me were Auburn, Tennessee, Florida, and Florida State. My dad had played at Auburn, but I always considered Florida my home state. Alabama was my parents' home state. I had grown up in the state of Florida, and this was my home, plus I figured a degree from Florida would be better than anywhere else. I remember that when I signed, the coach who was recruiting me for Auburn said, "I can't believe you're going to that mess down in Florida."

They had switched to Coach Doug Dickey the year before [in 1970], and there was a lot of controversy swirling around. But that was where I wanted

Burton Lawless started at guard for Florida from 1972 to 1974. He was named second-team All-SEC by the Associated Press as a junior in 1973 and senior in 1974. After graduation, Lawless was drafted in the second round of the 1975 NFL Draft by the Dallas Cowboys and played five seasons for the Cowboys and one season for the Detroit Lions.

to go and I am thrilled to this day that is where I went. Believe me, when I showed up on campus in 1971, I wasn't looking at it as a stepping stone to the NFL. I was just a wide-eyed kid, who didn't know what he'd gotten himself into. There were more people on the University of Florida campus than there were in my whole county.

The first quarter I was there, I didn't know how to study. I made a D, two C's, and dropped a class. I was a scared little freshman coming from a small town, and it was all new to me. I decided right then and there I was going to learn how to study and make grades or I was going to go home.

To make matters worse, on the second day of two-a-days, I got hurt. I had played with a fractured shoulder my senior year of high school and didn't even know it. Calcium had built up in there, so I had to have surgery and missed six weeks of my freshman year. I was able to come back and play in two games, freshman games because freshmen weren't eligible then. I was playing tight end, but in the spring they moved me to tackle for a while and then to guard. That was the best move of my life. I still wasn't real big, but I was quick and I always had been able to move my feet.

Pretty soon, I was starting at 235 pounds. But back then, there was nobody on our line that weighed more than 260. In 1972 we had some big wins and some really tough losses. We clobbered Florida State 42–13, but lost close games to Auburn and Georgia. We beat Miami but lost the last game of the year to North Carolina 28–24 in Jacksonville.

Still, it was a huge deal to me to be starting. When you're going through it, you don't realize what a big deal it is. Just a chance to play, it was great. But it was tough losing all those games. We went 5–5–1 my sophomore year, and big things were expected for the 1973 season.

In 1972 we had this running back come out of nowhere—Nat Moore. He was amazing. But he got hurt early in the 1973 season and we struggled. We were 2–4 after losing four straight, and they made the switch to Don Gaffney at quarterback before we went to Auburn. Now Florida had never won at Auburn. Never. They were going to put the burden on the running game, which was fine with me. My parents were at the game, and it was a huge game for me. We won 12–8, made history. And then we won our next four games.

That was good enough to get us into the Tangerine Bowl against Miami of Ohio. The game was played in Gainesville, but we spent a couple of weeks in Orlando just playing around. We didn't take it seriously. And when the game came, it was freezing, 29 degrees. That team should have never been on the same field with us. We were so much better than them. But they beat us 16–7 on our home field. That was a bad deal, but it was our fault for not being prepared.

We were supposed to be really good my senior year, in 1974, but it was another season of unfulfilled potential. We won our first four games running the wishbone that we installed that year. We beat Maryland in Tampa with Tony Green killing them on the draw play, and we beat LSU. But then we went to Vanderbilt and lost 24–10. They weren't as big as us, weren't as good. But we couldn't do anything right that day. It seemed surreal all day, like you couldn't believe it was happening.

We bounced back to win three in a row, including a win over Auburn on national television. They were ranked fifth in the country. That was a big game for me. I remember feeling great after that game. But then we went into a downhill spiral. We lost to Georgia by a point when we missed a two-point conversion. Then we went to Kentucky and lost before closing the season with a win over Miami.

That was good enough to get us into the Sugar Bowl, where we faced Nebraska. We should have beaten Nebraska. We couldn't punch it in from the 1-yard line and then they drove down the field and beat us 13–10. So it was a down way to end my career, but I still loved my four years at Florida.

Whenever I speak to anyone, I always thank the people who gave me the opportunity at Florida. Those were the best four years of my life. It was a huge adjustment for me coming from a small town, but once I adjusted, it was great. I feel so proud and happy and blessed to have been a Gator football player. It was the best decision I ever made.

I'll always be a Gator. My 13-year old boy is a big Gators fan. He wants to go to school there when he's ready. You form bonds that last forever. When Hurricane Charlie hit my hometown, Ralph Ortega, who played linebacker for us, sent a generator to me while I was helping my dad rebuild his home. That rekindled our friendship. Last summer, we went down to the Everglades with Darrell Carpenter, who was a defensive tackle. I'm still really close to a lot of the guys I played with at Florida and I still root for the Gators.

Burton Lawless, a native of Bessemer, Alabama, started at guard for Florida from 1972 to 1974. He was named second-team All-Southeastern Conference by the Associated Press as a junior in 1973 and senior in 1974. After graduation, Lawless was drafted in the second round of the 1975 NFL Draft by the Dallas Cowboys. He made an immediate impact as a rookie on "America's Team," starting 10 games at guard, including a start against the Pittsburgh Steelers in Super Bowl X. He played five seasons for the Cowboys and was a member of three teams that played in the Super Bowl. Lawless helped the Cowboys beat the Denver Broncos 27–10 in Super Bowl XII in the Louisiana Superdome on January 15, 1978. After playing one season for the Detroit Lions, Lawless planned to return to the NFL in 1982 with the Chicago Bears. But on May 7, 1982, a steel plow fell on Lawless at his Texas ranch and broke his neck. Lawless was paralyzed for 17 days, but miraculously he made a full recovery. During his rehabilitation, Lawless was moved to a hospital in Waco, Texas, and liked it so much he settled there. He is a spotter for the public address announcer at Baylor football games.

NAT MOORE

Running back

1972—1973

Wᴴᴱɴ I ᴡᴀꜱ ᴀ ᴋɪᴅ ɢʀᴏᴡɪɴɢ ᴜᴘ ɪɴ Mɪᴀᴍɪ, where I moved from Talla-hassee when I was five, it was more parks and street ball than anything else. We would travel from neighborhood to neighborhood, and they would come to us. It was like we had this unofficial league. Basketball was my game because I had real quickness, but I stopped growing. So by the time I got to Miami Edison High, I was playing football and basketball and running track.

I had a big year at Edison High School as a senior, breaking records and running for 1,000 yards, so there were plenty of recruiters coming around. The Big 10 schools were coming to South Florida to improve their team speed and they were all after me. But I messed up my test scores. Today when I talk to kids, I tell them they have to understand that it's not just what you do in the classroom. You have to understand how to take tests. Because of my tests scores, I was a non-qualifier. At the last minute, I took a scholarship offer from Tennessee-Martin because I wanted to keep playing football and I wanted to get away from home. I led the conference in rushing, but I was homesick and it was difficult for a black athlete because it was the first year they had us there, which made it a little uncomfortable.

I also had a daughter to support back in Miami, so I decided to come home. I wasn't giving up because I had shown what I could do, but I had to go back to Miami and earn a living. I took a job driving a delivery truck and took some night courses. I decided to play some basketball for Miami

Nat Moore led the Gators in rushing in 1972 with 145 carries for 845 yards and nine touchdowns. He played 13 seasons for the Dolphins and set nearly every franchise receiving record. He now is a color analyst for TV replays of Florida football games.

Dade–South Community College. I played point guard and set a school record for assists. I wanted to get back to football, but I was thinking I might be able to get into a Division I-A school on a basketball scholarship.

My coach told Doug Dickey about me and the Big Ten schools were back on me. Wisconsin wanted me badly, but it was just too cold. So I decided on Florida. If I couldn't play football there, I could always play basketball. And they had integrated the football team a couple of years earlier, so I knew I'd be comfortable. They had me on the scout team in 1972 and they wanted me to give a picture of the opponents for the defense. But I kept messing them up. A running back in a game wasn't going to give them a picture. That's what I kept telling them. So they moved me to the varsity offense.

I was able to get on the field a little in the early games and scored a touchdown on a pass in the opener [a 21–14 loss to Southern Methodist]. But when we played Florida State, Coach Dickey had come to recognize that I could make some plays, and that ended up being a special game for me. I didn't know a lot about the SEC schools, so FSU was the big one for me. I scored on a 42-yard touchdown run and later in the game made a move on their defensive back that left him reaching for air on a short touchdown run. We did a great job of blocking the play, but you know that everybody is not going to get blocked. I was one-on-one with the guy in the hole, and when that happens you have to make the guy miss. I went more than 100 yards in the game [a 42–13 victory] and it was a real validation for me that I could play at this level. From there, everything just kind of snowballed and I had a great year.

91

It was a good season in 1972 because with John Reaves and Carlos Alvarez graduating, nobody expected much from us. It seemed like we were everybody's homecoming game that year. We didn't have a lot of seniors, four I think, so everybody had to go out and prove themselves. I had a big catch for a touchdown on a screen play against Auburn [a 26–20 loss] and a long run against LSU [a 3–3 tie]. Mostly for me, it was just great to be back out on the field playing football again. God blessed me with an ability to run the ball. My natural instincts from all of those years playing on the streets took over. We didn't have a big offensive line, but they were very good at creating seams. And I had the best fullback in the country in Vince Kendrick. He was the smartest player on our team.

It was all set up for us in 1973 to have a big year. But it turned out to be a frustrating year. People were talking about me as a Heisman Trophy candidate, and I had changed my number from 39 to 33. I was ready for a big season and mostly I wanted us to win the SEC. But I hurt my ankle against LSU [a 24–3 loss] and then my knee against Alabama [a 35–14 loss]. I suffered a chipped tibia and missed five games. To have those injuries in my senior year was frustrating because Coach Dickey had built the offense around me. It was really frustrating to sit in the stands and watch my team lose. They did change quarterbacks to Don Gaffney and put a nice winning streak together at the end of the season. I came back and tried to help, and we ended up playing in the Tangerine Bowl, which was played in Gainesville that year, and lost on a bitterly cold night to Miami of Ohio [by a 16–7 score].

When I came to Florida, I really wanted to be part of the first SEC Championship—to bring it back to Gainesville—but we fell short of the goal. I do believe we set a foundation for some great Gators teams that followed. I think back to those days and I'm most proud of being a part of a fine football team that showed we were part of the revival in the state of Florida. From that point on, the three Florida schools started to play good football, which was a salute to the kids who played high school football in the state of Florida.

To be a Gator was always special to me and to see the Gators dominate like they have over the last 20 years has been great. All of the state schools have done so well that it's a stamp of approval for the football programs in the state of Florida. I had a great time at Florida and still have a great time as a Gator.

Nat Moore, a native of Miami, transferred to Florida in 1972 after playing at Division I-AA Tennessee-Martin and Miami-Dade South Community College. After returning to Miami to care for his daughter—he drove a delivery truck to earn a living—Moore burst onto the scene during the 1972 season. He led the Gators in rushing that season with 145 carries for 845 yards and nine touchdowns. Moore's senior season was cut short by injuries, but he was still drafted in the third round of the 1974 NFL Draft by the Miami Dolphins. He played 13 seasons for the Dolphins and set nearly every franchise receiving record, which were later broken by Mark Clayton and Mark Duper. Moore was a favorite target of Dolphins quarterbacks Bob Greise and Dan Marino and finished his pro career with 510 receptions for 7,546 yards with 74 touchdowns. He is perhaps best remembered for his "helicopter" catch against the New York Jets in a 1984 game. Moore was hit on opposite sides by Jets defenders, sending him spinning into the air before he held on for a critical first down. Moore was named NFL Man of the Year in 1984 for his charitable work, and in 1998 he established the Nat Moore Foundation, which assists disadvantage youth in Miami-Dade County. He works as a color analyst for TV replays of Florida football games.

DON GAFFNEY

QUARTERBACK

1972–1975

I GREW UP IN JACKSONVILLE, FLORIDA, and I was being recruited by some of the historically black colleges. Ironically, some of the schools that people believed were recruiting me actually did not. There were a couple of things going on at that time. The following year, freshmen would be eligible to play varsity football for the first time. Also, that was the beginning of the NCAA rules that allowed you to have only five official visits to different schools that were recruiting you.

Tennessee State recruited me extensively, but the only other predominantly black school that really made an attempt was Texas Southern. Believe it or not, Florida A&M didn't really recruit me. The coaches from Florida A&M came to see my father, but only after I had already announced my decision to go to Florida. My high school coach was a former Rattler, and I was waiting for an official invitation from Florida A&M but never received one.

My final college choices were Florida, Florida State, Miami, Tennessee, and Notre Dame. I got into some trouble when I went to Miami. I went on my visit and wanted to come back early. I didn't give them the time they deserved, and I wouldn't give them a decision when I went there. When I got home, Fran Curci, the Miami coach, sent me a $24 phone bill. I'd been on the phone talking to my mom and dad and my girlfriend and spent more time talking to them than I did going out and enjoying the Miami campus. I met with Fran Curci, and he told me that I was a "Stud." I'll never forget those words because that's the same thing the Florida State coaches called me. What that really told me was they thought I could play another position. Whenever someone suggested that to my father, he knew he couldn't trust them. My father was very, very angry every time that would happen. He wanted to be sure I'd be given a fair chance to play quarterback.

My choosing the University of Florida, particularly during that time, caused some hardship. That was a time when historically black colleges like Grambling, Florida A&M, and Tennessee State were considered national powers. The Rattlers were getting their fair share of great athletes, including some players from my high school [Raines High in Jacksonville]. At the time, SEC schools were only beginning to recruit black athletes. So there were a number of people that still didn't believe the University of Florida or the Southeastern Conference were ready for a black quarterback. They thought I had some decent talent, but that I was wasting it by going somewhere that wouldn't allow me to use it.

I visited Tennessee, which is where Doug Dickey once coached, and they had Condredge Holloway, who was a great black quarterback. It was a big deal when Holloway signed with Tennessee. It was a big deal to me, and I didn't even live in Tennessee. I liked Tennessee and even more so when they signed Holloway. It showed me they were willing to sign a black quarterback and let him play. I saw Holloway play when he was a freshman. I went there on my official visit and saw the freshman game. I knew Holloway could play. I knew I couldn't go to Tennessee and compete with Holloway, who would have been ahead of me.

I followed the Gators my entire life. I followed all the Florida schools. But Florida was the closest SEC school to my home, and Jacksonville was Gator country. There was the Florida coach's show on TV and I always watched all the highlights. I had a feeling for the Gators. Coach Dickey convinced me Florida and the SEC were beginning to embark on a new renaissance. I liked Tennessee because Coach Dickey was there, and then he went to Florida. I loved the Gators. To me, it seemed like an omen when Coach Dickey went there.

When I went to Florida in 1972, David Bowden was the starting quarterback. I had seen him play a couple of times. I heard about him and he was everything that I'd heard about. It still wasn't enough to deter me, though. Meeting David and seeing him up close really convinced me I could play at that level. When I arrived at Florida, it was David's first season as a starter, and he won the SEC passing championship. Of course, at the time, I was more concerned with establishing myself in the order. We had a lot of quarterbacks and a lot of talented guys who came in with a lot of fanfare.

My favorite teammate was Chan Gailey, who later became the Georgia Tech coach and is now back in the NFL. Chan was my coach and teammate. Chan is probably as responsible for my success as anyone, including Coach Doug Dickey and Jimmy Dunn, who was my quarterbacks coach. Chan was very unselfish and helped me learn what the heck was going on. If Chan had not been there, I would have struggled a lot more than I did, and who knows what would have happened.

I played in four games during my freshman season in 1972. I remember playing the least against Alabama [a 24–7 loss in Tuscaloosa]. I played three plays and we went absolutely nowhere. One play was a pass play in which I was sacked. But Coach Dickey gave me a chance to play for the first time, and I was really shell-shocked at the time. I'd just turned 18 and was playing for the Florida Gators against Alabama and across the field stood Bear Bryant. I remember playing against Mississippi State, LSU, and Miami. I didn't play against Florida State during my freshman season, and I remember I was very disappointed. But I dressed out the entire year until I was injured in the ninth game of the year. I injured my right shoulder and went ahead and had surgery and they shut me down.

95

I had some serious concerns about me being able to get back on the practice field the following spring. I didn't want to redshirt, but I knew it wouldn't kill me if they made me sit out. It certainly would have helped me academically to have that extra year. I was on pace to graduate and wasn't having any problems in the classroom. But I wanted a chance to challenge for the number two quarterback job. With the season David was having, my goodness, it was going to be difficult to win the job. Nonetheless, I had surgery in December and was concerned about being ready for spring practice in April.

Ironically, being held out of the off-season program helped me learn many different things. I was able to learn the mental parts of the game. Of course, at the time, I didn't know we'd change the offense the following season. In 1973 there was some debate as to who the backup quarterback was going to be going into the season. I think I played okay, and I knew I'd get stronger and be a formidable challenger in the fall. But I knew I needed to be the second or third quarterback going into the fall, or it would put some tremendous pressure on me the following spring. We put in the veer offense during the spring, which was good for me, because I didn't have to throw it as much coming off the shoulder surgery. Ironically, we didn't use the veer offense at all when the season started. I couldn't figure out why that happened.

During the midpoint of my sophomore season in 1973, we really ran into some problems. We lost our best player, running back Nat Moore, for quite a while. We were depending a great deal on David and Vince Kendrick, who was our big running back. We just weren't able to get it done because it was too much pressure on David. When you don't have a sufficient running game, it gives defenses the opportunity to really tee off on you. David wasn't extremely mobile, but he could throw it. My God, could he throw the football! We hung on for as long as we could, but we went through a stretch where we lost four games in a row. [After beating Kansas State 21–10 and Southern Mississippi 14–13 to start the season, the Gators lost four consecutive games to Mississippi State, LSU, Alabama, and Ole Miss.]

I took over as the starting quarterback in the middle part of my sophomore season. There were a lot of things that contributed to that decision. We were operating under some tough circumstances and needed more speed. There were a couple of guys who could throw the ball as well as I could, but I was more mobile. During the Ole Miss game [a 13–10 loss in Gainesville], David was pounded pretty good late in the game. He showed a lot of toughness because he really took a blow. But on fourth down, I think he lost track of where he was and what was going on. [Late in the game, on a fourth-down play, Bowden believed it was first down and threw the ball out of bounds to stop the clock. After his snafu, the Rebels took possession and held on to win the game.]

David always had quite a bit of latitude in the play-calling. Coach Dickey was signaling in plays, but David had the latitude to change the play. There was a lot of confusion. I was standing right next to the coaches when it happened. In hindsight, we should have called timeout. It was a bad experience for David. It was a bad experience for all of us, really. We were under a lot of pressure. We were playing our homecoming game, and Ole Miss really wasn't that strong of a team. There was a tremendous amount of pressure on David. He took a lot of ribbing for that play. Really, what caused my start and his demise was the fact that we were playing that game at home and lost.

After losing to Ole Miss, we were getting ready to go play at Auburn and had a week off before the game. We had put in that veer offense back in the spring and we changed our offense altogether during that off week. About

Don Gaffney, a native of Jacksonville, Florida, was the first African American to play quarterback at the University of Florida. Gaffney became the Gators' starting quarterback midway through the 1973 season and started as a junior and senior. He led Florida to three bowl games during his career: the 1973 Tangerine Bowl, 1974 Sugar Bowl, and 1975 Gator Bowl.

three minutes before we took the field to play Auburn, Coach Dickey told me I was going to be the starting quarterback. It was after Coach Dickey had given his last instructions. Just before our team prayer, he put the football in my hand and said, "Don, you've got it." I think he waited that long to protect me. I really do. He didn't want to give me too much time to think about it, so I'd sleep the night before and wouldn't be worried. I didn't have time to be scared—it was time to play! I felt good going in there. I felt good going through warm-ups. I didn't realize the pressure of playing at Auburn, because we'd already been on the road before. Who knows what I would have felt if we were playing at home. I like to think I would have done okay, but I'm not sure how things would have turned out.

We beat Auburn 12–8, and they were ranked pretty high in the polls. It gave me a lot of confidence. We were ecstatic after winning the game. We were happy for a lot of reasons. A lot of us didn't understand that Florida had never won at Auburn before. We were young. We had a lot of sophomores playing for the first time. A lot of black players were playing for the first time.

But Coach Dickey always reminded us that we were just one football team. Even though I was happy we'd won the game, I felt bad because I felt responsible for our defense losing its shutout. I fumbled the ball inside our 5-yard line with only seconds to go. Auburn scored with, like, two seconds left. What I should have done was gone down, but I was trying to make something else happen. That's just the way I played. I was always aggressive. But I learned from that experience. It was a terrible mistake.

We played Georgia in Jacksonville the following week. That couldn't have been a better script for me, you know? When we were flying home from Auburn, Coach Dickey got on the intercom on the plane and congratulated us again. He said, "Men, you did a wonderful job. You worked hard." Then Coach Dickey reminded us that Georgia had just knocked off Tennessee, and that Jacksonville Stadium would be a packed house. Georgia had beaten Tennessee on the road, and Florida had beaten Auburn on the road. Tennessee and Auburn had still been in the hunt to win the SEC. Georgia was a little bit better than people thought they were.

Honestly, I had played in that stadium in Jacksonville so much it was like being at home. The one thing I can remember is I looked around, but didn't see any faces. I saw fragments of faces, but the Georgia crowd didn't bother me. The noise was tremendous. The wind didn't bother me because I'd played there so much. I understood how to throw the football in that stadium, even more so than in Gainesville. The game was played late in the evening because of TV, so it was cold and the wind was really blowing. Georgia was beating us 10–3 in the fourth quarter, and the Bulldogs had a long drive and were trying to eat up the clock. Somehow, our defense came through. I was standing on the sideline and didn't have a parka on or anything, and I was just anxious to get one more shot. I knew the next drive had to be flawless.

Really, I knew that last drive was it. I had to show my teammates that I belonged, and we had to show that we could come back and win. I knew if we didn't get it done, it was over. After our defense stopped Georgia, we had a TV timeout, and it seemed like we stood out on that field forever. I remember saying to the guys, "We have to go!" We had called the first play of the drive on the sideline, so we sat there on the field during the timeout and thought about what we had to do. It seemed like forever. And as soon as we finally got out there, I almost threw an interception. Lee McGriff made a great play to break up the pass. He didn't get it, but they didn't get it, either.

I knew I had to settle down. You can't talk the game without playing the game, and I had to convince my teammates I could lead them. I had to trust they would do what they're supposed to do, and I had to do what big-time quarterbacks are supposed to do, which is to get the play, get it called, make the right read, make the right decision, and get it done.

We started that last drive at our 15-yard line, but we eventually moved down the field pretty well. On fourth down, I threw a pass to Lee McGriff, and he made one of the greatest catches I've ever seen for a touchdown. I wasn't surprised because I'd seen Lee make catches like that all the time in practice. Lee McGriff was one of the best receivers I ever played with. He was always practicing to make the tough catches. We had guys work on sideline catches and things like that, but Lee used to extend his body to make a catch every time you threw it to him.

The play seemed like it was in slow motion, and at that point I realized I was beginning to grasp college football. When I let that ball go, Lee came out of nowhere to get it. I knew where he was supposed to be, but I didn't see him. He went up and clutched the ball, and all I was concerned about was him hanging on to it when he came down. The safety was draped all over him, so that's why I had to throw it away from him. I didn't mean to throw it that high, but Lee made a great play. I saw him come down and roll over and then he lifted the ball up, which was kind of his trademark. Then I heard the crowd, and I knew it was a touchdown.

I started running down the field, and I looked over at Coach Dickey and he was holding up two fingers. We were going for a two-point conversion to win the game. I started running down the field and realized I didn't have the play! I turned around to get the play, but they were telling me to keep running because time was running down. I got the play and it was designed to go to Vince Kendrick, who was the first option. The play called for me to roll out to my left and come all the way back to Vince, almost swinging a pass to him. That play should have been wide open, but when I turned to throw to Vince, the strong safety came out of nowhere. But I think the play froze the cornerback and free safety. Lee popped open, but Henry Foldberg was wide open in the back of the end zone, too. Nobody was with Hank, and I'm still not sure what happened. Hank Foldberg was the third option. I threw it to Hank, who is 6'6" tall, and he has huge hands and a huge body. I threw it to Henry way down low, and he had to go down and get it. It was another great catch. Two guys made two tremendous plays and we won the game 11–10. It was a tremendous honor to be a part of both of those plays.

I didn't realize what we'd accomplished at the time. So much of my family is from Georgia, and living in Jacksonville we grew up watching that game. My dad always assured me all of us were going to go to college. We followed that game religiously. It was a big deal. We'd have to be at that stadium at 7:30 in the morning to sell drinks inside the stadium. We had to get there early because so many people were vying for those spots. I'd seen so many games in the Gator Bowl. I never missed the Georgia-Florida game, from the time I was 12 years old and on. From the time I was old enough to read the newspaper, we followed the Gators and SEC football in the paper.

We ended up winning our last five games in the 1973 season, which is what Florida fans called the "November to Remember." We lost to Miami of Ohio 16–7 in the Tangerine Bowl, which was played in Gainesville. I had been having back problems late in the season. I took a blow from an Auburn player in my first start and was really hurting the rest of the season. But I knew there was too much at stake to sit down. The injury caught up with me by the end of the season. It was so cold in December when we played the Tangerine Bowl. I took the first snap and that was all I could do. Robbie Davis ended up finishing the game at quarterback. He did well under the circumstances, but we weren't prepared to play under those circumstances and lost the game.

We opened the following season in 1974 against California and won the game 21–17. We went to Tampa the following week to play Maryland. I received a death threat before that game at our team hotel. To get a death threat at any time is kind of tough, but to get one under those circumstances was kind of odd. All we had done was win games to that point. It was a night game, which made it worse, because we had to wait all day to play. I had to stay out of sight. I was thinking, *This is kind of tough.*

I didn't realize the circumstances of what was happening until we got to Tampa Stadium. We were in the tunnel to go out on the field and there was just so much confusion going on in my mind. I didn't know what this meant. I didn't realize it, but there were just some people that did not want me to be the starting quarterback at Florida. What I remember most was Coach Dickey was just so calm, and some of my teammates were upset about it. At first, the coaches didn't want any of my teammates to know, which would have been a mistake. Coach Dickey and the coaches handled everything so well. We had to talk about it.

I remember being tired, and I'm not sure if it was because I was scared or what. It was a long, hard, exhausting day. I remember talking to so many people. My mother was upset. My dad was there, and he didn't normally spend the whole day with me on a game day. I knew something had to be wrong for him to be there. I was trying to keep my mind on the ballgame, though. When I got to the stadium, I remember going out for warm-ups. As soon as I stepped on the field, I was booed terribly. I couldn't understand it. Someone said to me, "Those aren't all the Gator fans." When we went back out on the field for the game, what made it worse was there was no booing until we got the ball on offense.

Maryland got the ball first, and I had to stand on the sideline wondering if something was going to happen to me. I don't know that I sat there wondering if someone was going to shoot me. But there are some weird people out there, you know?

We got on the field, and as soon as our offense got on the field, the booing started again. That was kind of tough. One of the guys who was most upset about it was Lee McGriff. Lee was from Tampa and he stepped out of the huddle and said, "Why don't they just shut up?" I really respected him for that. He didn't like it at all. Nobody was saying anything in the huddle. I remember thinking to myself, *This is not good.* It was going to be a real distraction and we couldn't afford to lose to Maryland. We were a much better team. We were an extremely good football team during my junior season. We should have won it all.

After the first couple of series against Maryland, I remember Coach Dickey putting his arm around me on the sideline. He said, "It's going to be a little too tough for you." I said, "Yes, sir." It was too tough. I couldn't go out there and concentrate on what I needed to do. I didn't want to sit down, but I couldn't complain about it. It was just for the best that I came out of the game. Jimmy Fisher went into the game and played fabulously.

As good as he was, it created another controversy. The irony was that it was my junior year and it should have been David Bowden's senior year. David wasn't with us on that trip, and he was another Tampa kid. It was my junior year and it hurt for something like that to happen. To be at a point in your life when things should be wonderful, and to get a death threat in a public facility, it was just so hard to understand. Times were tough. This was the early 1970s, and you just didn't know what was going to happen. I wish it hadn't happened. I wish I hadn't received a telegram that said, "If you step on the field, you're going to die." It was just so hard to understand why it happened.

My teammates were so tremendous in their support. It didn't matter if you were black, white, whatever. My family was very supportive, too. My grandmother hit a guy with her purse during that game. She was so upset this guy was booing me. I had a large family from Jacksonville, and every time I started a game in the state of Florida, there were a lot of family members there. I bet you we had 30 or 40 family members at the games. Against Maryland, this guy sitting in front of my grandmother says to her, "You know, that guy Gaffney was a good football player until he started taking those drugs." She heard it and, my goodness, she hit him with her purse! She said, "My grandson doesn't use drugs!" The guy apologized and said he didn't know I was her grandson. It was so funny. She was a little, short lady. I found out about it the next day, and I think I needed to hear something like that at the time.

We played Mississippi State at home the following week and we had a huge game. We won 29–13, and I had a huge game. It really quieted things down. We went on a tear after that Mississippi State game. They were getting Jimmy Fisher ready to play, and he needed to be ready because I played such a physical style of football that I was getting hurt. Some people took it the wrong way and thought they were taking snaps away from me. Before the 1974 season ended, I think I was playing as well as any quarterback in the country. But we made one switch I really regret. We switched to a wishbone offense, which put the emphasis on the running backs and took it off the quarterback. We had good running backs, but we had a tremendous stable of receivers. We always had good receivers at Florida. Of course, I had to make another adjustment, which I did. We ran the option well and, at one point, we were leading the SEC in total offense. We finished 8–3 in the 1974 regular season and lost to Nebraska 13–10 in the Sugar Bowl.

We opened my senior season in 1975 and lost to NC State 8–7 early in the season and then lost to Georgia 10–7. We went 9–2 during the regular season, and it was a disappointment. Turnovers and mistakes just killed us in those two losses. We had the football late in the game against NC State and were running down the clock to kick a field goal, but we lost a fumble on first down. Against Georgia, it was the same thing. We lined up to kick a field goal, and David Posey, who was probably our MVP, slipped on the Gator Bowl turf and missed the kick. We lost to Georgia 10–7. We should have scored more points.

I thought that team my senior year was the best team I played on at Florida. I think I became the player they thought I'd become under some very trying circumstances. I was very grateful to have a chance to play at Florida. I played with some great players and had some excellent coaches. I had a great career. I think we proved that African American players could survive socially and athletically and are capable of performing at a high level under great pressure. When we were there, every little thing that happened might have been the first time that somebody who looked like me did it. It paved the way for others to follow us. There were no questions about whether we could do it anymore.

Don Gaffney, a native of Jacksonville, Florida, was the first African American to play quarterback at the University of Florida. He arrived at Florida in 1972 and immediately worked his way onto the field. Gaffney became the Gators' starting quarterback midway through his sophomore season in 1973 and started as a junior and senior. He led Florida to three bowl games during his career: the 1973 Tangerine Bowl, 1974 Sugar Bowl, and 1975 Gator Bowl. Gaffney was named second-team All-SEC by the Associated Press as a senior. Three of his brothers, Derrick, Johnny, and Warren, and a nephew, Jabar, also played football for the Gators. Gaffney later served on the Jacksonville City Council and Florida State Legislature and is now a law professor at Edward Waters College in Jacksonville.

The
EIGHTIES

NEAL ANDERSON

RUNNING BACK

1982–1985

I WAS ACTUALLY BORN IN DOTHAN, ALABAMA, just across the border from Graceville, Florida, which is where I grew up. Graceville's hospital opened the day I was born, but they couldn't handle delivery of babies. So after I was born, they moved me to the new hospital.

Growing up in Graceville made you tough. There wasn't a lot there, no red light or fast food places, no Boys Club. Everyone worked at the mill. Life was tough, and I developed a mean streak, which really helped me play football. Plus, I could run. The older guys in town would always tell me my dad was faster, but I was pretty fast. So I started playing football in seventh grade, and by the time I was a sophomore, I was starting for the varsity. I always knew I'd be a star. When I was in middle school, I signed the yearbook "Neal 'Superstar' Anderson."

In high school, I could pretty much run for as many yards as I wanted. I dropped baseball to concentrate on football and broke all of the school records. So when it came to recruiting, it was going to be crazy. I tell people all the time that it makes me laugh when I hear about all of those recruits getting money or cars or stuff. My family went into debt during my recruitment. We had these famous coaches coming to our house, and my parents wanted to make sure it looked nice, so they went out and bought stuff to make the house look nice.

Neal Anderson was a starting running back for the Gators for four seasons, from 1982 to 1985. He led the Gators in rushing in three consecutive seasons and still ranks third in school history in career attempts (639), rushing yards (3,234), rushing touchdowns (30), and 100-yard games (14).

In a town like Graceville, to have Bear Bryant and Pat Dye walk into your house was a big deal. There would be a buzz all over town when any of the head coaches came in. The one hotel there was sold out all the time, but I always suspected that one of the schools was buying all of the rooms to make the other coaches stay somewhere else. I'm not sure which school it was. There were a lot of people who thought I'd go to Southern Cal because of their tradition of great tailbacks, but that was too far away, and I wanted my mom and dad to be able to watch me play. So it really came down to Auburn, Alabama, and Florida. It was hard to tell Coach Dye and Coach Bryant that I wasn't coming. But it came down to me wanting to go somewhere and be the first to win a championship.

Florida had never won anything. Everyone thought I had lost my mind going to Florida instead of Alabama or Auburn. It was an easy transition, but I was at the bottom of the depth chart my first season at Florida in 1982. I was hardly playing and I knew I could play at that level. They couldn't tackle me. But even when we had a bunch of injuries, Florida decided to go with a one-back set, and I would still be on the bench. That was the last straw. I went to Mickey Andrews, who was a defensive coach but recruited me, and told him that I was finished. I was leaving. If we're down to one tailback and I still can't play, this isn't the place for me.

The next day, they told me I was starting. I guess they believed me when I said I was leaving. That first start came at Kentucky, where we had some problems in the past. Our game plan was to run the ball with James Jones playing fullback. He did a lot to help me get ready and he was pounding on my helmet before the game to get me fired up. Maybe Kentucky didn't know about me and didn't pay attention. I was getting great holes to run through, thanks to James and the offensive line. I just kept picking up yards. We won the game 39–13. After the game, the reporters told me I had 197 rushing yards. I couldn't believe it. My dad still has that game ball.

After that game, I just kept rolling. It was great. Coming from such a small place, I had a lot of doubters. I didn't know what to expect in the SEC. I was playing with so many great players—Lomas Brown, Wilber Marshall, John L. Williams—guys who were stars and went on to be NFL stars. We didn't win the national championship but we had a lot of fun.

In my sophomore year in 1983, I led the team in rushing with 835 yards and nine touchdowns. We had another great team, but fell just short of winning the SEC. Then came 1984, my junior year. Early in the season, there were NCAA investigators around Gainesville. I felt like it was a slap in the face that they never talked to me. They were talking to walk-ons and trainers, but not to me. I kind of just watched it all take place. When I was being recruited, there were some schools that offered me different things. But the NCAA investigators never talked to me. I felt slighted. Maybe they knew I wouldn't have taken anything.

But even with our coach, Charley Pell, being fired after three games in 1984, we played as hard as ever. I have a hard time understanding anyone who doesn't play hard, no matter what is going on. You get on that field and your competitiveness comes out. I'm always going to be ready to play. It helped that Galen Hall took over as interim coach. He saw that the offense wasn't broken and stayed with it. Galen had come from Oklahoma, and everyone thought he was going to put in the wishbone, but he stuck with the program.

We kept winning in 1984 and had a showdown with Auburn in Gainesville late in the season. My teammates called me "L.A." for Lower Alabama, and Auburn was a school I considered attending during recruiting. So it was a big rivalry for me, especially because they had Bo Jackson. It was on national television, and I had a big game. We won 24–3. The next week, we played Georgia and finally beat them 27–0. People still come up to me to talk about that game and when we get together, that's the game we talk about. And when we beat Kentucky 27–0 to win the SEC championship, that was a special moment.

That's why I came to Florida, to win the SEC for the first time. I remember on the plane ride back, the plane went over the stadium and it was packed with people waiting for us. You could feel the energy from the Gators fans. The next spring, the SEC stripped us of the title, but we didn't care. We knew who the best team was in the conference. It didn't bother me at all. I didn't play for what was written in the newspapers. I played for my teammates.

109

During my senior season in 1985, we were ineligible for the conference title, but that didn't stop us. We got all the way to No. 1 in the rankings for a week before Georgia beat us. I had my first 1,000-yard rushing season. We finished the season with a 9–1–1 record. We won it on the field, and everyone knew we were the best in the SEC and maybe in the country.

My time at Florida has always been special to me. I have nothing but fond memories of playing for the Gators. I got a great education, got my degree. On and off the field, I wouldn't trade it for anything. I met my wife there, the mother of my three kids. It stays with you your whole life. I travel a lot and I'm always running into Gators fans. There is a group of us who played together at Florida, who still go on a golf trip every year. No matter where we go, people come up to us and want to go back in time.

Neal Anderson, a native of Graceville, Florida, was a starting running back for the Gators for four seasons, from 1982 to 1985. He led the Gators in rushing in three consecutive seasons and still ranks third in school history in career attempts (639), rushing yards (3,234), rushing touchdowns (30), and 100-yard games (14). Anderson was named first-team All-SEC by the league's coaches and the Associated Press as a senior in 1985. After graduation, Anderson was a first-round draft pick by the Chicago Bears, where he eventually succeeded legendary running back Walter Payton. Anderson ran for more than 6,000 yards and 70 touchdowns during an eight-year pro career. He still ranks second in Bears history in career rushing yards, behind only Payton, and was a four-time Pro Bowl selection. Anderson owns a peanut farm in Williston, Florida, and is part owner of seven banks in the area.

KERWIN BELL

QUARTERBACK

1984–1987

I GREW UP IN MAYO, FLORIDA, which was a really small town, so I didn't get a lot of attention from college recruiters. We won a state championship at Lafayette High School during my junior season in 1981. That was before the Internet and everything else, so I only had one college coach see me play. He was the defensive line coach from Valdosta State in Georgia. I'll never forget after one of our games, he told me if I didn't get a scholarship from a bigger school, they wanted to offer me a scholarship. So I was set in my mind that if I didn't get a scholarship from a bigger school, I was going to go to Valdosta State.

I got a lot of letters from colleges during my junior and senior seasons in high school, but nobody had offered me a scholarship when it was time to sign in February 1983. Even Valdosta State backed out before signing day, so I had no offers to play football in college. I decided I wanted to walk on because I felt like I could play somewhere. My wife, who was my girlfriend at the time, was a big Gators fan, so I started going to Florida games with her family. I really liked Gainesville and decided that's where I wanted to go to school.

I walked on at Florida in the fall of 1983. Mike Shanahan, who is the head coach of the Denver Broncos, was the offensive coordinator at Florida under Charley Pell. He really liked me and told me I'd have a chance to play at Florida one day. I'll never forget the first day of practice, I walked into the locker room, and they had the depth chart posted on the wall. I was the eighth-string quarterback and there were only eight quarterbacks there. I was literally at the bottom. I redshirted in 1983, which was Wayne Peace's senior year. I ran the scout team the entire season, and I felt like leaving a few times because you got beat up in practice so much. But I ended up staying and moved up to fifth-string during spring practice in 1984 because three guys graduated.

Before the 1984 season, it was four scholarship players and me competing at quarterback. Coach Pell told me, "Kerwin, we can only look at four quarterbacks, so we're going to let the four scholarship players compete for the job." I wound up playing in the spring game as a third-stringer for one of the teams. I had one series in the spring game and led our team 80 yards for a touchdown in four plays. After the spring game, Coach Pell said I was a dark horse candidate for the starting job.

We came back in the fall of 1984, and Donnie Whiting, who was a pretty good player, flunked out of school because he didn't get his grades during summer school. I moved up to the top four quarterbacks and competed with the three other guys from the first day of fall practice. The Monday before the first game, which was against Miami, the defending national champions, Coach Pell told me I was the backup quarterback behind Dale Dorminey, a fifth-year senior. I was excited just to be the backup after being eighth-string the year before. At least I knew I wasn't going to get hit in practice anymore.

After I was named the backup, Dorminey blew out his knee at the end of practice that night. He was running a play right before the end of practice in a goal-line situation, and our fullback fell right into him. We didn't think it was too bad at first, because Dale got up and walked off the field. I moved up to the number one huddle in practice. I remember Ricky Nattiel told me, "Kerwin, you're going to have to grow up in a hurry." I didn't think Dale was injured too seriously until that night. I was in the dining hall, and Coach Galen Hall, the offensive coordinator, told me, "Kerwin, Dale is out for the season. You're going to start." I'd just grabbed a tray of food. I put it back because I couldn't eat. I was so nervous. I had four days to get ready to play the defending national champions. For the next four days, I watched as much film as I could to get ready for the game.

We had a great football team in 1984. We had three first-round NFL picks in the backfield: Neal Anderson, Lorenzo Hampton, and John L. Williams. We went back and forth with Miami and went ahead in the second half before losing 32–20 in Tampa. Probably what solidified my job, really, was the last series of that game. We converted two fourth downs during the drive, and I threw a touchdown pass to Frankie Neal with about 30 seconds to go. With just that one drive, I think the team really started believing in me, and that gave me a chance to be the starter for the rest of my career.

We tied LSU 21–21 in Gainesville the next week, and then beat Tulane 63–21. Coach Pell was fired after the Tulane game. We'd just blown out Tulane. We knew we had a good football team. The rumor was Coach Pell was going to get to finish the season, but they made the decision to go ahead and fire him. There was an off-week after the Tulane game, and Coach Hall came in as interim coach. I think Galen was the perfect fit after what happened. Galen is a very humble person. He went in with the idea that Coach Pell was doing the right things as far as running the team.

Galen wasn't a guy who felt like he had to come in and do something on his own. He believed things were going well and we had a good football team, and he was humble enough to just fit in and keep the ship going in the right direction. I remember the players were really frustrated with what happened. We had a couple of players-only meetings, and we built the mentality that it was "us against the world," so to speak. We felt like we were wronged with the way they'd taken away our coach in the middle of the season, and we wanted to prove to everybody that we could persevere through this. We really built the attitude that we were going to prove everybody wrong on the football field.

113

We won our last nine games in 1984 and finished with a 9–1–1 record. We beat Kentucky 25–17 on the road to win the SEC title, which was the first time Florida had won it. I don't remember much about the game. When I think back to that moment, the only thing I remember is the flight back home. When we got to Gainesville, the pilot dipped the plane over Florida Field to let us see what was going on. We saw a wave of orange and blue in the stadium. All the fans were in the stadium waiting on us. When we landed, we had a continuous line of fans from the airport to the stadium. There were cars parked everywhere and people were in the streets. When I think back to that moment, I don't even think about the game. I just remember the madness back in Gainesville and the celebration after that win.

I don't know if we were playing for Galen to get the job. I think we were just playing for ourselves, really. We just wanted to prove everybody wrong. We wanted to prove we were going to stay together and make a statement on the field. I remember that being the attitude of the team. We felt Galen was letting us do what we did best. He tried to keep everything the same. I don't think we started really thinking about what was going to happen with Galen until the end of the season. We didn't know if he was going to keep the job or not. We'd heard Steve Spurrier was up for the job. As a quarterback, that's pretty enticing to think of what might have happened if he'd gotten the job then. We'd watched Steve coach the Tampa Bay Bandits, and they'd thrown the ball around quite a bit. But Galen had done a fantastic job with our team and was a great play caller. He deserved to get the job after holding the team together. We'd accomplished a lot during his first season and felt like we could accomplish a lot in the future if he were there.

When I became the second-string quarterback in 1984, Coach Pell told me they didn't have a scholarship for me because they'd already used all their scholarships for the season. But he promised me I'd get a scholarship in January, so I knew one was coming. I grew up on a family farm, and we grew tobacco and raised cattle and all those things. If it was a financial hardship for my father to pay for school, I didn't know about it. My parents said, "If this is what you want to do, we're going to send you down there." I was an invited walk-on, so I lived with the football players in the dorms. I never thought much of it, but I'm sure it was a sacrifice to a point for my family to send me to school.

During my junior season in 1986, we beat Georgia Southern 38–14 and then lost four games in a row. I tore meniscus cartilage in my left knee against LSU. The doctors told me I'd probably miss the rest of the season, but I really wanted to come back for the Auburn game. We were playing Kent State and then Rutgers, which wasn't very good back then, and then we had an open date. So I basically had a month to get ready to play Auburn. I didn't want to miss that game. I just continued to work out and tried to get my knee as ready as I could. I talked them into letting me practice the week of the Auburn game, and I really don't think they wanted to let me do it. They put a big knee brace on me, and I went out there. I was still in some pain, but I was really trying to hide the pain from everyone else. I think they realized I couldn't perform the way I really needed to, so Coach Hall told me, "Kerwin, I'll let you dress out for the game, but you won't play unless it's an emergency situation." I was kind of disappointed going into that game.

We played Auburn at Florida Field and turned the ball over, like, six times in the first half. People remember me bringing the team back in the fourth

By the beginning of his freshman season in 1984, Kerwin Bell was named Florida's starting quarterback and never relinquished the job during the rest of his college career. He led Florida to its first SEC championship in 1984 with a 9–1–1 record, although the SEC stripped the Gators of the title the following year.

quarter, but the MVP of that game was our defense. Auburn was ranked No. 5 in the country and they got six turnovers in the first half, including a lot of them on our side of the field. Somehow, our defense held them only to 14 points in the first half and we were only down 14–0 at halftime. After another one of our turnovers right before halftime, Pepe Lescano, our third-string quarterback, walked over to me and said, "Kerwin, I think you might be going in pretty soon." Auburn had Aundray Bruce and Tracy Rocker on defense. They were really getting after Rodney Brewer, who was the quarterback in the game. I looked at Lescano and said, "Pepe, I don't know if I want to go in there or not. It looks dangerous out there!" I knew I wasn't 100 percent and couldn't get away from them.

Sure enough, Galen put me in the game on the next series. I felt terrible trying to throw the football. I was favoring my knee, but the passes kept being completed. We were down 17–0 going into the fourth quarter, but I really got some confidence with a couple of good drives in the third quarter. We scored a touchdown right at the start of the fourth quarter to make it 17–7. We kicked a field goal to make it 17–10, and Auburn got the football back and went on this long drive. Brent Fullwood, their running back, was amazing, and we couldn't stop him. But with about two minutes left, he fumbled, and our defense recovered the ball.

A lot of people don't know this, but Ricky Nattiel had separated his shoulder on the drive before the last one. I threw a pass out in front of him, and the defensive back drove his shoulder into the ground. He had a third-degree separation, which is the most serious one you can have. Dr. Pete [Indelicato] told him he wasn't going back into the game. But Ricky jogged back onto the field for the last series, and he made an amazing catch on a corner route, which got us to Auburn's 5-yard line. He made a great play with his arms stretched out, and I'm still not sure how he was able to do it with a separated shoulder. Then we threw a fade route from the 5-yard line, a play we were pretty good at running. They were in man-to-man coverage, and Ricky was so fast he ran right by the cornerback. I just tried to throw the football to a spot, and he ran right up to it for a touchdown.

I was living in the moment, and for whatever reason thought we were going to kick the extra point to tie the score. I thought since we were down 17 points and came back, we were just going to tie the score. But Coach Hall called timeout, and I went over to the sideline. He told me we were going for two points. We had a play where we cleared everybody out, and wanted to get Ricky on an option-type route where he could just work his way into an open area. As I dropped back to pass, they really took him away. My second progression wasn't open, either, and I started to feel pressure. I just took off running. Everybody said it took a long time for me to get to the end zone, but I eventually got there and scored. We won the game 18–17.

116

We beat Georgia 31–19 in Jacksonville the following week. Ricky still had that third-degree shoulder separation, and most people wouldn't have played the following week with that injury. But Ricky was really, really tough. A lot of our pass routes that week were designed for Ricky to catch the ball and go out of bounds. It worked most of the day, and he didn't get hit a lot. Vince Dooley, Georgia's coach, played a lot of zone coverage and didn't pressure you a lot. The year before, when Georgia beat us 24–3 in a game that knocked us out of the national championship hunt, they blitzed us to death. Every time we were close to their 20-yard line, they blitzed us and we had no checks or answers. I think I threw for 400 yards against Georgia in 1985 (408), but we scored three points and couldn't get into the end zone. In 1986 we knew they were going to try to do the same thing and had a plan. We checked off and went to maximum protection, and Ricky was in man coverage and made three great catches for touchdowns.

We finished the 1986 season against Florida State, which was probably the first time they were athletically better than us. The NCAA sanctions were starting to catch up with us, and we didn't have a lot of depth. Deion Sanders was a cornerback on that FSU team. Of course, he was always a talker. He was a freshman the year before, and we threw all over him and won the game 38–14. It rained in Tallahassee during the 1986 game and flooded the field. Early in the game, Deion came up to me and said, "Kerwin, you're not going to do it again today." I told him, "Deion, we've got the rest of the game to do it again." We came back late in the game and threw a touchdown to Ricky on a post pattern, which was his last catch as a Florida Gator. We won the game 17–13.

We finished 6–5 in 1986 after starting 1–4, but we really didn't have a lot of confidence going into my senior season in 1987. When you see the talent level drastically change like it did, you don't have a lot of confidence. Anybody could see the difference. In 1984 our second- and third-stringers could play with our starters. In 1986 and 1987 we had guys starting who probably would have never started in the SEC. In 1987 we knew we were going to have to depend on some guys who really weren't ready to play. We felt like we were trying to get through the probation period and get Florida back to where it needed to be. We finished 6–6 during my senior season in 1987, but got to a bowl game and lost to UCLA 20–16 in the Aloha Bowl.

Playing at Florida really provided me with memories for a lifetime. You have all these great memories from your past that you'll remember for the rest of your life. A lot of them aren't about playing football. It's like coming back to Gainesville that night in 1984, when we won the SEC title at Kentucky. Seeing so many older people who were part of the Gator Nation for years and who had never experienced a championship is something I'll never forget. It was amazing to see it have that kind of an effect on people. Twenty years later, we're really remembered by a couple of events. People don't remember much about us, but they remember the Auburn game in 1985, the 96-yard touchdown pass to Ricky Nattiel against Georgia in 1984, and the two Florida State victories. Those memories are what will last a lifetime.

Kerwin Bell walked on Florida's football team in 1983 as an unheralded quarterback from Lafayette High School in tiny Mayo, Florida. Bell started his college career as the Gators' eighth-string quarterback. By the beginning of his freshman season in 1984, Bell was named Florida's starting quarterback and never relinquished the job during the rest of his college career. He led Florida to its first SEC championship in 1984 with a 9–1–1 record, although the SEC stripped the Gators of the title the following year. Florida went 9–1–1 in Bell's sophomore season in 1985. Bell is perhaps best remembered for coming off the bench with a knee injury in 1986 and leading the Gators to a come-from-behind 18–17 victory over Auburn. He also threw a 96-yard touchdown to Ricky Nattiel in Florida's 27–0 win over Georgia in 1984. He was named SEC Player of the Year in 1984 and left Florida as the SEC's all-time leading passer with 7,585 yards. After college, Bell was drafted in the seventh round by the Miami Dolphins in the 1988 NFL Draft. He spent seven years playing quarterback in the Canadian Football League and World League of American Football and also played one season with the NFL's Indianapolis Colts. Bell is currently the football coach at Division I-AA Jacksonville University in Florida.

TRACE ARMSTRONG

DEFENSIVE END

1988

ATTENDED JOHN CARROLL CATHOLIC HIGH SCHOOL in Birmingham, Alabama. There was a coach, Chip Wisdom, who was recruiting me to play football at Georgia. He took a job at Arizona State during the middle of recruiting season, and he called me up and asked me to come play out there. For a kid growing up in Birmingham, going to Arizona State was a big adventure. I loved Arizona State and liked the people and the defense and all those things.

I was kind of an unusual prospect in high school. I was probably 190 pounds when I played my senior year. By the time I got to college, I was probably 210 pounds. Florida State, Houston, Southern Mississippi, Auburn, Alabama, and most of the schools in the South recruited me. But I saw Arizona State as an adventure. It was a completely different part of the country and I'd never been to the desert before.

I went to Arizona State in 1984, which was the first year of Proposition 48. At the time, the NCAA standard was a straight 2.0 grade-point average to be eligible to play as a freshman. They didn't take into account test scores or anything else. I went to a really small parochial school that used a different grading system, and the NCAA really didn't know how to handle it. The NCAA had some problems coming up with what my grade-point average actually was, even though I'd taken calculus and other tough subjects at this parochial school. The NCAA was trying to tell me I might not be an academic qualifier. While the whole issue was getting sorted out, Arizona State allowed me to practice. Eventually, practicing was what ended up getting me ruled ineligible.

When the NCAA reinstated me for the 1985 season, they gave me an option of playing at Arizona State for three years and appealing for a fourth season. They said I could transfer to any other Division I-A school and be eligible right away. I decided to stay at Arizona State. I thought the NCAA would figure the thing out and fix it and do it right, but they never did. I would have redshirted during the 1984 season anyway, but it was tough. I had to go out and watch practice every day and sit there for three hours. I was working out and doing everything else on top of that. It was a very difficult year, but I learned a lot about life. It really made me focus.

When I signed at Arizona State, the coach was Darryl Rogers. He left after my freshman season and went to the Detroit Lions. John Cooper came in and was with me for three years. I had a great relationship with Coach Cooper and still do. There were a lot of great coaches on that staff. Cooper had Jim Colletto [now the Detroit Lions' offensive coordinator and former Purdue head coach], Pat Henderson [now running backs coach at Kansas], and Bill Young [now defensive coordinator at Miami, Florida]. There were guys on that staff who have really gone on to do some great things in college football.

120

That was an immensely talented football team at Arizona State, but we really didn't know how talented we were. Really, history proved how talented we were. There were guys on that team like Eric Allen, Randall McDaniel, Danny Saleaumua, and David Fulcher, guys who all had tremendous NFL careers. There were quite a few high draft picks to come out of that bunch. But we were still learning how to win. Coach Cooper was still building a program and building a mindset. [The Sun Devils finished 8–4 in Cooper's first season in 1985, losing to Arkansas 18–17 in the Holiday Bowl.]

We won the Pac-10 Conference and went to the Rose Bowl in 1987. It was really a tremendous experience. The Rose Bowl had a lot of prestige and to go into a stadium like the Rose Bowl and play in front of 100,000 people was almost too much to try and comprehend. We were a bunch of young kids and really didn't realize what was at stake. [Arizona State beat Michigan 22–15 in the Sun Devils' first appearance in the Rose Bowl.] When I went there, I thought Arizona State had a chance to win, which we did. We won a Rose Bowl and went to a bowl game every year I was there, which was back when it was still difficult to go to a bowl. [The Sun Devils finished 7–4–1 in Armstrong's junior season in 1987, beating Air Force 33–28 in the Freedom Bowl.]

Trace Armstrong played only one season at Florida after transferring from Arizona State in 1988. Armstrong made quite an impact in his short time with the Gators, earning All-Americas and All-SEC honors as a senior. He led Florida with 19 tackles for loss in 1988, despite playing much of the season with a serious knee injury.

Prior to the Freedom Bowl in 1987, I applied to the NCAA for my extra year of eligibility. They denied the appeal and said I could transfer to any other Division I-A school or declare myself eligible for the NFL Draft. I called Rex Norris, who had been my defensive line coach with Darryl Rogers. Norris was coaching with the Detroit Lions, and I asked him where I'd go if I declared myself eligible for the draft. Norris checked with some personnel people and they said I'd probably go in the third or fourth round. He told me I should stay in school. At that point, I really had no idea where I was going to go or what I was going to do. I asked Norris where I should go to school, and he recommended Florida because he and Galen Hall had coached together at Oklahoma during its glory years.

It was really strange. I had the opportunity to take five recruiting visits, just like I was a high school senior. I ended up visiting Georgia, Florida, and Penn State. The people at Florida really sold me on the school. When I got to Gainesville, one of the deans from the school of liberal arts met me and had a graduation plan in place for me. He showed me what credits would transfer to Florida and how I'd get my degree. I really liked Galen Hall. I thought he was a neat guy and a good coach. Tim Cassidy was the recruiting coordinator, and I really liked him. I'd been a three-year starter at Arizona State and had some success as a player. One of the things I really liked about Florida was they stressed that I wasn't coming there and starting over. They weren't going to treat me like a freshman or sophomore. That willingness to accept me as who I was as a player was another big part of my decision to transfer to Florida.

We had a great defense at Florida. I had two other great defensive linemen, Jeff Roth and Rhondy Weston, playing with me. It was a great defense. We had a really good group of young linemen, like Brad Culpepper and Tony McCoy. It was just a great practice environment. We all pushed each other relentlessly and we all got better. I think we elevated each other throughout that spring and the following season. But we struggled offensively that season. Emmitt Smith was nicked up a lot, and we were trying to figure out who the quarterback was going to be. We had Kyle Morris playing quarterback some, and Herbert Perry played quarterback some. We were a good team, but not a great team.

We beat LSU 19–6 in Gainesville to improve to 5–0. Winning that LSU game was huge. Tommy Hodson was their quarterback and he was a Heisman Trophy candidate. I remember he hadn't been sacked in six games, and they were talking about how great LSU's offensive line was. I think we had three sacks in the first half in that game. That was a really high point of the season. Brent Musburger did the game, and it was nationally televised. The defense played really well. I still have a picture in my home office of Rhondy, Jeff, and I walking off the field together with our arms around each other. That was just one of those great days that you'll never forget.

We played Memphis the next week, and they were really a better football team than people gave them credit for. They beat us 17–11. Then we went up to Vanderbilt, of all places, and lost 24–9. Those were tough losses. We played Auburn and lost 16–0. We had a chance to win the game, but we just couldn't score. Auburn had a very good defense, too, and we couldn't muster anything on offense. We lost to Georgia 26–3 in Jacksonville and just couldn't score again.

We came back and beat Kentucky 24–19 in Lexington. We finished the regular season against Florida State, and that was really the disappointing game. We just didn't play well at all. They were a very talented team. That was the game in which Deion Sanders rode up to the side of the field and got out of a white limousine for pregame introductions. I went over and told our receivers, "I don't care if you catch a ball. I just want you to knock the heck out of him the entire game." They actually did a pretty good job of that. We lost the game 52–17.

We finished the season against Illinois in the All-American Bowl in Birmingham. I missed that game because I'd had my second knee operation. I had the first surgery right after the Vanderbilt game because I'd torn cartilage in my knee. Dr. Pete [Indelicato] did the surgery on a Monday, and I played that following Saturday against Auburn. I actually played pretty well, but it was not a good idea. I ended up having to have my knee scoped again after we played Florida State. From that Vanderbilt game through the rest of the season, I'd have my knee drained every Monday and then have it drained again Friday, after going through a week of practice. I did that for five or six weeks. After the last game, I had to have surgery again, and having two surgeries in the same season was just too much.

It was disappointing to miss the All-American Bowl because the game was played in Birmingham. We'd all worked hard that year. Although the All-American Bowl wasn't a marquee bowl game, it was a bowl game and it was my senior year. It was your last chance to get to play with your buddies. It was difficult to watch, but there was just no way I could have gone out there and played and helped the team. Huey Richardson stepped in for me and, of course, had a great game against Illinois. Huey went on to be a great college player. [Florida beat Illinois 14–10 to finish the 1988 season with a 7–5 record.]

Galen Hall was fired as Florida's coach the next season, after I'd left for the NFL. It was disappointing; especially with the way it was handled. I don't know if Galen's career as a coach ever recovered. He left and was effectively black-balled in college football. I think his next job was as a graduate assistant at Penn State. Galen was a good man and a very good coach. He cared deeply about the players. He'd have the seniors and their girlfriends over to his house once a week during the season. He was just one of those guys who had an open-door policy. He got to know all the players and if there was a problem, he was always looking for a way to help.

I really enjoyed my time at Arizona State and played with some great guys and coaches there. It was in a great part of the country, and I had some success there. But I consider myself a Florida alumnus. I know that confuses a lot of people, but I think the reason I feel so strongly about Florida is because I got a chance to experience a school that does it right. They do it right athletically, in how they treat their players and their approach to the game. They do it right on the admissions and academics side, where they support the student-athlete. When I went to Arizona State, we were a very good football team. But being a football player out there was almost like a mark against you. It was really difficult to get the classes you wanted in school, and it was almost a burden to be a football player. I went to Florida and had a bunch of people who were great people and were willing to do anything they could to help. It just makes for a great environment.

After I left Florida, I remember very clearly my rookie season in the NFL. I was all beat up and tired and sore. I thought, *Gosh, I'll be lucky if I make it four years in this league.* I did have some fairly significant injuries during my career, but I always found a way to come back from them. To play 15 years is like an eternity in the NFL. I was very fortunate to have some great people helping me, and taking care of myself was a big part of my longevity.

I think my greatest asset was probably perseverance. I was always willing to get there early and stay late and out-work or out-last the competition. I was a late developer in high school, so it took me a couple of years of really hard work in college to get to the point where I could physically go out there and play and match up a little bit. It was that kind of work ethic, having to scratch and having to dig, that I carried with me throughout my whole career. Even when I was going into year 14 or year 15 in the NFL, I was still training six hours a day every day, just like I did when I was a 19-year-old kid trying to get some playing time at Arizona State. It was the character development and lessons I learned as a young guy that stuck with me my entire career.

Trace Armstrong, a native of Birmingham, Alabama, played only one season at Florida after transferring from Arizona State in 1988. Armstrong made quite an impact in his short time with the Gators, earning All-American and All-SEC honors as a senior. Armstrong led Florida with 19 tackles for loss in 1988, despite playing much of the season with a serious knee injury. Armstrong was a first-round draft choice (No. 12 overall) by the Chicago Bears in the 1989 NFL Draft. He played for the Bears, Miami Dolphins, and Oakland Raiders during a 15-year pro career. Armstrong led the AFC with 16½ sacks during the 2000 season and finished his career with 106. When Armstrong retired after the 2003 season, he was among only 21 players in NFL history to record 100 quarterback sacks during their career. Armstrong, who was president of the NFL Players Association for eight years, lives in St. Louis and works as a sports agent, representing several NFL and college coaches and TV/radio broadcasters.

The
NINETIES

KIRK KIRKPATRICK

TIGHT END

1987–1990

I GREW UP IN TAMPA AND ATTENDED Brandon High School. When I was in high school, the University of Florida was on NCAA probation. But Florida was still a popular choice. Florida never really had a great football program, but they won the SEC title in 1984 when they were on probation. They played a couple of games in Tampa Stadium, which was close to my home.

I was recruited by all the major schools, from Notre Dame to Florida to Florida State to Miami. But I just really liked Florida. Looking back on it, I really don't know what I was thinking at the time. Florida never threw to the tight end much back then, but I just really wanted to go to school there.

I went to Florida in 1986 and redshirted, which was fairly popular back then. It seemed like everybody redshirted. Very rarely did a freshman not redshirt. I really needed that year to get stronger and add some weight. I needed to get used to the fast game of college football. I weighed 215 pounds when I got there. The most I probably weighed in college was 230 pounds when I was a sophomore. By my junior and senior seasons, I was a lot leaner. I couldn't keep weight on during the season.

I played a few games during my redshirt freshman season in 1987. I caught my first pass against Tulsa [a 52–0 victory]. I mostly played on special teams and lettered, but I didn't play much on offense during that first season. I started a few games as a sophomore in 1988 and caught eight passes. The 1987 season was when the sanctions from the NCAA probation really started to set in. There might have been only 15 players in my recruiting class. That was one of the reasons you really wanted to go to Florida—you thought you were a part of a special group because there weren't that many scholarships to give.

Florida had a ton of tight ends, though. The tight end wasn't that involved in the passing game when Galen Hall was the coach. I went in there, and we had a ton of big tight ends who were much bigger than me. The thing that really stood me out from them was I was more of a receiver. The other tight ends were all just big blockers. They could catch passes, too, but most of them were not receiving-type tight ends.

I was never that close to Galen Hall. I think Galen was probably a really good offensive coordinator and positions coach, but I think he was a little bit out of it as a head coach. I didn't really know that many people who were that close to Galen. His offense was the Penn State–style offense. We ran and passed a little bit, but it was a balanced offense. We had a few offensive coordinators come in and promise to pass the ball, but it never worked out. We had Lynn Amedee, who might have been probably the worst offensive coordinator we had. He came in from Texas A&M and had a big ego, and we didn't do anything. We had so much talent, though.

129

We opened the 1989 season and beat Ole Miss 24–19. We beat Louisiana Tech [34–7], Memphis State [38–13], and Mississippi State [21–0]. We were 3–1 going into a big game against LSU at Baton Rouge. Ironically, that was the game when Galen Hall was fired. I had no idea he was being fired. Looking back on it, it probably created more turmoil for us. Everybody's job was on the line. Gary Darnell, the defensive coordinator, took over as the interim coach, but none of the assistants knew if they were going to keep their jobs. I'm sure all of the coaches were getting their résumés ready and didn't think they'd be back. It became a very loose team.

After beating LSU [16–13], we beat Vanderbilt [34–11] and New Mexico [27–21]. But then things kind of fell apart. We lost Kyle Morris, our quarterback, who was suspended from the team. Shane Matthews was suspended from the team, too, but he wasn't a big-time quarterback yet. It was a season filled with turmoil, and Emmitt Smith was pretty unhappy, too. Whitey Jordan was his position coach, and they were very close. For all practical purposes, Emmitt ran the team that season. Emmitt was a good guy, had a good head on his shoulders, and was a good leader. He was an all-around great

Kirk Kirkpatrick was a starting tight end for the Gators from 1988 to 1990. After catching only 27 passes in his first three seasons, Kirkpatrick caught 55 passes for 770 yards and seven touchdowns as a senior, which set season-high marks for any Gators tight end.

player. We lost four of our last five games, including a 34–7 loss to Washington in the Freedom Bowl.

We had heard rumors that Steve Spurrier might be coming on as our coach, but we knew for the most part that the coaching staff was gone. There was a little bit of anarchy because everybody on the team knew the coaches weren't coming back. When you have a bunch of 18- and 19-year-old kids, they're going to take advantage of the situation. I'm not sure anyone really cared about playing in the Freedom Bowl. There were a lot of guys showing up late for practices, meetings, and curfew checks—things that had never happened before.

I had never met Coach Spurrier before. I knew he threw the ball a lot. Growing up in Tampa, I knew he was the first quarterback for the Tampa Bay Buccaneers. I just heard a lot of great things about him. I knew he had a great offensive mind. With Spurrier coaching, Duke had just won the ACC championship in football. Duke! It was crazy. He came in, and everybody was really excited. The first time we met him, everyone was really impressed with him. Before he came in, information was very suppressed at Florida— things were very strict, and the little things were always more important. Spurrier got there and concentrated more on the big things. He got more out of the talent than anyone else did.

Spurrier came in before the 1990 season and probably had less talent than we had in 1988 and 1989. Yet, we had such a big turnaround. We probably had less talent because we had just lost Emmitt Smith and all those great play- ers. He looked at our team and asked, "How are you guys losing to Auburn? How are you guys losing to Georgia? You have more talent than those teams." He gave us some swagger and confidence.

It wasn't anything magical for me. He just said we were going to throw to the tight ends. Before my senior season, Steve said I was one of the best receiving tight ends he'd ever had. That made a big difference for me. I'd never been told that. Under Galen, you never got much recognition. He never complimented you much, so I didn't know if I was a good tight end or a bad tight end. I knew I could catch the ball, but I wasn't used in that respect. Spurrier came in and said, "We're going to throw to the tight end." I just believed him.

The defense used to kick our butts in practice every single day. If you remember back then, Florida's defense in the late 1980s was always ranked in the top three in the nation. We had great defensive backs, great linebackers, and a great defensive line. We had a really, really good defense and great tal- ent on offense, but we could never score. When Spurrier came, all these plays just started working. The offense just clicked. Spurrier's plays are really easy to learn, but they're hard to defend. I never found them that complicated, and

I think most people wouldn't. Everything is off a basic tree, and once you learn the fundamentals of Spurrier's offense, you can start adding new plays. His offensive philosophy is put together extremely well—it's not all fragmented like the other offenses people would bring in. Spurrier invented his offense, and I'm sure it's an off-shoot of one of the earlier San Diego Chargers–type offenses, but he refined it and made it his own. Players of great athletic ability and not-so-great smarts can learn his offense. That's how he got the most out of his offense.

All of the sudden, we went from doing poorly on offense to holding our own or dominating our defense, which was still pretty good. Spurrier just came in and gave us a lot of confidence. Plus, he was a Florida guy, and he was one of the first coaches who came in and was very proud to be a Florida alumnus. It was the first time we'd seen somebody show their loyalty to the University of Florida. He was proud to be a Gator, and showed it in everything he did. At the end of games, we'd go sing the Alma Mater. He was just a good Gator.

Spurrier surprised a lot of people when he named Shane Matthews the starting quarterback before the 1990 season. Shane hadn't done anything up until that point—he was a redshirt sophomore and had come into the spring as a fifth-string quarterback. Shane threw such a catchable ball and was so poised that he beat out everybody because he didn't make many mistakes. He always threw the football exactly where it needed to be. If you look at Spurrier's offense, the quarterbacks with the strongest arms weren't necessarily going to win the job. It was the quarterbacks who knew the offense the best and threw a catchable pass who were going to get it.

I'll never forget the first game of the 1990 season. We were getting ready to play Oklahoma State at the Swamp and it was a 3:30 pm kickoff. We were getting ready to go to the pregame meal about noon. Spurrier had just finished running and was in the swimming pool. I could have sworn I saw him drinking a beer. He was just so relaxed. He looked at us and said, "Okay, you ready to run some ball plays today?" I was with a group of guys and said, "Yeah, of course." Florida was always so uptight in the past. You would have thought we were getting ready to go into Normandy or something. It was just so serious and dead quiet. If you were acting out or laughing or something, people would get on you and say, "You're not taking the game seriously enough." That's just how serious it was. But with Spurrier, we were prepared as we needed to be, but he wanted to have some fun. It was a lot looser. I responded to it more, and everybody else did, too. He came in with a swagger and had a much better feel for it.

We went out and beat Oklahoma State 50–7. I don't think we ever scored 50 points in a game before Spurrier got there. It was all Spurrier. We were relaxed and had a good time. We went to Alabama the next week, and that was huge. Spurrier said that Alabama was the turning point for the program, and I think he was right. That was a typical Florida game where the defense would have played well and the offense would have played crappy. We would lose by a touchdown to 10 points. But we went into Alabama, which was coming off a pretty good season, and won the game 17–13. It was a hard-fought game and it was the first close SEC game we won. Going against Alabama in Tuscaloosa and winning, it was just a big turning point for us. It just felt different.

We beat Furman [27–3] and Mississippi State [34–21]. After the Furman game, the SEC said Florida wasn't eligible to win the SEC title. As a protest, we all painted our shoes black. It really wasn't fair because none of the players at Florida were involved in the NCAA violations. It made no sense whatsoever. We were quite upset about it. The Gainesville murders were going on at the same time during the 1990 season, and that kind of took the steam out of what we were doing. We were doing things that normally would have been huge news everywhere, but the murders happened and we were put on probation for something that happened when most of us weren't even there. There were a lot of things happening that were out of our control, but we responded by going out and just playing solid football every single week.

133

We went to Baton Rouge to play LSU in a nationally televised game on ESPN. It was kind of Florida's coming-out party. The 1990 team kind of gets lost in the shuffle. We were doing things that no Florida team had done before. It was kind of a turning point for Florida football. We were winning games we'd never won before. We beat LSU 34–8 and thumped them pretty good.

Near the end of the season, we were really clicking. We felt really good about ourselves and just played fantastically. Shane was playing great, and the offense was playing really well. Auburn came in and was undefeated and ranked No. 4 in the nation. Auburn had been kicking our butts for a few years, and it was Senior Night. We just beat them up pretty good, 48–7. It had been a while since Florida had beaten Auburn, and for us to throttle them like that was really a statement. Pat Dye apologized to his fans for the way Auburn played. We followed that game by beating Georgia pretty badly, 38–7. Very rarely had Florida won both of those games in the same season. When we played Georgia, Steve just went to another level.

Steve Spurrier is the reason Florida is where it's at today. He's the biggest Gator of anybody, as far as I'm concerned. If it wasn't for Coach Spurrier, Florida wouldn't even be on the map. And I don't even talk to him—I've probably talked to him twice in the last 18 years. But he is the reason Florida is what it is today. He came back in 1990 and brought that program back from the dead and made it what it is. Urban Meyer is living off that now and so have all the players ever since.

I'm very proud of that 1990 team. I don't think we get enough credit. I'm glad to be a Gator. I was very fortunate to play for Coach Spurrier for one season, and that was enough. It was unfortunate we didn't get to play for an SEC title or play in a bowl game, but I'm still proud of what we accomplished. It hurts as the years go on because you don't have the reunions for the SEC championships and things like that, but it's just the facts of life. It was just a really exciting time to be a part of Florida. That senior season really went by fast. I still maintain the 1990 team kind of turned it on for this generation.

Kirk Kirkpatrick, a native of Tampa, Florida, was a starting tight end for the Gators from 1988 to 1990. An under-utilized tight end in his first three seasons on the team, Kirkpatrick flourished after Steve Spurrier returned as his alma mater's coach in 1990. After catching only 27 passes in his first three seasons, Kirkpatrick caught 55 passes for 770 yards and seven touchdowns as a senior, which set season-high marks for any Gators tight end. He was named All-SEC by the Associated Press and league's coaches and second-team All-American by the AP, United Press International, *Sporting News*, and *Football News*. After graduation, Kirkpatrick spent time with the Los Angeles Rams and Tampa Bay Buccaneers in the NFL. Kirkpatrick lives in the Tampa area and owns several business ventures.

BRAD CULPEPPER
DEFENSIVE TACKLE
1988–1991

I GREW UP IN TALLAHASSEE, and my father played football at Florida. Obviously, I liked Florida because my dad played there. But growing up in Tallahassee, I watched Florida State, and they always had good teams. They played in the Orange Bowl in 1979 and 1980, when they had quarterbacks Jimmy Jordan and Wally Woodham. I liked Florida State growing up, and I wasn't going to go to Florida just because my dad went there.

So I went through the recruiting process and visited Florida, Florida State, Notre Dame, Alabama, and Auburn. Of course, I didn't want to be a farmer, so I didn't go to Alabama or Auburn. I kind of wanted to get out of my hometown. I really didn't want college to be an extension of high school, and that's kind of what eliminated Florida State in my mind. It was down to Florida or Notre Dame, and the girls at Florida were much better looking than the ones at Notre Dame. That's kind of what did it for me.

We had a good football team at Leon High School, where I played in Tallahassee. We ran into a buzz saw in the playoffs during my senior season when we played Escambia High School, which had Emmitt Smith at running back. We were the number-one-ranked team in the state and we were a passing team. When we played Escambia High, we played in a torrential downpour, and they ended up beating us in the state playoffs. Escambia High ended up going on to win the state championship. The same thing happened to us during my sophomore season. We were a good team, but we just didn't have much luck in the state playoffs. I ended up being a freshman at Florida with Emmitt, which was kind of interesting.

I really liked playing baseball in high school. Florida had talked to me about being a relief pitcher in college, but it was pretty much football all the way for me. Had I focused on baseball in high school, I'm not sure how it would have turned out. I threw 90 miles per hour as a sophomore in high school. But by the time I left high school, I was about 250 to 260 pounds. That's not the ideal pitching weight. Had I been 220 or 230 pounds, I probably would have concentrated on baseball. But football was my gig. Looking back on it now, I definitely should have gone out and thrown some relief innings for the Gators, but it would have been hard to balance football, academics, and baseball. That's so hard to do.

Before I went to Florida as a freshman, I contracted some kind of infection in my spine. The doctors couldn't diagnose what was wrong with me, and I had fevers for about two straight months. Some of the fevers would spike to about 104 degrees and the rest of the time I had constant low-grade fever. My back was killing me, and I wasn't sure what was wrong. The doctors in Tallahassee weren't sure what was wrong, so I ended up going to Shands [Hospital] in Gainesville. Anytime you have an infection in your body for that long and they can't diagnose it, it's bad news. They put me on IVs for about six weeks: three weeks in the hospital and three weeks at home. Fortunately, I've never had any lingering effects from it. I'm 38 years old now, and my back doesn't bother me at all.

Because of the illness, I ended up losing about 40 pounds. I was a blue-chip recruit as an offensive or defensive lineman. But when I showed up at Florida, I weighed about 215 pounds. I actually lost about a half-inch in height because the infection ate through my spine. When I arrived in Gainesville, I'm sure the coaches were like, "We didn't recruit that kid." Needless to say, I was redshirted that first season in 1987.

Because I had lost so much weight, the coaches immediately moved me to the defensive line. If I hadn't gotten sick, I'm sure I would have ended up on the offensive line, playing center or guard. Instead, they were like, "I guess we have to put him on defense because he's too small to play anything else."

Fortunately, moving to defense worked out for me. That move ended up putting me in the Florida Hall of Fame, really. It paid my bills by playing in the NFL for nine years. Honestly, I liked defense better than offense. I thought my body type was better suited for offense before I got sick. Once I got sick, I put my weight on much better. I ended up being leaner and quicker. At 215 pounds, I learned how to use my quickness because, obviously, I couldn't rely on strength anymore. As my career went forward, I was able to add weight and get stronger. By the time I left Florida, I was probably 250 pounds or 260 pounds and could bench press 550 pounds.

Galen Hall was Florida's coach when I got there in 1987. I really liked Galen Hall. He was a great coach. He was a great person. We'd sit down at lunch and just talk. We had a good recruiting class, which was Florida's first full class in a few years because it was coming off NCAA probation. Emmitt Smith was the star of that recruiting class. On defense, we all played pretty early in our careers because we didn't have a lot of depth because of the probation.

We went 6–6 in 1987 and always had a pretty good defense. Offensively, we just struggled for whatever reason. We were playing Florida State at the end of the 1987 regular season. We had a 6–4 record at the time. They came to us before the game and said, "If you win the FSU game, you'll go to Shreveport, Louisiana, and play in the Poulan Weedeater Bowl. If you lose the game, you'll go to Hawaii for the Aloha Bowl." Needless to say, we lost the game 28–14. I didn't mind. I got a free trip to Hawaii. We lost to UCLA in the Aloha Bowl 20–16, but actually played the Bruins pretty well. Troy Aikman was on that UCLA team.

137

As a redshirt freshman in 1988, I played a lot and ended up starting against Illinois in the All-American Bowl in Birmingham, Alabama. We played Illinois, which had Jeff George at quarterback. Trace Armstrong was hurt, so that game ended up being my first start. On the first play from scrimmage, I shed a block from the center. They ended up handing the ball to the fullback, and I hit him right at the line of scrimmage. I was like, "Man, I got him!" The guy ended up driving me about eight yards. My first tackle was an eight-yard gain, after I think I hit him about a half-yard behind the line. Welcome to the SEC and college football, buddy. We won the game 14–10, and everybody went out drinking afterward. Instead, I went back to the hotel and was soaking in the bathtub. I was so beat up.

I started about every game as a sophomore in 1989. A lot of us were sophomores who were starting. We started out the 1989 season and were really hot. We lost to Ole Miss 24–19 to start the season, but then won six games in a row [over Louisiana Tech, Memphis State, Mississippi State, LSU, Vanderbilt, and New Mexico]. After we beat LSU [by a 16–13 score in Baton Rouge], Florida fired Galen Hall as coach for some things he'd done with

Brad Culpepper helped lead the Gators to a 9–2 record in 1990 and the school's first official SEC title in 1991 as team captain. Culpepper was the recipient of the Draddy Scholarship Trophy in 1991, which is presented to the country's premier football student-athlete.

Jarvis Williams. I think he was paying some child support and paying coaches out of his own pocket, which was against NCAA rules. It seemed like kind of benign stuff, but Florida had just had the problems with Charley Pell [who was fired early in the 1984 season for breaking NCAA rules].

We had no idea about what was happening with Galen before the LSU game. It was a really big game at LSU. The score was tied 13–13 late in the game, and we were driving for a game-winning field goal. Our regular kicker was John David Francis. But for whatever reason, Galen put Arden Czyzewski in the game to kick the field goal. Arden had come in with us as freshmen, and we were all like, "Oh, my God! This guy can't make anything!" But he ended up nailing the game-winner at the horn. I think Galen knew he was going to be fired before the game. He was really, really emotional. The next day, it was announced Galen was being fired because of the allegations.

A week later, our quarterback, Kyle Morris, was kicked off the team for being involved in some on-campus gambling ring. We were down to our last quarterback, who was Donald Douglas. It was great for our opponents. We had no passing game after losing Morris. We lost at Auburn 10–7, when Reggie Slack threw a touchdown to Shayne Wasden in the back of the end zone really late in the game. Our quarterback had one completion in that game. We lost to Georgia 17–10 in Jacksonville. We had a really good team in 1989, but after losing our coach and then our quarterback, we really ended up struggling. Gary Darnell, the defensive coordinator, ended up becoming our interim coach. We lost four of our last five games and got beat pretty badly by Washington [by a 34–7 score] in the Freedom Bowl.

139

Steve Spurrier ended up getting the job before the 1990 season, and everybody was pretty excited about him coming back. Steve just had instant credibility. He won the Heisman Trophy at Florida and won an ACC title at Duke. Who would ever think somebody could do that? He had early success at Florida, and guys just bought into it.

Steve revolutionized college football. He really did. I give him all the credit in the world. He kind of took what Galen had and made it better. He put in that offense that just spread everybody out. I think a lot of teams have copied it now with the spread offense. But in the 1990s, I think every single coach in the country who was successful kind of copied Steve's offense, at least the SEC coaches did. It was "three yards and a cloud of dust," and then everybody started passing it once Steve came to Florida.

Steve came in and told us, "You've got to believe you can be champions. You've got a good defense, and I'm about to fix your offense." He was a great coach. As far as a person, if you sat down to talk with him, he either talked about football, himself, or golf. But as a coach, he knew the game, had us prepared, and made us believe we could win. He gave us all the confidence in the world.

When Spurrier came in as the coach, most of us playing on defense had redshirted and played a lot as freshmen and sophomores. Spurrier inherited a really good defense, and, of course, he took Shane Matthews out of a trash heap and made him a star quarterback. Our offense really came around, and Errict Rhett was a really good running back. We ended up winning the SEC in Spurrier's first season in 1990. We lost to Tennessee 45–3, but then ran through the rest of our SEC games. We won the SEC, but then they took the title away from us because of the NCAA sanctions for what Galen Hall had done. It didn't involve any of the coaches who were there. It didn't involve any of the players who were still there. Yet, we were still getting the penalties, so we couldn't officially win the SEC title. Steve still got us rings that said, "Best in the SEC." We really were the best team in the conference that season.

During my senior year in 1991, we went undefeated in the SEC and won the school's first official SEC championship. We dominated everybody. We beat Alabama 35–0. We shut out LSU 16–0. At the time, winning the SEC for the first time was really the biggest thing ever. But it's kind of been watered down over the years. I remember when I was in high school in 1984, the Gators won the conference under Galen Hall. They beat Kentucky on the road to win the title, and I remember the team flew back down over Florida Field when they returned to Gainesville. They had an impromptu pep rally at the stadium, and I remember reading about it in the newspaper. They played "We Are the Champions," and it was just a huge deal to win the conference. Of course, the SEC stripped Florida of the 1984 title because of the NCAA violations. It was kind of the same feeling during my senior season. We won it against Kentucky at home, and had a pep rally and people stayed and cheered.

Now, of course, Florida has won seven SEC titles and won national championships in 1996 and 2006. Danny Wuerffel won four straight SEC titles. You look at it now, and it's like, "Maybe we were making a big deal out of nothing," because they've done so much after we left. But at the time, we'd never won it. That's a long time—it's 80 years of history without ever winning a title without an asterisk. We were the greatest team in Florida history, at least that's what we considered ourselves. It was the biggest deal then.

Really, the biggest game we had in 1991 was against Florida State at the end of the season. The Seminoles had beaten us four straight years, in 1987, 1988, 1989, and 1990. They were really good in 1991. They had quarterback

Casey Weldon, who was the runner-up for the Heisman Trophy. They were ranked No. 1 in the country for most of the season, but had just lost to Miami 17–16 on their first "wide right." We were probably double-digit underdogs, but ended up winning the game 14–9 in a great game at Florida Field. It was my last game as a senior, and we ended up holding their potent offense to only nine points. It was a close game. It was hot. It was, like, 100 degrees in November. Casey took Florida State down to our 10-yard line late in the game. We'd all played a long time and we were all tired. He rolled left, then rolled back around right. He threw a pass, and a couple of guys knocked it down. That's the game people still talk to me about.

That Florida State game was the biggest game of my senior year. It was huge. I was not going to lose to the Seminoles again. The year before, 1990, we had a really good team. We went up to Tallahassee, and they beat us 45–30. Casey Weldon had a huge game against us. That 1991 game against FSU was my last bite of the apple. Growing up in Tallahassee and being somewhat of a Seminoles fan, I'd heard for four years how we weren't good enough to beat them. Urban Meyer has asked me to come back and speak to the Florida team a few times, and I've talked to them about the FSU game. I tell them the measuring stick of how you do as a Gator is how you do against Florida State. We're all the same guys—each of us could have gone to FSU or gone to Florida. The whole thing is: do you get better or do they get better? The measuring stick is that senior year. If you beat them, you got better during your career. If they beat you, they got better. That's the way we took it as seniors at Florida. If we beat them, we were better than Florida State during our careers.

141

We ended up getting our defense all banged up in that Florida State game in 1991, so we went into the Sugar Bowl against Notre Dame really thin. Notre Dame was kind of underrated. They had about 15 first-round picks and won only nine games that season. They had Jerome Bettis, who ran all over us. We had a bunch of guys hurt. They had Rick Mirer at quarterback, Derek Brown at tight end, Aaron Taylor on the offensive line. They were loaded. They kind of snuck up on everybody and beat us in the Sugar Bowl 39–28.

I like to think I was on some of the teams that really got Florida started. I ran into Urban Meyer at a hunting camp last summer. They were having their coaches' retreat at the hunting camp, and I saw Charlie Strong, who was an assistant at Florida when I played there. I was about to leave and saw Charlie. He told me I had to meet Urban. Urban kind of eyeballed me because

I'm only 205 pounds now and a lot smaller. He looked at me and asked, "You're Brad Culpepper, who was the All-American?" He asked me if I was on the 1996 team, which won the national title. I told him, "No, but let me tell you something. Every one of those guys came to Florida because of what we did in 1991. They were all in high school in the early 1990s and came to Florida because of what we did. We set the stage." Urban was like, "Man, you've got to come speak to my team!"

I have children now, and they're rabid Gators fans because their dad played there. It makes me proud seeing them enjoy being Gators. I think that's what makes me most proud. I'm not a guy who really dwells on my past. I was fortunate to be at Florida and then play for the Tampa Bay Buccaneers for six years. It was good to live in this area. It's fun to go to games now and show my kids the plaques and pictures they have hanging up around the locker room and stadium. It's nice to see they're proud of their old man. They love it. It hits home with my kids, which hits home with me as well.

Brad Culpepper, a starting defensive tackle for the Gators from 1988 to 1991, grew up behind enemy lines in Tallahassee, Florida. But Culpepper followed in his father's footsteps when he chose to play college football for the Gators. Bruce Culpepper was captain of Florida's 1962 team. Brad Culpepper was named All-American by the Associated Press, *Sporting News*, *Football News*, and Kodak during his senior season in 1991. He had 21½ tackles for loss in 1991 and finished his career with 47½ tackles for loss. Culpepper helped lead the Gators to a 9–2 record in 1990 and the school's first official SEC title in 1991 as team captain. He played on three Florida teams that played in bowl games: the All-American Bowl in 1988, the Freedom Bowl in 1989, and the Sugar Bowl in 1991. Culpepper was the recipient of the Draddy Scholarship Trophy in 1991, which is presented to the country's premier football student-athlete. He later received a master's degree in sports administration and law degree from Florida. Culpepper was a 10th-round draft choice of the Minnesota Vikings in the 1992 NFL Draft. He made his mark in the NFL with the Tampa Bay Buccaneers. In five seasons with Tampa Bay, Culpepper had 33 sacks, ranking among the highest totals in franchise history. Culpepper now lives in Tampa with his wife and three children and has a highly successful law practice.

SHANE MATTHEWS
QUARTERBACK
1989–1992

EVER SINCE I WAS BORN, my dad was a high school football coach. Obviously, that helped me quite a bit. I grew up being the ball boy, and as soon as school was out, I was out at practice with him. I was around football my entire life—not only football, but it carried over to baseball and basketball, too. I was always the bat boy for the baseball team until I was old enough to play. I think being around sports at such a young age—and coming home at night and seeing my dad watching the old film reels going against a blank wall—helped me understand the game of football.

We grew up in Cleveland, Mississippi, and moved to Pascagoula, Mississippi, after my sophomore year of high school. At the time, Pascagoula High School was the largest high school in the state. Our first year, we were 4–6 and weren't very good. My senior year, we went 15–0 and won the state championship. We had an unbelievable football team. We had Kez McCorvey and Terrell Buckley, who played at Florida State, and we had four or five guys go to Mississippi State and two more go to LSU. A couple of guys went to SWAC schools. If you counted the sophomores, juniors, and seniors on that team, we had more than 30 guys go on to play college football.

It was very difficult playing for my father. I'm an only child. We had a rule in my family that once we got home, we couldn't talk about football. My dad was also the high school's athletics director, so he saw every one of my basketball games and every one of my baseball games. We would talk about those games a little bit, but we never talked about football. We never talked about the outcome of games or how I played. It was always done in the meetings, on the field, or in the field house. He just wanted to be a dad to me when he was home. My parents wanted a family atmosphere at home. Sometimes we talked about Ole Miss football because my father played there and my mother was a cheerleader there. I grew up going to every Ole Miss game. After our games on Friday nights, we'd load up the car and go to Oxford, Mississippi, Baton Rouge, Louisiana, or wherever the Rebels were playing on Saturday.

Everyone thought it was kind of a forgone conclusion that I was going to Ole Miss. The Ole Miss coaches recruited me, but probably not the way they should have. They probably thought they had me in their back pocket. Texas A&M recruited me pretty hard because Jackie Sherrill was the coach and he was from Mississippi. Texas A&M started recruiting me before my junior year of high school. LSU was only three hours from Pascagoula, and the coaches there recruited me pretty hard. I was recruited by the majority of SEC schools, except Alabama. I would have loved to have gone to Alabama. I'm kind of weird because I'm a big uniform guy, and I loved Alabama's uniforms more than any other uniform in college football. They were simple uniforms, and I just loved them. I loved Alabama's tradition, but they didn't recruit me. Florida State recruited me because we went to their summer camps. We took about 12 guys from our high school team to Tallahassee, and Kez and Terrell ended up going there.

I officially visited Texas A&M, LSU, Florida, and Florida State. I didn't need to visit Ole Miss. The Rebels were running the veer offense under Billy Brewer at the time, and it just wasn't for me. I wanted to play big-time college football. Our high school stadium seated about 15,000 people and it was packed every night. So we were used to playing in front of big crowds. I'd go to games at Ole Miss, and its stadium seated about 35,000 people at the time. It just didn't seem like it was that big of a jump. Then you'd go to games at Tiger Stadium in Baton Rouge or Florida Field, and it was a huge difference. Plus, in the time it took me to get from Pascagoula to Oxford, I could pretty much get to Gainesville. I was as far south as you could get in Mississippi, and Oxford was pretty much as far north as you could get.

My parents went with me on every one of my visits. I'd fly to the schools, and they'd drive and meet me there. My mom always wanted to do a list of pros and cons after we got home from every school. The only reason I visited Texas A&M was because of a coach named Lynn Amedee. He had been recruiting me since my sophomore year. Then Lynn was hired at Florida, and that's kind of how the Gators got into the mix. I really liked LSU because my best friend, Frankie Godfrey, was going there. He was my center in high school, and they were trying to get us as a package deal. I was kind of built like LSU quarterback Tommy Hodson, and they kept telling me, "You're the next Tommy Hodson." Florida State was in the mix, too, because of its tradition, and they were really winning at the time. Florida State was recruiting quarterback Charlie Ward at the time, though. I still tell all my buddies, "You guys wouldn't have even known who Charlie Ward was if I'd gone there!" After I went to Florida, we did the list of pros and cons, it wasn't even close as far as academics and athletics. Florida was the best place for me.

I got to Florida in 1988 and redshirted. I was 165 pounds when I signed my scholarship. I tried everything in the book to gain weight. I was never a big weight lifter or workout guy. Spurrier didn't like his quarterbacks to lift weights. I was a bulking 180 pounds when I graduated from Florida. My redshirt season wasn't bad—it was a learning experience. It was kind of neat being away from home for the first time, and it was just kind of fun. I knew I wasn't going to play in any games, but I got to travel to a couple of road games. We played Ole Miss in Jackson, Mississippi, and I caught a lot of crap from people in the stands. They were calling me a traitor and all that stuff.

145

I started the 1989 season about third or fourth on the depth chart and wasn't playing at all. I actually thought about transferring back to Ole Miss. All of my buddies from high school who didn't play football were frat boys at Ole Miss, and Oxford has the best looking women you'll ever see. I thought I'd never play at Florida and knew I could go to Ole Miss and play. But we had a rule in our family that whenever you started something, you finished it, no matter what it was. My parents told me, "We don't care if you ever take a snap at Florida. You're going to graduate from there." That's why I ended up staying.

After five games in the 1989 season, Galen Hall was fired as our coach. Being a guy that wasn't playing, it really didn't affect me, I guess. I think he got a raw deal because he was fired for something that happened a few years earlier. Galen was a great coach. He was a different kind of coach. He was quiet and didn't say a lot. He was one of those coaches who would sit up in the tower. Gary Darnell, our defensive coordinator, took over as interim coach the rest of that season.

Shane Matthews guided Florida to its first official SEC title by finishing 10–2 in 1991. Matthews was named SEC Player of the Year in 1990 and 1991 and finished with 9,287 passing yards and 74 touchdowns.

I was roommates with Kyle Morris, our starting quarterback. We got into some trouble after Galen was fired. I used to get a bunch of parking tickets on campus because it was so hard to find parking. We started gambling through some of the fraternities, and I was trying to get enough money to pay my parking tickets. One of the other quarterbacks found about it and called his dad. His dad called the school, and that's how the whole thing blew up. They found out about it and told us to stop, but the other player's dad wanted us to be punished. So they suspended us for the rest of the season. It was a good learning experience for us.

Steve Spurrier was hired to replace Galen before the 1990 season. Steve reinstated Kyle and I to the team. Growing up an Ole Miss fan, I knew every thing about SEC football. But to be honest, I had no idea who Steve Spurrier was, not even after spending two years at Florida. Up until that time, they didn't have his Heisman Trophy stuff displayed anywhere because Florida hadn't done anything in football. During that Christmas break, I was back in Mississippi watching bowl games with my dad. We watched Duke's bowl game against Texas Tech in the All-American Bowl. We saw Steve's offense and I said, "Man, this is right up my alley."

Spurrier told everyone in the first meeting that nobody had a starting job. He said there might be a pecking order, but the starting jobs were up for grabs. I started that spring about fifth or sixth on the depth chart. A couple of guys got hurt, and I slowly started working my way up the depth chart. I played well in a few scrimmages. John Reaves, who was helping with the quarterbacks, picked me to play on the Orange team during the spring game. I threw three touchdown passes. Kyle, who was the returning starter, threw four interceptions.

I just felt comfortable in that offense. Spurrier's offense is so quarterback-friendly. If you have an understanding of how to play the game, he doesn't make it real difficult. There are a lot of offenses I've been in that just didn't make sense to me. I have a memory where I can look at a play that's drawn and memorize it just like that. Seeing it once is all I need, and I immediately know where everyone is going. There are some offenses where I can sit there and say, "This just doesn't make sense." But I could take 11 guys and teach Steve's offense to them in three or four hours, and they'd know the base offense. It was that simple.

Steve named me the starting quarterback a week or two before our 1990 opener against Oklahoma State. Obviously, I was really excited. I'm sure the

Gator Nation and all the big-money boosters were like, "What the hell is Spurrier thinking? He's taking a guy who has never taken a snap and never thrown a ball and named him the starter?" Kyle had played quite a bit, and Spurrier was choosing a guy who had never played before. But he'd told everyone at the Gator Club meetings that whoever his starting quarterback was would be the All-SEC quarterback. I think Steve understood that I was a coach's son and he liked having a guy on the field that thinks like he does. It's amazing how much he and I think a lot. But it was kind of surprising that he would choose a 170-pound kid who didn't have much of an arm to open up his legacy at Florida.

I remember being in the locker room before the Oklahoma State game. I was getting dressed and was nervous. Coach Spurrier came up to me and asked, "Shane, what do you want to open up with?" Every quarterback wants to throw the ball, but I told him, "Coach, let's open up with a little screen pass and get the confidence going." He said, "Shoot, no, we're going to throw it down the field." I still remember the play: trips left, Z short, blue slide, Z cross. I dropped back, and Ernie Mills was wide open for a 25-yard gain. I threw another long pass to Ernie on a steamers play for another 20 yards. I think we scored in about five plays. It was outstanding. Not only did you have a new quarterback, but you had the hero of Florida football coaching in his first game. Here comes the "Fun 'n' Gun" offense. Everybody was expecting to see the ball in the air, and to go down the field like that with no incompletions, it was a great moment. I had a pretty good game for my first start, and we won 50–7. That first start was special.

We played at Alabama the next week. A lot of people at Florida say beating Florida State to win the national championship in 1996 was the biggest win in Florida history. But that Alabama game was the turning point in Florida football history. Because of Alabama's tradition and Florida's history of never being able to win SEC road games, that's where it turned. There were still a lot of questions about me. I remember we were backed up to our own goal line at Alabama, and Coach Spurrier called a long post pattern to Ernie. I was like, "Are you crazy? These guys have been killing me all day, and you want me to take seven steps?" But I hit Ernie perfectly, and it would have been a 99-yard touchdown if Ernie hadn't been tripped by the turf monster. Will White had three interceptions in the game for us. It wasn't a typical Spurrier offensive display. Alabama shut us down pretty good on offense, but we still found a way to win 17–13.

That Alabama win kind of started the snowball effect. We beat Furman [27–3], Mississippi State [34–21], and LSU [34–8]. We were 5–0 and feeling pretty good about ourselves. We went to Tennessee and wore those blue pants that Spurrier wanted to bring from Duke. I don't think we ever wore them again. Tennessee was loaded with Dale Carter, Chuck Smith, and Jeremy Lincoln. The score was 7–0 near the end of the first half, and we drove down the field. I threw a pass to Kirk Kirkpatrick, who was probably one of the best tight ends in SEC history. He ran a curl route, and there probably wasn't a guy within 15 yards of him, and he dropped it. We had to settle for a field goal, and it was 7–3 at the half. We were feeling pretty good, and kicked off in the second half to Dale Carter, who went about 90 yards for a touchdown. It was a disaster from there, and we lost 45–3. Spurrier took me out of the game, and Kyle and a couple of other quarterbacks played. None of them played very well, and Spurrier told me, "I'll never take you out again."

We bounced back and beat Akron [59–0] and then beat Auburn [48–7] in a night game on ESPN. We always had a lot of success against Auburn. I never lost to Auburn in four years at Florida. Then we played Georgia in Jacksonville. As a player, Spurrier never had much success against Georgia. He knew that game would determine which team would win the SEC. For whatever reason, Spurrier just hated Georgia, and it showed. Florida was 11–1 against Georgia when he was the coach there. He always thought Florida went into that game with the better talent, but always found a way to lose. I think he was so sick of hearing the Georgia people that he just stressed we were going to beat Georgia no matter what.

We finished 9–2 during the 1990 season and actually won the SEC. But the NCAA put Florida on probation, and we weren't allowed to win the title. After the Alabama game, we found out about the sanctions, and a couple of guys decided we were going to spray paint our shoes black. We ended up finishing first in the SEC, and that started Spurrier's legacy there.

We came back in the 1991 season and were undefeated in the SEC. Our only losses were against Syracuse and Notre Dame in the Sugar Bowl. It was very gratifying. It was the first official SEC championship in Florida history. We played Florida State at the end of the season, and it was the most physical game I've ever played in. It was supposed to be this big offensive explosion, but it ended up being a defensive struggle. Florida State had a great offense with Casey Weldon. We had a great offense. In about the fourth play

149

of the game, I took a shot while throwing the ball, and my knee was shot. I played the rest of the game, but had torn cartilage in my knee. I walked out of the locker room on crutches, and Casey walked out of FSU's locker room on crutches. We won the game 14–9. It was the best college football game I ever played in.

We went to New Orleans to play Notre Dame in the Sugar Bowl. I'll be honest, we had a lot of fun in New Orleans. We were still ready to play and were up 13–0 in the first half. They couldn't stop us, and we were going right down the field. But then they made some adjustments on defense and were rushing only one or two guys. I'd never seen so many guys covered. They also realized we'd lost some key defensive linemen to academic problems. They just started running Jerome Bettis, and we couldn't stop him. With the way they were defending us, we probably should have run Errict Rhett a little bit more. But Coach Spurrier got a little antsy and wanted to throw it. I didn't play that well coming off the knee injury, but Notre Dame had a good team. We were better but didn't execute and lost the game 39–28.

We lost a lot of players before my senior season in 1992. We lost most of our defense and all but one guy on the offensive line. We started two true freshmen, Reggie Green and Jason Odom, at offensive tackle. They ended up being great players, but they were right out of high school. It was a rough year for me. My mother passed away from breast cancer right before the start of the season. We were 1–2 after losing to Tennessee and Mississippi State. The Mississippi State game was a disaster. I threw five interceptions, and it took me right out of the Heisman Trophy race. The Mississippi State crowd was all over me. They ran the option with Sleepy Robinson, and we couldn't stop them. We lost the game 30–6.

I was proud of that season. Even though we represented the East Division in the first SEC Championship Game, we weren't very good. In my opinion, the 1992 team was probably the least-talented team Spurrier had at Florida. We started the season terribly, but found a way to get into the SEC Championship Game. We played Alabama, which had the best defense I'd ever seen in college football. They were beating us 21–7, but we came back and tied the score. Our defense got us the ball back, and I threw an interception to Antonio Langham, who ran it back for a touchdown. We lost the game 28–21. It was fun to be in that SEC Championship Game, but the way it ended was brutal. The only good thing to come out of it was that Alabama went on to win the national championship. If we had won the game, Florida State would have played for the national title. We finished 9–4 during my senior season, which wasn't bad. In fact, it was probably Spurrier's best coaching job at Florida.

Playing for my dad at the high school level, there was tremendous pressure—everybody thought I was playing quarterback because I was the coach's son. I think that actually helped prepare me to be able to handle Coach Spurrier. I think there are certain guys who can handle him and certain guys who can't. I'll be real honest, all of his criticism was constructive. But I kind of let it go in one ear and out the other. If you let it get to you, it could really affect your play. I think the people who handled it the best were myself, Danny Wuerffel, and Rex Grossman. I think most of the other guys had issues with him.

Spurrier's wife always said it was scary how he and I were so similar. We're both very competitive. He's an avid golfer, and so am I. I like to compete, no matter what it is. During a lot of games, I knew what play he was going to call before he called it. I think it was just the way he prepared us. He's different from most coaches because he ran the quarterback meetings. The more you watched film with him, the more you knew about how his brain worked. Being around football my whole life, it just came naturally for me.

It is an honor to be the first quarterback that started Spurrier's legacy at Florida. What Steve did at Florida was amazing. I don't think people around the country truly realize what he did. They see Florida being a top-five team for the last 20 years, but before then, Florida was nothing. People don't realize that. Florida always had good teams, but they couldn't win the big games. That's one of the things he stressed in his first meeting—the only way we were going to win championships was to win SEC road games and beat Georgia. He did all of that.

There is a little bit of jealousy, not only for myself, but for guys who played on the 1990, 1991, and 1992 teams. Because we played on TV and established that offense, guys like Wuerffel, Jacquez Green, Ike Hilliard, and Fred Taylor came to Florida. We kind of laid the ground work for the 1996 national championship.

But I wouldn't change a thing. I tell kids all the time that playing 14 years in the NFL was a blessing for me, but I'd trade every dollar I ever made to go back and start all over at Florida. The experience of playing in that stadium and playing in other SEC stadiums, there's nothing like it. The three years I played at Florida and for Steve Spurrier were the three best years of my life.

> Shane Matthews, a native of Pascagoula, Mississippi, was Steve Spurrier's first starting quarterback at Florida. As a sophomore, Matthews guided the Gators to a 9–2 record in 1990. The Gators had the best record in the SEC in 1990, but were ineligible to win a conference title because of NCAA sanctions. The following season, Matthews guided Florida to its first official SEC title by finishing 10–2 in 1991. Matthews was named SEC Player of the Year in 1990 and 1991 and was fifth in Heisman Trophy voting as a junior. He broke 50 Florida records and 19 SEC marks during his three-year starting career and finished with 9,287 passing yards and 74 touchdowns. He signed with the Chicago Bears as an undrafted free agent in 1993 and played 14 seasons in the NFL, starting games for the Bears and Washington Redskins. Matthews lives in Gainesville, Florida, and was named coach of the Florida franchise in the fledgling All-American Football League.

TERRY DEAN

QUARTERBACK

1991–1994

I GREW UP IN NAPLES, FLORIDA, and was the first player to commit to play for Steve Spurrier after he was named Florida's coach. I got to know him during my junior year of high school. I attended the Duke football camp that summer, when Steve was the coach there. Of all the camps I attended, he helped me understand the game and the motion of throwing the football better than anyone else I'd worked with. I developed a good relationship with him during that camp, and when he got the job at Florida, he called me that day. I knew that in all likelihood Florida was the school I was going to go to.

At the time, Florida had the potential to get the death penalty from the NCAA and was getting ready to get hit with some sanctions. They really didn't know what they were going to get hit with. I was originally from Birmingham, Alabama, and grew up an Auburn fan. We moved to Florida when I was about 10 years old, but I'd always wanted to play for Auburn. It was down to Florida and Auburn, but I just kind of felt like Florida was going to do more to develop me and send me on to the next level.

Once I got to Florida in 1990, I was redshirted as a freshman. I sat three seasons behind Shane Matthews, who was the starting quarterback. It was a tough time for me. My relationship with Spurrier had deteriorated almost immediately once I got there. He was very difficult to play for, and I really struggled with my confidence and just not knowing if I was going to play. It was a tough time. I guess I learned more about myself during that time than I did about anything having to do with football.

Shane left Florida after the 1992 season, and I went into the 1993 season expecting to be the starting quarterback. Danny Wuerffel was only a freshman at that time, and I thought I'd earned the job. But it was pretty apparent that Danny was an immediate favorite of Steve's, and I knew I'd have to play well or it wouldn't last. Danny and I kind of alternated at quarterback during the 1993 season. We alternated during the first game [a 44–6 victory over Arkansas State] and went up to Kentucky for the second game. Both of us were throwing picks against Kentucky, and he'd keep yanking each of us. Danny threw a touchdown to Chris Doering at the end of the game [a 24–20 victory], and so Danny was the quarterback from there.

We played Auburn on the road and lost 38–35. Steve brought me in for the next-to-last play of the game and put me at receiver. He was going to run a double pass to me, and that was the only play I had in the game. It was pretty disappointing because the game was at Auburn, and I had a lot of family there. My grandmother had passed away that week, and I went to her funeral after that game. My father and I had also scheduled some time to go down to Troy State. I wanted to look at the school and saw it as a place to maybe transfer to. Honestly, I don't think I ever came that close to transferring. I would have had to finish the season at Florida, and it was pretty apparent that Danny was going to be Spurrier's choice. Had I not played again that season, I probably would have transferred. It's funny how things work out.

We played Georgia in Jacksonville in 1993 and there was a torrential rain storm. Danny was really struggling to throw the wet ball because he had small hands, so Steve put me in the game. I was trying to throw it as hard as I could, really to irritate Steve more than anything else. It had really gotten to the point where my relationship with Steve was completely gone. I barely talked to the guy and almost had an ambivalent attitude about it. I came in and just played without a care in the world. I kind of developed that attitude toward him. If he jumped on me, I just turned away and didn't let it bother me like it always had. We beat Georgia 33–26, and I was excited about being able to come in and help us win. I didn't know what it meant, but I knew it was going to help me.

We played Southwestern Louisiana the next week, and I threw six touchdowns but got hurt [in a 61–14 victory]. We went to South Carolina, and I don't even think I dressed to play in the game [a 37–26 win]. I started against

Terry Dean helped guide the Gators to two SEC championships as a junior and senior. He threw for 255 yards in the Gators' 41–7 thrashing of previously unbeaten West Virginia in the Sugar Bowl, which capped an 11–2 record in 1993. It was the winningest season in Florida football history to that point.

Vanderbilt [a 52–0 shutout] and I think I got benched twice during that game. I threw an interception, and he put Danny in. Danny threw an interception, and he put me in. It was musical chairs at that point. You knew if you went into the game and threw an interception, you were coming out of the game. It was as difficult as you would think it was. You knew if you made a mistake, he was going to yank you and put the next guy in. Fortunately, you knew he was going to do the same thing to the next guy, so you just kind of waited around for that to happen. I was a little bit more of a slinger than Danny was. Danny was a pretty conservative guy and threw safe and shorter routes. We had Jack Jackson, Willie Jackson, and Harrison Houston at receiver, so I liked to let it fly. Sometimes, you had to take the good with the bad.

The Florida State game in 1993 was the loudest I'd ever heard anything in my life. Steve pulled Danny after we fell behind, and we scored and scored again. All of the sudden, we were only down seven points early in the fourth quarter. I threw a touchdown to Jack Jackson in the corner of the end zone. He won an ESPY award for the catch he made, kind of flipping it over his shoulder to catch it. I remember being on the field and our fullback, Chris Bilkie, ran up to me. His face mask was right up to my face mask, and he was yelling at me, but I couldn't hear anything. It was so loud, and the ground was actually vibrating. We held them, and on third-and-eight, Charlie Ward swung a swing pass to Warrick Dunn. My roommate, Michael Gilmore, ran up to make the play, but he was stiff-armed. Dunn bust down the sideline for a 70-yard touchdown, and that kind of finished it. We lost the game 33–21.

Danny hurt his knee against Florida State, so I was able to start against Alabama in the SEC Championship Game [a 28–13 win] and against West Virginia in the Sugar Bowl [a 41–7 victory]. The SEC Championship Game was kind of my fondest memory at Florida. Growing up in Alabama and growing up an Auburn fan, I hated the University of Alabama. I'm very close to my family, and my father hates Alabama. To go through what I went through that year, and then to beat the team I grew up watching my dad pull against, was pretty special. We were able to do it in Birmingham, where I was born, and it was the pinnacle for me. It's the best memory I have from playing there. We played West Virginia in the Sugar Bowl, and they still had a chance to potentially win the national championship. We kind of set the tone early. We smacked them around and then just put the wood to them. That was a fun game.

I thought I had done enough as a junior to win the starting job as a senior in 1994. But Steve said during the spring that it was going to be an open competition. I won the job in the spring and went into the season as the starter. It had gotten to the point where his antics really didn't bother me anymore. We went into the season ranked No. 1 in the country and truly had the best team in the country. It's a shame it turned out the way it did because we should have won the national championship.

We hammered people early and often during the 1994 season. We beat New Mexico State 70–21 in the opener, and I threw seven touchdowns in the first half. Steve put Eric Kresser, one of our backups, into the game, and he threw a touchdown. We beat Kentucky 73–7 in Gainesville the next week.

156

It was kind of a revenge game for me because Kentucky was where I really lost my job the year before. I threw five touchdowns in that game, and we were just rolling. We were a machine at that point. We went up to Tennessee and won 31–0. We knew we had a good team, but to go up to Knoxville and win like that was really a statement. Of course, I can also say I'm 1–0 against Peyton Manning, which isn't a bad thing to say. Everything was just clicking that night, and our defense was great. To shut them out at their home was a pretty special night.

We beat Ole Miss in Oxford 38–14 and then beat LSU 42–18 in Gainesville. The LSU game was kind of where it fell apart, and I'm not sure why. I had a pretty good game against LSU, but not a great one. I went in the Sunday after the LSU game and was watching film preparing for the Auburn game. Coach John Reaves, the quarterbacks coach, came into the room. Then Steve came into the room and asked John to leave. He closed the door and just jumped on me and cussed me. I was really baffled. I left the room and called my dad and said, "I think I just played my last game at Florida." Spurrier told me in that room, "If you play bad against Auburn, I'm going to bench you." Spurrier was our quarterbacks coach, offensive coordinator, and head coach, so we were with him every minute in practice. He told Coach Reeves during practice that week, "You know, these quarterbacks aren't listening to me. You're going to coach them this week." Spurrier literally didn't talk to me the whole week. On the Friday before the Auburn game, we were going through our walk-through, and Spurrier came up to me and put his arm around me. He told me, "You know, I just want to tell you, if you play bad against Auburn, I'm going to put Danny in the game."

We went to the hotel that night and I told Michael Gilmore, "This is going to be my last game at Florida." He told me I was insane. At that point, I was among the potential leaders for the Heisman Trophy. But I just knew it was over, and it became kind of a self-fulfilling prophecy. I was just in a fog in that Auburn game and knew it was going to happen. I was just waiting for it to happen and, sure enough, I kind of fell right into the trap. I played poorly against Auburn, and Danny came in off the bench. We lost the game 36–33.

After the Auburn game, I didn't play much more at all. We were playing Southern Miss late in the season, and it was kind of a weird moment for Steve. He put me in the game, and I threw a quick hitch to my brother, Jason, who was a walk-on. That's still one of the plays I remember from my career at Florida, getting into the game and being on the field with my brother at the same time. Why Steve gave me that moment, I have no idea. It was a nice moment for me and my brother.

When Florida won the 1996 national championship, I was happy for Danny. I grew up a Christian like Danny did, and even with all the things we went through, I was never mad at Danny. I never held a grudge against him. If it had to be anybody in the world, I'm glad it was Danny who won a national championship. He's a great example and a great Christian guy. I never had any problems with Danny. My problems were with Steve.

I have a lot of respect for Urban Meyer. He's really done a lot to reach out to former players and bring them back. I never would step foot up there when Steve was the coach. I wanted nothing to do with the program. Urban came in and created some programs to bring back former players. I think it's smart business on his part. I'm glad to be involved with Florida football again. I am an avid Gators fan and follow the recruiting and get on the blogs and everything else. I've become sort of a junkie with it.

I'm a big believer that God had a plan for my life and I went through these trials to grow as a person. A lot of people ask me if I regret going to Florida and wish I would have gone to Auburn. The answer is no. I met my wife at Florida. If I'd known how my life would turn out, being back in Naples and having a great life, I wouldn't have changed anything. I really wouldn't change anything about it. I had some high highs and some low lows, but the whole experience made me what I am today.

158

Terry Dean, a native of Naples, Florida, was the Gators' starting quarterback during parts of two seasons, from 1993 to 1994. Dean helped guide the Gators to two SEC championships as a junior and senior. He threw a school-record seven touchdowns in a 70–21 victory over New Mexico State on September 3, 1994, and threw six touchdowns in a 61–14 win over Southwestern Louisiana on November 6, 1993. Dean's 39 career touchdown passes still rank eighth in Florida history. Dean was named most valuable player of the 1993 SEC Championship Game, completing 20 of 37 passes for 256 yards with two touchdowns in the Gators' 28–13 win over Alabama. Dean threw for 255 yards in the Gators' 41–7 thrashing of previously unbeaten West Virginia in the Sugar Bowl, which capped an 11–2 record in 1993. It was the winningest season in Florida football history to that point in history. Dean is an investment banker and lives in Naples.

SHAYNE EDGE

PUNTER

1991–1994

I WENT TO FLORIDA IN 1991 and was part of Steve Spurrier's second recruiting class. I grew up in Lake City, Florida, and graduated early from high school and participated in spring practice at Florida in 1991. I guess you would say my recruiting class consisted of myself, Jimmy Owens, and Alfred Smith. There were three of us who graduated from high school early and went to Florida for the spring.

Florida had an immediate need for a punter, which is one of the reasons I went there. I'd gone to a couple of Florida games the year before, and Arden Czyzewski was the punter. He had a couple of 25-yard punts, and I thought if I couldn't punt there, I didn't need to go anywhere else. Clemson recruited me to be its quarterback because we ran an option offense at Columbia High School in Lake City. Georgia Tech recruited me to play defensive back, and so did Georgia. But Florida and Tennessee wanted me to punt, and my dad really wanted me to go to Tennessee. My dad loved the mountains and wanted to move up there. I went to a football camp at Tennessee during the summer before my senior year, and Johnny Majors brought me into his office and offered me a scholarship. My dad was like, "We gotta go. We gotta go to Tennessee. We might not get another offer."

I definitely wanted to play quarterback, but I thought cornerback was a better position for me. At Florida, I knew there was no way I was going to play quarterback or cornerback and get to the next level. I knew I could go to Florida and punt for four years and hopefully make it to the NFL. As a kid growing up, that's what you dream about, to play in the NFL. I knew if I went to Florida, I'd have that chance. Of course, I did not know that I wouldn't punt that much. I think during my junior year, I didn't even qualify for the best average in the SEC because we didn't punt enough. Coach Spurrier wasn't about punting. There were a couple of times we went for the first down on fourth-and-four or fourth-and-five from our own 30-yard line. I'm thinking, "Boy, I'm ready to go." I'd start running out on the field, and Coach Spurrier would say, "No, no. Shayne come back! Get off the field!"

I wore a No. 6 jersey when I first got to Florida. I practiced that whole spring wearing No. 6. One day out of the blue, Coach Spurrier came up to me and said, "Shayne, No. 6 isn't treating you very well. We're going to put you in No. 14." I was No. 14 from that day on, and I guess it worked pretty good because I punted pretty well.

We opened up the 1991 season against San Jose State and we didn't punt in the first half. Coach Spurrier came in the locker room at halftime, and we still didn't know if Judd Davis or I were going to do the punting. We'd had a good competition in camp. Spurrier came up to me at halftime and said, "Shayne, you've got the first one." On the first punt, I went out there and shanked it about 31 yards. I pretty much knew the next punt would be Judd's. But Coach Spurrier came up to me as I was running off the field and said, "You gotta get that nervous stuff out of your system. You've got to punt it like you're capable of punting." My second punt was 62 yards in the air. I got a standing ovation from the crowd, and Coach Spurrier met me right there on the field and said, "Great job." From then on, I was Florida's punter.

I'll never forget the Tennessee game during my first season. Tennessee was ranked No. 4 in the country when we played them, and Dale Carter was their punt returner. He was leading the nation in punt returns. I averaged 54 yards per punt in that game, and we beat them 35–18. Larry Kennedy intercepted a pass and ran it back for a touchdown. The Florida State game was big in 1991. We were both ranked in the top five. We beat FSU 14–9 in Gainesville. We almost lost the game because I hit a bad punt late in the game. I averaged, like, 45 yards a punt, even with the bad punt, but Terrell Buckley returned a punt about 30 yards late in the game. Luckily, our defense tipped away a pass to Matt Frier in the end zone at the end.

With Coach Spurrier, it was all about winning championships. Coach Spurrier will tell you that 1990 team won the SEC and started it all. But they were on probation and weren't allowed to win it. But that success carried over to 1991, when we won the school's first SEC title. The biggest thing to Coach Spurrier was winning the title at home against Kentucky [a 35–26 victory]. It was a really big deal. He made sure all the players stayed on the field. As a matter of fact, we even went back on the field after our postgame meetings to celebrate with the fans some more.

We played Notre Dame in the Sugar Bowl in New Orleans, and it was a fiasco. Notre Dame beat us 39–28. They had Jerome Bettis, and when I played with him with the Pittsburgh Steelers, he gave me fits about that game. Coach Spurrier being Coach Spurrier, he was going to throw the ball. It didn't matter how many people they dropped back in coverage, he was going to throw it. He let the seniors have a good time the week before that game, too. We practiced like we were supposed to, but he wanted to make sure the seniors enjoyed the experience. The curfew was pretty lax that week, but I guarantee you he locked us down pretty good when we went to bowl games after that.

We opened the 1992 season against Kentucky and won 35–19. We flew to Tennessee the next week and lost 31–14. It really rained during that game, and we almost crashed flying home to Gainesville. Then we went to Mississippi State and got beat up pretty good, 30–6. Shane Matthews was still a Heisman Trophy candidate going into that game, but he threw five interceptions. The Mississippi State fans were throwing dog biscuits at us. Coach Spurrier went up and down the sideline, telling everybody to put their helmets on so we wouldn't get hit by dog biscuits.

We were struggling, but turned it around and won our next seven games in a row. We beat LSU [28–21], Auburn [24–9], Louisville [31–17], and Georgia [26–24]. I never played well against Georgia, for whatever reason. I'm from Conyers, Georgia, and always wanted to play well against them. Coach Spurrier hated Georgia and still does. I think he'd rather beat Georgia than any other team in the country. You could always tell it was Georgia week with Coach Spurrier. He'd be more fired up for that game than any other game during the season. He hated Florida State, too, but he was always ready to go for Georgia. I've never seen anybody get so fired up to play Georgia.

After losing two of our first three games, we were 8–2 and ranked No. 6 in the country going into the Florida State game in 1992. We had a couple of

Shayne Edge was the Gators' starting punter from 1991 to 1994. He punted 182 times during his career, third-most in Florida history, and his 42.5-yard career average ranks fourth in school history.

fake punts in that game. We always had fake punts drawn up, but Coach Spurrier seldom used them. He believed more in his offense than he did in me faking a punt. He'd just always go for it. We drew up a fake punt before the Florida State game and went through it every day in practice. We got ready to run it in Tallahassee, and I threw the ball the wrong dad-gum way. We still got a first down because of pass interference, but we would have scored a touchdown if I'd done what Coach Spurrier told me to do. We lost the game 45–24.

We played Alabama in the first SEC Championship Game in Birmingham. The score was tied 21–21 late in the fourth quarter. Monty Duncan, one of our wide receivers, ran the wrong route, and Shane Matthews threw it to where he was supposed to be. Antonio Langham intercepted the pass and ran it back for a touchdown. We lost the game 28–21. Coach Spurrier never let Monty forget that play. Coach Spurrier always hated to lose, but he really hated to lose like that. Earlier in the game, I tried to run a fake punt, but I mishandled the snap and tried to get back to the line of scrimmage. I didn't make it. Coach Spurrier yelled, "Shayne, get the ball off! I don't care what you do! Get the ball off!" During crucial times in games, he'd always come over to me and say, "Listen, I don't care what you have to do. You get the ball off! Kick it down the field 30 or 40 yards and be done with it!"

We came back and beat North Carolina State 27–10 in the Gator Bowl. That was the Fog Bowl. It was really foggy, and Coach Spurrier told me during warm-ups, "Shayne, see how high you can kick it up there. If you get it up there high enough, they won't be able to see it coming down! They'll fumble it, we'll pick it up and go score!" It was always about scoring with him.

We got off a really hot start during my junior season in 1993. We beat Arkansas State [44–6] and Kentucky [24–20]. Danny Wuerffel threw a late touchdown to Chris Doering to help us win the Kentucky game. Judd Davis had a chance to kick a long field goal in the game, but Coach Spurrier decided to go for it. We threw five or six interceptions in that game. We beat Tennessee [41–34] in Gainesville. We played Mississippi State and won 38–24. I had a couple of roughing-the-punter penalties in that game. They'd barely hit me, but I'd fall down and get the penalty. Anytime you could get a first down for Coach Spurrier, he'd be happy. So I'd always fall down and act like they broke my leg. Spurrier would walk about halfway onto the field and give me a thumbs up. Then he'd turn around and start calling his plays again.

We went to LSU and won 58–3. Eric Kresser, one of our backup quarterbacks, came into that game in the fourth quarter and checked off to a middle play, a streak route. The LSU fans gave him fits. We were up 51–3 at the time, and Kresser threw a 60-yard touchdown. The crowd was booing us like crazy, and Coach Spurrier yelled, "It wasn't me! It was him! I didn't call it!"

We lost to Auburn the next week, 38–35. We should have won that game. Then we went to Jacksonville to play Georgia. That Georgia game was the Mud Bowl. Coach Spurrier gave me a tip before that game. Judd and I were kicking in the pouring rain, and Coach Spurrier came up to us and told us not to wear socks. He said, "If you wear socks, they're going to get wet, and you're not going to be able to kick the ball. Take your socks off!" I was like, "What?" Judd kicked four field goals. He wore socks because he was a sissy. Eric Zeier was driving Georgia for a touchdown late in the game. He threw a touchdown, but Anthone Lott called timeout right before the play. We won the game 33–26.

After the Georgia game, we blew out Southwestern Louisiana [61–14] and beat South Carolina [37–26]. We beat Vanderbilt [52–0] and then got beat by Florida State again [33–21]. Late in the game, we had cut the score to 26–21, and Kevin Carter had just batted down a second-down pass attempt. They threw a little flare out to Warrick Dunn, and Tamarick Vanover clipped Anthone Lott. Dunn ran around him and scored on a 70-yard run. That was the loudest I'd ever heard the Swamp. I've never heard the Swamp that loud. You couldn't hear anything.

After losing to Alabama in the SEC Championship Game the year before, we came back and beat the Crimson Tide 28–13 at the end of the 1993 season. Late in the game, we had a fourth-and-13 and ran a fake punt. I ran for 20 yards and a first down. I could have run out of bounds, but I tried to cut it back and score. I can remember lying on my back and talking trash to whoever hit me. It was a linebacker who had knocked the dog crap out of me. I got up, and Spurrier didn't even blink an eye. That's the way he always was. If he got a turnover or a big play, he was going for a touchdown on the next play. I still don't know how Jack Johnson caught a touchdown. Terry Dean threw it too far in front of him, but Jack caught the pass for a 43-yard touchdown. I can remember on the plane ride back home, Spurrier came up to me and said, "Shayne, those media boys kept asking me if your run was a designed play. I told them it was because they don't know any better." I wasn't supposed to run it.

West Virginia was undefeated when we played them in the Sugar Bowl at the end of the 1993 season. They had an outside shot at winning the national championship. It was kind of like that Sugar Bowl against Notre Dame in 1991. We didn't think Notre Dame should have been playing in the game, and that's kind of the way West Virginia felt about us. But Monty Grow hit their quarterback, Darren Studstill, so hard in that game he didn't know where he was. He hit that man so hard his face mask was going down the side of his face. We won the game 41–7.

During my senior season, in 1994, we opened the season and were really rolling on offense. We beat New Mexico State [70–21], Kentucky [73–7], and Tennessee [31–0]. That Tennessee game was one of our best games, and Terry Dean really played well. We had some goal-line stands at the end of the game to keep the shut out. They tried a couple of field goals at the end of the game just to put points on the scoreboard, and they missed both of them.

We were ranked No. 1 in the country after that Tennessee game and beat Ole Miss [38–14] and LSU [42–18]. Terry Dean threw an interception in that LSU game, and Coach Spurrier told him if he ever threw another interception, he was done. It was kind of weird. Going through it as a player, both quarterbacks were definitely capable of getting the job done. It was amazing to watch Terry go from first-string and Heisman Trophy candidate to fifth-string. After starting for two years, he was left messing around with the kickers during practice. He knew he wasn't going to get in the games, so he'd be over there messing around with us. He knew he was never going to step on the field again. We lost to Auburn 36–33, and that knocked us out of the No. 1 ranking. Danny Wuerffel came off the bench and threw a couple of touchdowns. We should have won the game. It was the beginning of the end for Terry. Afterward, we had guys in the locker room crying and moaning. Coach Spurrier said, "Who's crying? It's a game! Don't be crying!"

We kind of took out our frustration on Georgia the next week. It was the first time in a long time we played Georgia in Gainesville. We won the game 52–14. We beat Southern Miss [55–17], South Carolina [48–17], and Vanderbilt [24–7]. We went to Tallahassee to play Florida State, and it might have been the worst moment of my career. They said it was a tie, but we got handled pretty good in that game. We were up 31–3 in the third quarter, and Jason Odom, one of my best friends, told me we were going to lose. I said, "What? Have you looked at the scoreboard, buddy?" He said, "Spurrier has gotten conservative. He's not attacking anymore." All we did in the second half was punt. I had a punt in that game where I almost got into a fight with Peter Boulware. It was a high snap, and I ran off to the right and missed a guy. I got off the punt, but Boulware still came at me. I knocked him down, and, of course, I liked to run my mouth a little bit and was talking trash to him. The punt rolled 56 yards, and I thought we were going to win the game. They had bad field position, but they went right down the field like we were nothing. The game ended in a 31–31 tie. I think that game hurt Spurrier more than any loss we ever had in the time I was there. It was bad.

We played Alabama for the third straight season in the SEC Championship Game, but they played the third one in Atlanta. We trailed 23–17 late in the game, and Wuerffel threw a little flare pass to Chris Doering. Doering threw a pass to Aubrey Hill to get down to Alabama's 2-yard line. Then Wuerffel threw a touchdown to Doering with about five minutes left. We won the game 24–23.

We played Florida State in a rematch in the Sugar Bowl in my last college game. That game was a big mess. We had a couple of guys get in a fight at a Sugar Bowl function, and they were a big part of our game plan. Darren Hambrick was one of the players who was suspended. We lost the Sugar Bowl 23–17.

I don't think I could have walked into a better situation than Florida. You were starting out in a program that was getting better game by game. You could see Coach Spurrier wasn't going to lose. He hated losing more than anyone I'd ever seen. I hated losing, too. It was just like he was playing in the games. That's why we were so good. If he had good players, how was a defensive coordinator going to outcoach him? It was fun playing for him.

Shayne Edge, a native of Lake City, Florida, was the Gators' starting punter from 1991 to 1994. Edge was a three-time All-SEC choice and three times was named All-American honorable mention by United Press International. He punted 182 times during his career, third-most in Florida history, and his 42.5-yard career average ranks fourth in school history. Edge's 76-yard punt against Vanderbilt in 1992 still ranks as second-longest punt by a Gator. After graduation, Edge played for the Barcelona Dragons of the World League of American Football and for the NFL's Pittsburgh Steelers during the 1996 season. He lives in Lake City, Florida, and teaches for Columbia County Schools.

CHRIS DOERING
WIDE RECEIVER
1991–1995

I GREW UP IN GAINESVILLE, FLORIDA, and I was a huge Gators fan my whole life. I went to everything, every sport. I'd go to gymnastics and baseball and, of course, football games with my family. I really was one of those kids who bled orange and blue.

When I was a kid, I even got my picture taken with Cris Collinsworth, who was my hero. I still have the picture. The newspapers in Gainesville had gotten hold of the photo when I made the team at Florida. It was kind of funny because we were similar players—tall and lanky with good hands. But I didn't play football when I was young because my mom and dad didn't want me to get hurt. I played soccer instead, which probably helped with my stamina later in life.

I finally got to play football in junior high as a place kicker and then in the last game they put me in at wide receiver. As a freshman, I was moved up to the varsity at P.K. Yonge High School and also played basketball. We won the state basketball championship during my senior year in 1991. I was playing well and I had a basketball coach in Randall Leath, who had played at Florida, who really pushed me to be competitive. And John Clifford, another former Gator, had put together a really good football program.

But when it came time to pick a college, nobody in Division I-A wanted me. It was devastating. I was such a big sports fan and wanted to be a Gator, but not only did the Gators show no interest, but nobody else did either. I had a couple of non-scholarship schools offer me a chance to play football, but what kind of offer is that? I thought about going to Kentucky Wesleyan, but my heart was breaking.

Nobody had ever told me I wasn't good enough. I was 6′4″ and only weighed 155 pounds. But I knew I could play at the next level. The funny thing is that one school that showed interest in me to be a walk-on was Florida State. I thought I might just do it, go there and show the Florida coaches they made a mistake. But I went to a Florida–Florida State baseball game, and their fans were doing the Seminole chop. I hated it. Really, it made me sick to my stomach. All those years of being a Gators fan, I couldn't switch. So I just decided, since my parents could afford it, I was going to go to Florida.

The good thing was that Steve Spurrier was the Florida coach and he liked guys who really wanted to be Gators. So I got preferred walk-on status and didn't have to try out for the team. Another thing he liked was guys who were in good shape. I won the 12-minute run, which was a big deal to him. So Spurrier noticed me during my first season at Florida in 1991. The coolest thing was that I got to go to the Sugar Bowl after the 1991 season [when Florida lost to Notre Dame by a 39–28 score] with the rest of the freshmen who were redshirting, even though I wasn't playing. We didn't feel like we were part of the team, but we did enjoy ourselves and got to be part of the bowl experience.

In 1992 I did get to play a little bit in the games. I caught my first pass at Tennessee [a 31–14 loss]. It was pouring down rain, and they were killing us. So Coach Spurrier put the scrubs in. Antwan Chiles threw me a short pass, and it popped up in the air, but I somehow caught it. I remember thinking I could never feel anything as good as catching a pass for the Gators in a college football game. Everybody was down on the ride home, but I was pumped.

The next year, in 1993, we were loaded at wide receiver with Jack Jackson, Aubrey Hill, and Willie Jackson. But just before the season, Coach Spurrier gave me a scholarship. I remember calling my parents to tell them. I was so excited because I had earned it. I think knowing that I had worked so hard made it that much more special. I also knew that if Coach Spurrier put me on scholarship, it meant I was going to play. He was running some four-receiver sets and I was catching everything in practice.

Sure enough, I caught two passes in the 1993 opener [a 44–6 rout of Arkansas State] and went to Kentucky the next week knowing I would play.

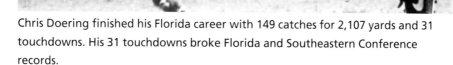

Chris Doering finished his Florida career with 149 catches for 2,107 yards and 31 touchdowns. His 31 touchdowns broke Florida and Southeastern Conference records.

Of course, that was one of the most amazing games ever. [Quarterbacks] Terry Dean and Danny Wuerffel both played, and neither one could quit throwing to the other team. But I caught a touchdown pass and now I had a new greatest ever memory. Little did I know what was going to happen.

We had the football and were down 20–17 on the scoreboard late in the game. We moved the ball to Kentucky's 28-yard line. Danny tried to hit me on a "steamers Y-Z" pattern but missed me. In the huddle, he called the same play, and I was wide open this time. The secondary went with Jack Jackson, which I would have, too. Danny laid it in there perfectly for the touchdown. I was wide open. Talk about an amazing feeling. It has stayed with me my whole life, the call [radio play-by-play announcer] Mick Hubert made, "Doering's got a touchdown! Doering's got a touchdown!" The next day, the headline in the *Gainesville Sun* said, "Doering does it."

Now, I was truly living my dream. I had seen so many games where someone had made a play like that, and this time it was me. We went on to have a great year in 1993 after we survived Kentucky. We finished the season with an 11–2 record and won the SEC and the Sugar Bowl [41–7 over West Virginia]. It was great to go back to Sugar Bowl and be playing, instead of being a hang-around guy, as Coach Spurrier used to call them.

The next season, 1994, we won the SEC again, but it was hard. Alabama was beating us the whole game in the SEC Championship Game, but Coach Spurrier pulled off some trickery. I threw a pass to Aubrey that set up a short touchdown pass from Danny to me in the back of the end zone. The night before the game, I had a dream that I caught the winning touchdown pass. That was surreal. We finished the 1994 season with a 10–2 record and lost to Florida State 23–17 in the Sugar Bowl, the third time in four years we played in New Orleans.

During my senior season, 1995, we went undefeated until the Fiesta Bowl. It was an incredible year. We were steamrolling through everyone and we had so many great receivers, like Ike Hilliard, Reidel Anthony, and Jacquez Green, but the ball kept coming to me. We played Georgia in Athens [while Jacksonville Municipal Stadium was being renovated], and I caught three touchdown passes on one drive. The first two were called back because of penalties. That was great putting 52 points on the Bulldogs [in a 52–17 rout, the first time a Georgia opponent ever scored 50 points in Sanford Stadium].

In our last regular-season game against Florida State in the Swamp, I caught a touchdown pass that gave me the all-time SEC record for touchdown catches in a career. You talk about a special feeling. To do it at home, on Senior Day, against our rivals, against the school I almost went to, that was surreal.

My senior season and my career ended with that blowout loss to Nebraska [62–24 in the Fiesta Bowl]. It was strange because I had a great game, but they were all over Danny, and we couldn't stop them. In our hotel room that night, it was weird because the whole season had been so great and then ended with such a thud.

I can look back and see my career as a real testament to perseverance and hard work. I was a nobody who became a somebody and I still encourage kids not to give up on their dreams. And being a Gator my whole life, it made what I accomplished at Florida that much better.

The thing is, you never stop being a Gator. I found that out coming out of high school and I find it out every day. You are always a part of the Gator Nation, and people look at you differently when you've played football for Florida. I'm lucky that I had great coaches along the way, especially Coach Spurrier. There's a guy who doesn't cheat, does things the right way, and makes you the best player you can be. I'm proud of what I was able to do at Florida and proud to be a Gator.

Chris Doering, who grew up near the Florida campus in Gainesville, began his college career as a walk-on receiver in 1991. By his second season on Florida's varsity squad, Doering had impressed coach Steve Spurrier enough to be awarded a full scholarship. Doering was only getting started. He finished his Florida career with 149 catches for 2,107 yards and 31 touchdowns. His 31 touchdowns broke Florida and Southeastern Conference records. Doering was named first-team All-SEC by the league's coaches and the Associated Press as a senior in 1995 and was named a second-team All-American by the AP. Doering was drafted in the sixth round of the 1996 NFL Draft by the Jacksonville Jaguars. He played parts of six seasons for the Indianapolis Colts, Denver Broncos, Washington Redskins, and Pittsburgh Steelers in the NFL, finishing his career with 42 catches for 476 yards and three touchdowns. After retiring from football, Doering, his wife, and two children returned to Gainesville, where he operates several business ventures and works as a college football analyst for Sun Sports.

JUDD DAVIS
KICKER
1992–1994

I HAD A ROUNDABOUT WAY OF GETTING to the University of Florida. I was born in California, but moved to Michigan when I was very young. I was a soccer player and a big Notre Dame fan. I loved the Irish, but my real heroes as a kid were the soccer players.

I played youth soccer and didn't really get interested in football until my dad dragged me out onto a field one day and held a football for me to kick. I boomed it, and he knew I would be a kicker. So I kicked some in middle school, but we moved to Ocala, Florida, before I started high school. You want to talk about culture shock. The way they talked in Ocala was different. I couldn't understand what they were saying some of the time. And for my brother and I, we had to start over making friends.

I started kicking for the Ocala Forest High School team, but I got hurt my junior year. I had a good senior year, but if you missed your junior year as a kicker, nobody knew who you were because recruiting started then. So nobody was recruiting me. I had buddies who said I should go to a small school, but that made me want to kick at a big school even more. I really wanted to go to Florida, but I had to get my academics in order. So I spent a year at Central Florida Community College.

I finally got to Florida in 1992, and Steve Spurrier was there. He had a kicker on the team already, so I went out for punter. But then they signed Shayne Edge, who was a tremendous punter. His second punt as a freshman went 61 yards, so it didn't look good for me. Then they signed Bart Edmiston, who was a high school All-American, to do the kicking. I really thought about transferring. It looked like my dream was dead.

Finally, I went into Coach Spurrier's office. I was full of bravado, but I knew I had to do something to get noticed. He just told me to keep kicking. I'm sure he wondered what I was doing in there. This was during the 1992 season, and we went to South Carolina. At halftime, we were sitting in the hallway eating something, and Bart had missed a chip shot in the first half. Coach Spurrier told me I was in. I was so pumped. I was nailing everything in warm-ups before the second half. I made a few extra points and won the job. I made a 47-yard field goal the next week against Vanderbilt and got a game ball.

So I was the kicker to start the 1993 season and I was having a great year. We went to play Georgia in Jacksonville, and it was raining harder than I ever saw it rain. There were huge puddles near our sideline. I didn't figure I'd be doing any kicking that day. But we kept having drives that stalled out, and they'd trot me out there. Shayne was my holder, and he'd make a little tee with the mud every time I kicked. I was a pretty good golfer, so I knew the best way to make sure I got it all was to go down and get it. After every kick, I'd look down at Shayne, and he'd have mud all over his face. But they kept going through the uprights. I made all four of the kicks I tried, and they were all important because we won 33–26. After the last one I made, Coach Spurrier came out on the field to congratulate me. That was big.

173

Everybody says that game won me the Lou Groza Award that year and they are probably right. The conditions were so bad and it was such a big game, for me to make all those kicks on national television got the attention of a lot of voters. It was an incredible honor to get that award and it means a lot to me to this day. They invited me to present the award in 2007, and it was really special to spend some time with the kickers who were finalists, playing golf and having dinner with them. And over the years I've gotten to know the Groza family, which has been really something.

During the 1993 season, we went on to win the SEC Championship Game in Birmingham [beating Alabama, 28–13] and won the Sugar Bowl against West Virginia 41–7. It was an incredible year, the start of a tremendous run by Florida in the SEC. In my senior year, 1994, I kicked well, but

As a junior in 1993, Judd Davis won the Lou Groza Award as college football's best kicker and was named All-American by UPI. He made 33 of 38 field-goal attempts inside 50 yards during his career and set an SEC record with 65 consecutive extra points made during the 1994 season.

we didn't try a whole lot of field goals. The offense was incredible, and we scored a lot of touchdowns. But I did kick a 52-yarder against Southern Miss, which was the longest of my career and made all 65 of my extra points, including the game-winner in the SEC Championship Game against Alabama [a 24–23 victory].

That was the game where Shayne and I decided we wanted to do something special, so after one of my kicks, we did the "Nestea Plunge"—just hit helmets and fell back to the ground. Everybody loved it and luckily we didn't get a penalty. So it was a good year, but I didn't win the Groza. No back-to-back awards, but we won the SEC again, which is what really mattered.

I look back on my career, and it really means a lot to me that I went from this skinny kid who wasn't supposed to play Division I football to being named the best kicker in the country. I'm really proud about what I was able to accomplish. During the four years that I played for the Gators, I really didn't have a grasp of what an honor it was to actually be out on that field in the Swamp. At the time, I just thought is was cool to be recognized every now and then, to be called an All-American and maybe get an article written about me from time to time. I had no idea how it would affect the rest of my life.

I remember right after the Florida-Georgia game in 1993, my dad pulled me aside outside of the locker room. He walked me away from all of the fans, friends, and reporters. He looked at me and very seriously told me to stop, look around, and really take a minute to appreciate the moment. He said that this would all be over faster than I could imagine and to cherish it. I remember thinking he was being kind of dramatic, but I listened to him. I never forgot what he said. It's amazing how I can remember that moment like it was yesterday, but 17 years have gone by in what seems like a week. He was exactly right.

Recently, I took my seven-year-old son down in the football locker room and showed him the pictures of me in the hallways. He couldn't believe his old dad was actually up there next to some of the greatest college football players in history. That moment with him trumped all others and I now know that I will forever be part of the so-called "Gator Nation."

Judd Davis, who grew up as a soccer player before moving from Michigan to Ocala, Florida, was one of the greatest kickers in Florida history. He took over the place-kicking duties midway through the 1992 season and kept the job the next two seasons. As a junior in 1993, Davis won the Lou Groza Award as college football's best kicker and was named All-American by UPI, the first Gators kicker to earn such an honor. The former walk-on completed his career with 225 points, the highest scoring total by a Florida player at the time. Davis made 33 of 38 field-goal attempts inside 50 yards during his career and set an SEC record with 65 consecutive extra points made during the 1994 season. He completed his career with a then-school-record 81 consecutive extra points made. After graduation, Davis tried out for a few NFL teams. He returned to Ocala, where he still lives today working as a real estate banker. He occasionally works with Gators kickers.

JASON ODOM
OFFENSIVE TACKLE
1992–1995

I WAS ONE OF THOSE KIDS WHO WAS A LOT BIGGER than the other kids my age. I started playing Little League football in 1982 in Bartow, Florida, with kids who were three, four, or five years older than me. When I finally got to where they went by age instead of weight and I was playing with kids my own age, I remember thinking, "This isn't fair."

Until I went to junior high, I never played the offensive line. I was always a skill player. I was fast and could move, so I played running back, quarterback, and fullback. But then they moved me to the offensive line, and I stayed there until my senior year. That is when I moved to fullback. The coaches decided to move me into the backfield to put me at the point of attack. I was a blocking kind of an H-back my whole senior season. I never did carry the ball. I asked my coach later why they didn't let me run with it, and he said they didn't want to take a chance that I might get injured.

But there was no confusion about what position I would be playing in college. Just from watching me, the coaches all knew I was an offensive lineman. I grew up a Gator, always a fan. Since I was eight years old I had been rooting for the Gators. But I wanted to do the diplomatic thing and open myself up to recruiting to all of the schools in the Southeast. I had been to Gainesville for a lot of games.

I took an official visit to Michigan, but I didn't like the presentation there. So I canceled the rest of my visits and committed to Florida before I made an official visit there. I knew in my heart I wanted to be a Gator. I had been to games during my sophomore and junior years of high school when Steve Spurrier was really getting it going there, and that just cemented it.

I was there when the Gators won their first Southeastern Conference title in 1991, cheering like crazy. I was the first commitment for that 1992 recruiting class, an amazing class that went on to win a bunch of championships.

When I got there to start school in 1992, I was a wide-eyed kid who didn't know what to expect. But I was eager to get in there and see what I could do. Rich McGeorge was the offensive line coach and he had me running with the first team right away. Ryan Taylor was a senior ahead of me. He hadn't started, but he was the next in line. Coach McGeorge told me, "We think you can play, but make sure you get the playbook down before we stick you in there."

They considered me a starter in 1992, even when I wasn't starting. I wasn't doing any scout team stuff. I was just trying to get a grip on the offense and what I needed to do on every play. They even worked with me on snapping the ball after practice to see if I might play center. I was on the extra-point and field-goal teams at the start of the season. I remember lining up for a field goal or an extra point against Kentucky, and three guys rushed on my side. They ran me over. As I came off the field, Coach Spurrier said, "Got your ass run over, didn't you?" I realized at that point I had to bring it on every play. Once I stepped on the field, that meant business.

Reggie Green was a true freshman playing left tackle in 1992, and we went at it every day. We would try to beat up on each other. I remember going back to the dorms after practice being beaten up, but we were just trying to make each other better. We played Mississippi State, and I didn't play a snap. That was the game where they were all over Shane Matthews, and he threw a bunch of interceptions [in a 30–6 loss]. The next game I was starting at right tackle, so we had two true freshmen starting.

We made a nice run at the end of the 1992 season and made it to the SEC Championship Game. I thought back to watching the Gators win it in 1991 and now here was our chance. That was a neat feeling, even though it didn't work out [Florida lost 28–21 to an Alabama team that won the national championship]. But in 1993 we beat Alabama 28–13 to win the SEC. And we beat Alabama again in 1994 [by a 24–23 score], and in 1995 we beat Arkansas [by a 34–3 score]. That was euphoric to win three SEC championships in a row.

The Gators played in the SEC Championship Game in each of Jason Odom's four seasons, winning SEC titles in 1993, 1994, and 1995. Odom was named All-SEC first team as a junior and senior. He twice won the Jacobs Blocking Trophy as the SEC's top offensive lineman in 1994 and 1995.

An opportunity to win championships is why I went to Florida. I couldn't have written the storyline any better. I can't put into words how exciting it was to be a part of that era.

When I was a junior, somebody came to me and told me I had won the Jacobs Trophy, which went to the SEC's best blocker. I didn't even know there was such an award. And they told me I was the first Gator since Lomas Brown to win the award, and that really was special to be mentioned in the same breath as Lomas. Being a Gators fan for so long, I knew how great he was and I've gotten to know him since then, which makes it even more special.

I had improved as a blocker because I had been given the opportunity to develop my upper body. I was never that strong, and in my freshman year I was just playing and not getting any stronger. But as I went along in my career, the game got easier for me. It became a lot more fun, especially the way we were going up and down the field.

In my senior year, in 1995, I won the Jacobs Trophy again. It's funny because they call it the Jacobs Trophy, but I never got a trophy. I got a parchment. Maybe someone has a couple of trophies somewhere, but I never saw them. I never got caught up in that stuff anyway. I just wanted to do my job and help us win, and we did win a lot of games. In my senior year, we went undefeated before losing to Nebraska [by a 62–24 score] in the Fiesta Bowl. That wasn't the way I wanted my college career to end.

It was a great group on the offensive line with guys like Jeff Mitchell and Donnie Young and, of course, Reggie Green. The funny thing was that the year after I graduated, they won the national championship. It was a little bittersweet because the seniors on that team were from the class I came in with, guys like Danny Wuerffel and James Bates. I was so proud of them, but I was also wishing we could have done it the year before. I got over it after a couple of hours. I was playing for the Tampa Bay Buccaneers then, and I remember watching Danny win the Heisman Trophy in a hotel room in Chicago. I was proud and happy for him.

Still, I can't imagine not being a Gator. I was literally living my dream. It sounds like a cliché, but as a kid you have a dream, and mine was to play for the Gators. Most people don't get a chance to live their dreams. You remember the odd little things like the whiffle ball tournaments we used to have in the locker room. For me, to stay in Florida to play college football was a true blessing. And the people around me, we developed this great chemistry. It's like a fraternity of people in a club that I'll always be a part of. And when you meet other Gators, it's a special bond.

Jason Odom, a native of Bartow, Florida, started on Florida's offensive line for four seasons, from 1992 to 1995. The Gators played in the SEC Championship Game in each of his four seasons, winning SEC titles in 1993, 1994, and 1995. Odom was named All-SEC second team by the Associated Press as a sophomore in 1993 and All-SEC first team as a junior and senior. He twice won the Jacobs Blocking Trophy as the SEC's top offensive lineman in 1994 and 1995. After graduation, Odom was a fourth-round draft choice in the 1996 NFL Draft, staying in the state of Florida and near his hometown of Bartow when the Tampa Bay Buccaneers selected him. Odom became a starter for the Buccaneers at right tackle and played four years until a back injury knocked him out of professional football before the 2000 season. Odom was involved in several business ventures and began training to become a deputy sheriff in Hillsborough County, Florida, in 2008. "I'm living another dream I had as a kid," Odom said.

BEN HANKS

LINEBACKER

1992–1995

IGREW UP IN THE OVERTOWN SECTION OF MIAMI and shared an apartment with six of my brothers and sisters, my grandmother and grandfather, my mother and an uncle. There were 10 of us in a two-bedroom apartment. At the time, I thought it was normal and didn't think much about it. We got along well and were comfortable.

It was normal to me then, but being older and a little wiser now, you understand that when you have a household that large, you should have more room. But back then, I thought it was normal and was comfortable with it. My grandmother and grandfather provided a roof over our heads and there was always food in the refrigerator. Being the oldest child, I really enjoyed that time with my brothers and sisters. Really, I think it allowed me to be the loving and caring person I am today.

Growing up in Overtown, you didn't think it was any rougher than the next neighborhood. Some of the same things that happened in other neighborhoods—drugs, killings, and shootings—happened in Overtown. There were positive things going on because people were doing a lot of positive things for the kids in the neighborhood. I really didn't think my neighborhood was any worse or better than the other areas in Miami. As I've gotten older, I've realized there is some violence in my neighborhood. But I wouldn't change the environment I grew up in for anything in the world because it made me the strong person I am today. It's allowed me to share a lot of different experiences and come back to my neighborhood and give back to the kids here. I can show them that there is a way out and you can better your life. I've shown them that you can leave and come back and provide for the kids who are looking for role models.

I really thought I was an average athlete growing up. I always played with older guys because I was taller than most kids my age. I played football, basketball, and tennis, and we'd swim and do a lot of other things. I played on the offensive line and defensive line in Little League football. I took pride in it. My friends would brag about how many touchdowns they scored, and I'd brag about how many pancake blocks I had in the games. When I got to high school, I realized I couldn't be a lineman anymore because I wasn't getting any bigger. I moved on to the skill positions and did well because I was used to the contact from playing on the line. When I got to high school and moved to linebacker and safety and receiver, the contact wasn't anything new to me. I developed a lot faster than other kids who weren't used to the contact.

We had a little place we called the "hole" in Overtown, where we played touch football. We'd get a soda can or a milk carton if we didn't have a football. We'd stuff it with paper or toilet tissue and fold it down. We'd throw it up in the air and play throw-it-up tackle. You can imagine 15 guys going for that one milk carton. The field was about 35 yards long, and you'd have to make the other 14 guys miss to score a touchdown. It gave you a lot of the instincts you'd need to make guys miss on a real football field. Those were some of the creative things we came up with to entertain ourselves as kids. If we didn't have a football, we didn't think it was the end of the world. We'd just find something else to do to stay out of trouble and have fun. Even if it was midnight, we'd always be out playing basketball on an eight-foot rim. We were just always competing against each other.

Going into Miami Senior High School, I wasn't eligible to play football as a freshman. I left Booker T. Washington Middle School, and my grade-point average was a 1.5. I failed two classes there, but I was still promoted to high school. I wasn't able to play football or any other sports to get my academics in order as a freshman. It hurt me not to be able to play with my friends because I was used to being active. At the same time it helped me because it made me realize I needed to get my grades up in order to play football and basketball. It provided me a lot of motivation to get things together.

My uncle, Sheldon Hanks, was the defensive coordinator and defensive backs coach at Miami Senior High. I remember in the spring before my 10th-grade year, there was a rising senior starting at safety on the varsity team. I took his job, and everybody said, "The only reason you're starting is because your uncle is the defensive backs coach." But I played well in the spring game and had an interception, and everybody else quit talking about it. Two of my uncles from my father's side of the family really played a big role in helping me get my life in order. My uncle, Clinton, had an apartment in our neighborhood, and when he got married, he allowed me to move into that apartment. A lot of my friends would stay in the apartment on the weekends. It was just like I was back at my grandmother's house. We'd have 10 guys sleeping in a one-bedroom apartment. Clinton and one of my other uncles helped pay the bills so I could live there. They'd come by and check on me and just chill out when they were in the neighborhood. My father was in and out of jail, and we didn't have much of a relationship, but his two younger brothers really picked up the slack and made sure I was taken care of. They were really there for me when it came to academics and athletics.

I had scholarship offers from Florida, Florida State, and Miami. Some other schools were recruiting me, but I wasn't going to leave the state of Florida. During the 1990s, the Florida schools were the cream of the crop in college football. You couldn't go wrong with any of the three. Miami was a powerhouse and Florida State was right there, too. Miami had just lost Jimmy Johnson, and Dennis Erickson led them to a national championship in 1991. Florida was just coming back to the top with Coach Spurrier, who had just taken over after leaving Duke. You saw the Florida program was on the rise. It was like I couldn't lose with any of those three programs. I thought I was going to go to Miami, but there was an incident during my senior year of high school that changed my mind. Some friends and I were coming home from a party, and some police officers harassed us and put us up against a wall. After that happened, I knew I needed to get away. I didn't want to go too far from home, but I knew I needed to get out of Miami and start a new chapter in my life. That's what really pushed me toward Florida, and Coach Spurrier was already doing a great job of recruiting me.

I took the SAT test seven times to get eligible to play at Florida. My friends can remember us being in SAT preparatory classes and a tutor would come in to work with us. The tutor had made a score better than 1,500 and had missed only one or two questions on the SAT. He was really smart. I'd taken the test four times before I started working with the tutor, and he showed us some strategies that really worked well. After working with him, my test score kept getting higher each time I took it. Eventually, I got the test score I needed to go to Florida.

When I got to Florida in 1991, they still weren't going to let me enroll in classes. At Miami Senior High, they had three English classes during my senior year. I took skills English, and Florida wasn't going to accept it as a core class. I found out later that Coach Spurrier went to bat for me with the university president, telling him I was a kid who worked hard and that I came from a tough environment and wanted to do well. As part of the agreement, I had to redshirt during the 1991 season. The president wanted to make sure that I had a semester to get acclimated to going to classes and doing well academically. My advisers told me if I got ahead of the game early, then college would be smooth-sailing. I took a math class and preparatory English class during the summer before my freshman year and made a B in the math class. Right away, I had a 3.0 grade-point average. It really helped me get started academically.

I moved into the starting lineup in 1992. Like during high school, I beat out a rising senior for the starting job. Myrick Anderson, who is still one of my good friends today, had started on defense during the 1991 season as a junior. Myrick was going to start as a senior, but he failed the conditioning run before the start of preseason camp. Coach Spurrier got mad at him and told him we weren't going to wait on him and that we had hungry young players who were ready to go. I was second-string going into the fall, and Spurrier moved me in front of Myrick to motivate him to get into shape. Spurrier didn't know I wasn't planning on giving the starting job back to Myrick, friend or no friend. I was able to hold him off and continued to get better and better each game. He never got the spot back, and I started for four years.

Coach Spurrier brought his No. 11 jersey out of retirement, and it was funny that he wanted me to wear it. At the time, being an 18-year-old kid, I was honored to wear it. Some people thought it might be too much pressure, but I saw it as an opportunity to bring exposure to myself. A Heisman Trophy winner was bringing his jersey out of retirement so I could wear it, so I knew there would be a lot of pressure on me. I didn't really feel the pressure because pressure had always been a part of my life. I saw it as a great opportunity and challenge. He never took it away from me, so hopefully I did a good job of upholding the number.

We opened the 1992 season against Kentucky at the Swamp. Some of my childhood friends came up to the game from Miami. They were there to support me, and it was my first game playing in front of about 90,000 fans. It was just exciting to start my first game. I was a little overwhelmed by the big crowd, but I played pretty well. I had a big hit on the sideline and there was a loud thump and everyone yelled, "Ooooh!" We ended up winning the game 35–19. We lost to Tennessee 31–14 the following week. It rained like crazy at Tennessee, and the plane almost crashed coming home. The plane dropped about 10,000 feet, and we had to make an emergency landing in Georgia. We had to get on another plane, and some guys weren't crazy about getting back on the plane. Ellis Johnson said there wasn't any way in the world he was getting back on the plane. He rode back with the equipment manager in a U-Haul van.

It was an up and down season in 1991. After we lost to Tennessee, we lost at Mississippi State 30–6. It was a terrible game. We came back and won our next seven games in a row. We lost to Florida State 45–24 at the end of the regular season, but Florida State was a better team than us that season. We were a young team and were just learning how to win. We went to the SEC Championship Game and lost to Alabama 28–21. We went to the Gator Bowl and beat North Carolina State 27–10. We ended the season with a 9–4 record.

We came back and won the SEC championship in 1993. We lost to Auburn 38–35 on a late field goal and lost to Florida State again, 33–21, in Gainesville. We were losing to Florida State pretty badly, but came back and cut their lead to 26–21. I was playing on all the special teams and was pretty tired. I came out of the game on defense late in the fourth quarter. I only wanted to come out of the game for two plays, but the guy playing behind me did so well that we left him in there. On third down, Warrick Dunn swung out of the backfield, and we had a blown coverage. Dunn outran Eddie Robinson down the sideline and ran 70 yards for a touchdown. It was the loudest I ever heard the Swamp. It was so loud you couldn't hear anything. Your ears were ringing it was so loud. We ended up losing the game 33–21.

We went back to the SEC Championship Game and beat Alabama 28–13 in Birmingham. It was good to beat them after losing to them the way we had the year before. We went to the Sugar Bowl and blew out West Virginia 41–7. West Virginia was undefeated and ranked No. 3 in the country. West Virginia was mad because they weren't playing for the national championship.

They weren't ready to play us, and we were all over them. Lawrence Wright had a really big game on defense.

We opened the 1994 season ranked No. 1 in the country because we had so many people coming back. We beat New Mexico State 70–21 and Kentucky 73–7 to start the season. We went up to Knoxville to play Tennessee and won 31–0. They had Peyton Manning and James Stewart. I actually sacked Manning in that game. We beat Ole Miss 38–14 and LSU 42–18, and were still ranked No. 1. Then we lost to Auburn 36–33 on another late field goal. That was the most disappointing game we played during my four years at Florida. I can remember Wilber Marshall coming back and talking to us that spring and he said, "I don't care what you do. Don't lose to Auburn!" To go out in the Swamp, knowing that they'd beaten us the year before after they called a personal foul on Lawrence Wright, it was the most disappointing loss we had. It was even more disappointing than losing to Nebraska for the national championship.

We came back and beat Georgia 52–14 in Gainesville and beat Southern Miss [55–17], South Carolina [48–17], and Vanderbilt [24–7]. We were 9–1 going into the Florida State game and still had a chance to get back in the national championship race. We were winning the FSU game 31–3 and just didn't finish it. We got into the fourth quarter and totally collapsed. The game ended in a 31–31 tie. I still wish Bobby Bowden had gone for a two-point conversion so the game hadn't ended in a tie.

We came back and beat Alabama 24–23 in the SEC Championship Game in Atlanta. Danny Wuerffel threw a late touchdown to Chris Doering to win the game. We lost to Florida State 23–17 in the Sugar Bowl. They had a lot of talent and they were a better team that day, but I don't think they were a better team throughout the season. I think they had added confidence because of the way they'd come back against us during the regular season.

During my senior season in 1995, we just rolled over everybody during the regular season. We were scoring, like, 60 points a game and really playing well on defense. We played Arkansas in the SEC Championship Game in Atlanta. We knew to get to the Fiesta Bowl and have a chance to play for the national championship, we had to win the SEC title. We'd been in that position before and didn't want to squander that chance as seniors. We knew we had to leave it all out on the field. We were up in the game early in the second half. I had a long fumble return for a touchdown against the

Razorbacks. We were winning the game, but Arkansas was putting together a drive and trying to regain some momentum. They had the ball on our 5-yard line, and I was playing outside linebacker. They were running an option play and wanted to run right at me and blow me up. I was able to hold my ground and gave the quarterback a fake, and he pitched it out. I was able to jump in front of the running back and grab the ball. I ran 95 yards for a touchdown. To look up at the Jumbotron on the scoreboard and see yourself running and no one close to you was a great feeling. A lot of my friends told me it took me forever to get to the end zone. We won the game 34–3 and went on to play Nebraska in the Fiesta Bowl for the national championship.

Obviously, the Fiesta Bowl was very disappointing. It was the ultimate game and the game you always wanted to be in as a player. It was a chance to win the national championship. We just didn't play well at all and lost the game 62–24. It was very disappointing, but we learned a lot from it, and the guys were able to win a national championship the following season. A lot of my friends still tease me when they see highlights of Tommie Frazier juking me on TV. I think it's something that's going to live with me for 20 years until people forget about that game. You've got to give Nebraska credit. We'd never played against an option team that good. Tommie Frazier was a great quarterback, and Lawrence Phillips was a very good tailback. They had a really big offensive line. We were never able to take Nebraska out of what they did.

I would like to say I proved a lot of people wrong and surprised a lot of people by going to Florida and graduating with a degree. I know there were doubters, including people at the University of Florida and people back home. They thought I'd end up coming home because there weren't a lot of success stories from my neighborhood. So many people before me left home and were back in a year after failing. They thought I'd fall into those same traps. For Coach Spurrier to go to bat for me in the beginning, I knew I couldn't let him down. To become the first person from my family to graduate from college was a great honor. I think it opened up a lot of eyes and made a lot of people proud. It was a great time in my life. I'll always be a Gator.

Ben Hanks, a native of Miami, Florida, was one of the greatest success stories in Florida football history. Growing up in an impoverished neighborhood, Hanks struggled to become academically qualified at Miami Senior High School. He was accepted to the University of Florida, but only after football coach Steve Spurrier asked university officials to give Hanks the opportunity to attend college. Hanks redshirted in 1991 to focus on his academics, then started at linebacker for four straight seasons, from 1992 to 1995. Spurrier even took his No. 11 jersey out of retirement and allowed Hanks to wear it. Hanks was a two-time All-SEC choice as a junior and senior. In the 1995 SEC Championship Game, Hanks returned a fumble 95 yards for a touchdown in a 34–3 victory over Arkansas. After graduating from Florida, Hanks played two seasons in the NFL for the Minnesota Vikings and Detroit Lions. After retiring from pro football, Hanks returned to his hometown of Miami and works as a youth coach and counselor in the same Overtown neighborhood where he grew up.

JAMES BATES
LINEBACKER
1993–1996

I GREW UP A TENNESSEE FAN. My dad played there, and my mom went to school there, and we finally moved there from Rochester, New York, when my dad got a job on the Volunteers staff. The coach at Seiver County High School, about 20 miles from Knoxville, wanted me to come play for him and promised my mom a job, which never materialized.

I was a safety for awhile, but they moved me to inside linebacker. We had some great games there, and I played one of my best against Knox County High School, which was Todd Helton's team. I think that was the game that got the recruiters interested in me.

Everyone assumed that I would go to Tennessee. Here I was living just outside Knoxville, my dad had been a player and a coach there. If you were being recruited by Tennessee, why would you go anywhere else? But Florida just seemed like the right fit for me for a lot of reasons. I was a Brian Bosworth fan, and I wanted to wear number 44, which was available. Tennessee was a little too close to home. I had moved a lot as a kid and I was getting a little restless. And Florida had this coach named Steve Spurrier, who was taking the SEC by storm.

I visited UCLA, Michigan, and Texas in addition to Florida and Tennessee. My dad told me to make my own decision. My mom wanted me to go to Tennessee. Coach Spurrier told me that all of the people up where I was living wanted to turn 60 so they could move to Florida. I hadn't thought about that.

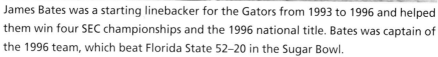

James Bates was a starting linebacker for the Gators from 1993 to 1996 and helped them win four SEC championships and the 1996 national title. Bates was captain of the 1996 team, which beat Florida State 52–20 in the Sugar Bowl.

I committed on my visit to Florida. Coach Spurrier told me to call my mom and let her know. When I told her, she said she'd see me when I got home and hung up. I pretended like she was still on the phone. She wasn't happy, but she eventually got over it.

I was so fired up about being a Gator I wore a shirt to all of my workouts up there with 9/19 written in magic marker. That was the date of the Florida-Tennessee game during my first year at Florida in 1992. My class was amazing, with Danny Wuerffel and all of the guys who would make history. I was so excited to get down to Gainesville, but I was a little light to be playing linebacker at a major college. They let me play a couple of games in 1992 before redshirting me, but that little taste of action lit a fire for me that was incredible. I'd be standing on the sideline, and it was driving me crazy not to be playing. I wanted to be a part of it so badly.

Once I got the chance to wrap my arms around it, it was so big. I always say I started two and a half years because I was in and out in 1993 and 1994 and then was full-time starter my last two seasons. I remember against Tennessee in 1993, I forced a fumble on a kickoff, and that was memorable because Tennessee was always my biggest game.

It's funny, but when I look back at big plays I had—the interception against Auburn in 1995 or the one against Tennessee in 1996—they seem to be in slow motion. To have been a part of the great tradition of Florida football was special and to have been a part of the most incredible run really makes you feel proud.

Every time my dad came to see me play, it seemed like I had a big game. Because he was a coach, he couldn't see me a lot, but I remember in 1994 he was there for the Georgia game. I had two interceptions against Eric Zeier and returned one for a touchdown. One of the coolest things to me is that we were able to experience Florida-Georgia from every angle. Because the stadium in Jacksonville was being renovated, we played in Athens and Gainesville and then twice in Jacksonville.

But the most amazing thing was what we did as a team over those four years. We just kept stacking up victories. We beat Tennessee four straight seasons, which was great for me with all of those people questioning why I would leave the Volunteer State. To own them and own Georgia and LSU, that's not supposed to happen.

When I get dressed for work, I always wear a ring, and to have five to choose from—four SEC championship rings and a national championship ring—is amazing. To have the option of picking the one that goes best with the tie I'm wearing, how many people have that choice?

The 1995 season was special to run the table like we did. Beating FSU that year was big because it got us off the slide. We were the first Florida team to go undefeated, but to end it the way we did, getting trounced by Nebraska in the Fiesta Bowl, was the worst thing I could imagine. You know how hard it is to get there and you know that chances are you won't get back.

I think that Nebraska loss made us hungry and we rolled right through the 1996 schedule until we went to Tallahassee. Losing that game, I don't think calling it a punch in the gut does it justice—it was a haymaker to the gut. We knew we were the better team. I felt like I'd been run over by a truck. We had taken the philosophy that there was a reason we didn't win it during our junior seasons. It was because we were going to win it as seniors. And then it was gone. And what was really hard was watching those Seminoles fans coming out of the stands taking pieces of sod home.

All we could do was focus on Alabama. But then things started to happen. The day of our SEC Championship Game, Texas beat Nebraska. We didn't think Texas had a chance. There were 300-pound guys running up and down the halls in their underwear. I would have hated to be a guest in that hotel. Now we knew we had a chance and there was no stopping us that night against Alabama.

It was the same type of deal at the Sugar Bowl. We were riding a bus to Gonzales, Louisiana, the night before the game and could barely see the game on snowy television sets. We got to the Holiday Inn, grabbed a bite and ran to the rooms to see Ohio State beat Arizona State. When they scored, Zach Piller did a split and ripped his corduroy pants. He knew I could sew a little, and I ended up sewing his crotch so he could wear those pants to the game.

We hammered FSU in the Sugar Bowl, but I missed the second half. A lot of people say I had a concussion, but I think it was a blood sugar thing. I just couldn't focus on anything I wanted to do. But it was amazing to watch us rolling on the field. There was a little bit of sadness that night because I realized it was the last time I'd ever play with those guys.

At the same time, we won the national championship to go with those four SEC titles. I took my kids to Florida Field recently, and I don't know if they felt what I wanted them to feel, but I know that some day they will. To see those years we won championships up on the wall is a special feeling for me, something that can never be taken away.

I was a part of the Florida Gators and I am a part of the Gator Nation. I can't tell you what that means to me. It makes every weight I lifted, every workout worth it. I'll always be able to say I played during an amazing time for Florida football. And I'll always be a Gator.

James Bates, a native of Sevierville, Tennessee, spurned the hometown Volunteers (his father, Jim, was an assistant coach at Tennessee) and signed with Florida in 1992. He was a starting linebacker for the Gators from 1993 to 1996 and helped them win four SEC championships and the 1996 national title. Bates was captain of the 1996 team, which beat Florida State 52–20 in the Sugar Bowl. He was named All-SEC by the Associated Press and the league's coaches as a senior. After graduation, Bates began work as a college football analyst and currently works as a play-by-play announcer and studio analyst for the Mountain West Conference Television Network. Bates and his wife, Tina, a former Florida swimmer, are raising their family in Gainesville, Florida.

DANNY WUERFFEL

QUARTERBACK

1993–1996

I WAS YOUR TYPICAL ARMY KID. About every three years we'd move some-where else, but I never had trouble making friends because I played sports. I think it also helped me to meet so many different people from different parts of the world and the country.

When I was in Colorado, I played quarterback in seventh and eighth grades, but it was time to move again. We had two options. We could go to Japan or Fort Walton Beach, Florida. We ended up in Fort Walton Beach, which was different. Right away, we're playing in a jamboree, a night game with all kinds of people. They love football in that town. I was a backup and also played basketball, which was really my best sport.

When Jimmy Ray Stephens arrived as the head coach at Fort Walton Beach High School, we just hit it off. I was the starter, and we went on to win the state title in my senior year in 1991. Because I had lived in so many different places, I had a lot of favorite teams. But while I was in high school, I was a Florida State fan. So I definitely was considering playing for Coach Bobby Bowden.

We had our state title game in Gainesville and we had a lot of success there. I had a sister at FSU and I also was considering Alabama. But there were a couple of things about Florida that I liked. Coach [Steve] Spurrier was hav-ing success there, and I knew what he could do with a quarterback. And I knew that if I wasn't playing football, Florida would be the school for me. I

Danny Wuerffel was a two-time All-American and became the Gators' second Heisman Trophy winner during his senior season in 1996.

really was more emotionally tied to FSU, but I thought it through and chose Florida.

I redshirted my first year, in 1992, when Shane Matthews was the quarterback, and then Terry Dean was the starter in 1993. But Coach Spurrier let me know I'd have a chance to play. I was just grateful. Sure enough, we were struggling against Kentucky, and I got my chance. But I was struggling, too. Coach Spurrier went back and forth, and I was in for the last drive. That was the game where Chris Doering came wide open on a steamer route, and I hit him for the game-winning touchdown [in a 24–20 victory in Lexington].

You know, it's kind of like having kids. Which one is your favorite? There were so many special moments for me. But that Kentucky game never slips through my mind.

There was another special moment the following year in 1994. Terry was the starter again, and we were ranked No. 1 in the nation. But in the Auburn game, Coach Spurrier put me in, and I was the starter from then on. We went to the SEC Championship Game for the third straight year and came back to beat Alabama 24–23. That's a game that will always stay with me because it had been such a battle to get there. Then to rally and throw the winning touchdown pass to Chris was special.

So in 1995 I was the starter, and we got on a roll. We scored 62 against Tennessee at home [a 62–37 victory] and won at Auburn [49–38], which had beaten us the two previous seasons. And we beat FSU [35–24], which had been a problem since I arrived at Florida. They had come back from 31–3 down the previous year to tie us [by a 31–31 score], and that was a tough one to take. So beating them on Senior Day for a lot of great players was really something.

We played in the SEC title game again in 1995 and handled Arkansas 34–3, which meant we'd become the first Florida team to go 12–0. And we were playing for the national championship in the Fiesta Bowl against Nebraska. It wasn't a great night. Nebraska was really good, one of the best teams ever in college football, and they had an answer for everything we tried to do. They clobbered us [62–24], and it was a really tough night for a lot of reasons. Not only did we lose and lose badly, but there were so many seniors on that team that I knew were not going to be coming back—guys like Chris and Jason Odom, guys I had really become close to. That season had been so special for all of us, and to end it like that was a tough, tough night. I'm just glad it wasn't my last game as a Gator.

That game also helped change our mindset. We had gone to that game as kind of Hollywood superstars going to the Fiesta Bowl. We knew we had let a great chance slip away and if we ever had another chance we had to make it count. In 1996 our offense really got going with Reidel Anthony, Ike Hilliard, and Jacquez Green, a great offensive line, and three very talented running backs in Terry Jackson, Fred Taylor, and Eli Williams. We were rolling through some pretty good teams. We went to Knoxville for a game that was really hyped up, and I hit Reidel on a fourth-down play for the first score. The next thing you knew, it was 35–0 [the Gators won the game 35–29]. And we stormed through LSU, Auburn, and Georgia.

That start set up a big game in Tallahassee, but we came up short [in a 24–21 loss]. There was a lot of talk about late hits, but it never really affected me. I tried not to personalize it. My dad told me he counted the number of times I was hit by FSU defenders, and it was 32. It felt like it. Coach Spurrier made some comments, but he was just trying to stick up for me. I was just disappointed that we had made another great run and that loss had ruined it. But we had to regroup to play a great Alabama team in the SEC Championship Game. We played a great game that night, scoring 45 points [in a 45–30 victory]. I threw a bunch of touchdown passes, but the credit goes to the receivers, who made me look good. We knew Nebraska had lost during the day and we'd get another shot at FSU in the Sugar Bowl.

The night before we played Florida State in the Sugar Bowl, Ohio State beat Arizona State in the Rose Bowl, which meant we'd have a shot at the national championship. There were a lot of guys yelling and running around, but we also knew we had to take care of business. That's the mindset we were taking this time in the bowl game, that this was a business trip. We also had a new weapon—the shotgun. And it worked beautifully. It gave me time to find my receivers. The play I'll never forget was Ike making that stop-and-go catch. It was a phenomenal play, but I didn't see it because I got knocked to the ground. I didn't know what happened until I looked at the big screen. I somehow lumbered in on a scramble for another touchdown. I always had dreams of diving into the corner of the end zone—just inside the cone—and it happened.

It was a great night, amazing to beat Florida State 52–20 and know you had accomplished your goal. The only sad part was that I knew it was our last game together. I was trying to find my teammates after the game, but there were so many members of the media on the field, I couldn't find any of them. But what a way to go out.

I really didn't understand the whole Gator Nation phenomenon when I started going to Florida. I didn't grow up in Florida. I just knew it was a great school with a great football program. But the more I was around it, the more I realize how special it is to be a Gator. I realized after spending time with other players, it meant more to them than just a school or just a football team.

Danny Wuerffel, a military brat who traveled the world before attending high school in Fort Walton Beach, Florida, became the greatest quarterback in Florida history and one of the most efficient passers in NCAA history. Wuerffel was a two-time All-American and became the Gators' second Heisman Trophy winner during his senior season in 1996. His coach, Steve Spurrier, won the Heisman Trophy in 1966. A two-time winner of the O'Brien National Quarterback of the Year Award, Wuerffel finished his career completing 708 passes for 10,875 yards, the fifth-best total in Division I-A history. His 114 touchdown passes set an SEC record and was second-most in major college football history, and his career passer rating of 163.56 also was the highest by a college quarterback. Wuerffel was a two-time academic All-American and also was recipient of the Draddy Trophy, which is presented to college football's top student-athlete. After graduation, Wuerffel was drafted in the fourth round by the New Orleans Saints. He played six seasons in the NFL, including one for Spurrier and the Washington Redskins. Wuerffel is now trying to rebuild his Desire Street Ministries in New Orleans, most of which was destroyed by Hurricane Katrina.

TERRY JACKSON

RUNNING BACK

1995–1998

I WAS BORN IN GAINESVILLE and went to P.K. Yonge High School. My father played at Florida, and my brother played for the Gators, so there really wasn't any doubt in my mind about where I wanted to go to school. It just came down to whether or not the Gators were going to offer me a scholarship. I decided if Florida didn't offer me a scholarship, I was going to go to another school and wasn't going to walk-on. I was getting a lot of pressure from the other schools to commit to them while I was waiting on a scholarship from Florida.

I ended up getting the last scholarship from Florida in February 1994. It's a good thing, because I wondered how I was going to go to another school and still root for the Gators. It didn't make too much sense to me. It really weighed on me, and that's why I was holding out for that last Florida scholarship. Ron Zook was recruiting me for Florida, and he told me, "Terry, hold on. I'm trying to get a scholarship for you. Just hold on." It was pretty late in the recruiting process when they offered me. Somebody else switched to another school, and Coach Zook called me and offered me. I was pretty excited at the time, to say the least. At the time, Duke was putting a lot of pressure on me to come there. I was actually pretty close to going to Duke. I figured if I couldn't go to Florida, I'd got to a school where I could become a doctor or a lawyer or something. I thought I might have played a little basketball there.

But I was always a Gator and wanted to go to Florida. I grew up going to Florida games. Even before my brother, Willie, played at Florida, my dad would take us out to watch the Gators play. We'd go out on the field after games and spend all day playing football on the turf and collecting cups. It was a blast. My father, Willie Jackson Sr., went to school there and was the first African American to play football, along with Leonard George. My mom went to school there, and we went and watched my brother play. It was just a thrill to see my brother play there. I knew my dad played there, but to actually see my brother in the games on the field where we used to play as kids was a really big thrill.

I went to Florida in 1994 and redshirted. I was a defensive back in high school, but the coaches brought me to Florida as an athlete. I wanted to play wherever I could come in and get on the field the fastest. I started out at the "Gatorback" position, which was kind of a hybrid linebacker. I was playing behind Ben Hanks and Darren Hambrick. They moved me to safety the following spring, and I had a pretty good spring playing in the secondary. Mike Peterson moved from safety to linebacker, and I moved from linebacker to safety.

Before the 1995 season, we had some injuries in the backfield. Fred Taylor and Elijah Williams were nicked up, so Coach Spurrier moved me to running back. He told me, "Terry, I told you I'd always give you a chance at running back." I went to offense and ran one draw play and made about three or four people miss and gained about seven yards. Spurrier said, "I have a running back," and that was it. I actually played a little bit on both offense and defense during my sophomore and junior seasons because of some injuries, but I mostly played running back.

201

We opened the 1995 season against Houston and won the game 45–21. I scored my first touchdown against Houston and got a little playing time, and that was very exciting. The next game against Kentucky, I expected to play a lot in the fourth quarter after we were blowing them out. But Fred and Elijah both got hurt in the first quarter, so I went in there. Once I got the ball and got in the game, I was ready to go. It was just very exciting to be "the guy" in the game. I felt like I could just run all night. [Jackson ran for 138 yards and three touchdowns in a 42–7 victory over the Wildcats.] We played Tennessee in Gainesville the following week, and both teams were ranked in the top 10. It was a huge game. I had a 66-yard run, and if there was instant replay back then, it would have been a touchdown. A guy caught me from

Terry Jackson played running back, fullback, outside linebacker, safety, and all special teams for the Gators in parts of four seasons, from 1995 to 1998. He helped the Gators win the school's first national championship in 1996, running for 118 yards and two touchdowns in a 52–20 victory over Florida State in the Sugar Bowl.

behind on that run. When the guy tackled me, I fell into the end zone. They thought I was a slow running back before that play, and my teammates still give me crap about that play.

We won the SEC Championship Game during my redshirt freshman season in 1995 and were really rolling over teams. We played Nebraska in the Fiesta Bowl, and it was a big wake-up call. We hadn't played a close game the entire season and pretty much blew out everybody we played. We felt that we should have won the national championship. We had worked hard during the off-season and knew we were a fast team. We didn't think Nebraska could run with us. We were a little cocky and went to the Fiesta Bowl and didn't give the game the attention it needed. When we got to Arizona, we partied a little too much and had too much fun. Nebraska was all business and came ready to play. Walking out on the field and seeing those guys, we thought we were playing the Arizona Cardinals. They were just giants. They were big guys with big muscles. We went into the locker room thinking, "They can't be that fast." On the first kickoff, they hurt two or three of our guys with hits. They beat us 62–24. We knew we had to be faster and stronger the following season.

I played running back, fullback, and linebacker as a sophomore in 1996. I just wanted to be on the field and didn't care where I played. I just wanted to play. We rolled everybody again until we lost to Florida State 24–21 in Tallahassee late in the season. We knew we were the best team in the country, but it was just one of those games where everything that could wrong did go wrong. We knew we were a better team than FSU, but they just beat us that day. There were some FSU teams that were more talented than us during my four years at Florida, but we were a better team in 1996. Certain things just didn't work out, and it was always difficult to play in Doak Campbell Stadium.

We knew if we got another chance to play FSU, we would be ready to play. We thought we might get another shot at them, but we didn't know if it would be for a chance to play for the national title. We beat Alabama 45–30 in the SEC Championship Game and went to the Sugar Bowl to play FSU [after Texas upset Nebraska in the Big 12 championship game and Ohio State beat undefeated Arizona State in the Rose Bowl, the winner of the Sugar Bowl would be declared national champion]. When we sat in our hotel rooms and watched Ohio State win, we knew we were going to play for a national championship. We were ready to play FSU again and knew what was going to happen. I ran for 118 yards and scored two touchdowns in the game. We won the Sugar Bowl 52–20 and won the national championship.

Growing up a Gators fan and watching the program evolve over the years, I really can't describe what it meant to be the first Florida team to win a national championship. When I dove into the end zone after a 42-yard touchdown in the fourth quarter, we knew that was the culmination of Florida's evolution from a pretty good team to the best program in the country. It was just total elation. We knew the game was over after that touchdown.

It was really fun to play in that offense because defenses couldn't key in on one single player. Any of our skill players could score. If defenses keyed in on Reidel Anthony or Ike Hilliard, the running backs would get 200 or 300 rushing yards. If a defense keyed in on the running backs, Ike and Reidel would go nuts. Fred Taylor was making big runs. We had so many guys who could burn you badly. It was a very unselfish offense because everybody knew they'd get their touches. We had a guy as talented as Jacquez Green returning kicks and blocking kicks. It was pretty exciting, and you enjoyed watching those guys play. You enjoyed blocking for them. If one of our receivers made a short catch, I was sprinting down the field to block for them because I knew they had a chance to score on any play. It was the same thing with Fred or whomever. Our linemen did a great job of protecting us and covering our backs, and it was just a great offense.

I moved to fullback the following season, in 1997. Fred Taylor was playing running back, and we were in the backfield at the same time. Elijah Williams had led us in rushing the previous three seasons, and they moved him to cornerback. That was just the makeup of our team. Whatever it took to help us win games, anyone was willing to do it. We just wanted to be on the field, and it didn't matter where we played. We just wanted to win championships, and we were very unselfish. It wasn't just me. Elijah moved over to defense, and it was something he hadn't done since high school. He was a marvelous cornerback and really helped us. I moved to fullback, but I was basically doing the same thing I'd done before. We wanted our best guys on the field at the same time, so it wasn't a big deal to me.

I played four games during the 1997 season and then tore the anterior cruciate ligament [ACL] in my right knee. I had a pretty good season going and then tore up my knee against Kentucky. It was very disappointing because I was having a good season and had enjoyed a pretty good career up until that point. I hadn't had any serious injuries or surgeries before then. When it happened, it really threw me for a loop. It was one of the worst injuries you could have. I didn't feel like I was really part of the team anymore because other guys were sweating and doing what it takes to make the team great. All I could do was watch, and I wasn't able to contribute after putting in all that hard work during the summer. It was pretty upsetting to me at the time, but looking back it was probably one of those things that happened for a reason.

I was able to come back for my senior season in 1998 after recovering from the knee injury. It meant a lot to come back as a senior, and I had a pretty good season going. But in the sixth game against LSU, I suffered a high ankle sprain and missed four or five games. It was another upsetting thing, but it's just part of playing sports. I had to deal with it and keep trying to get better. I was able to come back for the last game against Syracuse in the Orange Bowl and had a pretty good game [Jackson ran for 108 yards on 21 carries in the Gators' 31–10 victory over the Orangemen]. It was a fitting end to my career, but I was disappointed I couldn't help the team win a championship while I was hurt. I thought that 1998 team was probably the most talented team we had during my four years at Florida. Our defense was probably the most dominating defense we had during my entire time at Florida.

Playing for Coach Spurrier was a lot of fun. It was called "Fun 'n' Gun" and that's exactly what it was. Anything could happen, and we just had so much confidence. Spurrier's confidence rubbed off on all the players. He felt we could score on any play, and that's how the players felt. We believed in that, and it was fun knowing you could score on any play. We thought we should win every single game we played.

It was a dream come true to play at Florida and then to play in the NFL for seven seasons. I grew up playing the video games with Jerry Rice, Steve Young, Bryant Young, J.J. Stokes, and Terrell Owens playing for the San Francisco 49ers. Then to get to play for the 49ers and have a locker right next to those guys was pretty awesome. It was something my brother and I always felt like we were going to do, but to actually do it was an even greater feeling. It was definitely a dream come true.

I always wanted to come back to Florida and be a part of the coaching staff. Having grown up in Gainesville and played at Florida, I just thought it would be really awesome to go back and be a part of the program. I'm here at home and what else would I really want to do than be around Florida football? It's been really awesome to be around the guys, who are just like me when I was their age. To be able to help them find their way and live up to their potential is something I'm very grateful for.

Terry Jackson, a native of Gainesville, Florida, was a second-generation Gator, following his father, Willie Jackson Sr., and older brother, Willie Jackson Jr., to the University of Florida. Jackson played running back, fullback, outside linebacker, safety, and all special teams for the Gators in parts of four seasons, from 1995 to 1998. As a redshirt freshman, Jackson helped guide the Gators to the 1995 SEC championship. The following season, Jackson helped the Gators win the school's first national championship, running for 118 yards and two touchdowns in a 52–20 victory over Florida State in the Sugar Bowl. During his time at Florida, Jackson served as student body vice-president and was cocaptain of the football team. After graduation, Jackson was selected in the fifth round of the 1999 NFL Draft by the San Francisco 49ers and played seven seasons in the NFL. In April 2008 Jackson was named Florida's director of player and community relations and established a mentoring program for Gator football players and Gainesville youth.

TRAVIS McGRIFF
WIDE RECEIVER
1995–1998

My dad was playing for the Tampa Bay Buccaneers when I was born, but we moved to Gainesville when I was two. From an early age, I was surrounded by Gators sports. I knew my dad [former Florida receiver Lee McGriff] was a player who had a great career and that other members of my family had been athletes at the University of Florida. I think that's what made it so much more than the logical stuff of playing for Florida for me—the family history. I grew up so connected to that. I was always around it, from being a ball boy at middle school to being able to become what I had grown up watching.

I played all three sports at the Gainesville Boys Club and in the city league. I started high school at Buchholz High and was a quarterback, who mostly handed the ball off. My dad could see there wasn't much of a demand for a quarterback who handed the ball off, so I transferred to P.K. Yonge High School, where they liked to throw it with former Gator John Clifford coaching there. I loved it because I was able to throw the ball and play cornerback on defense. Every once in awhile, we'd throw deep and they'd put me at wide receiver.

I had a lot of schools looking at me to play different positions—quarterback, safety, and wide receiver. I went to Notre Dame's camp, but it was too cold there. It came down to Florida and Florida State, although looking back I wish I had taken more visits and enjoyed myself. I went to

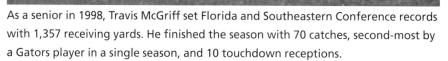

As a senior in 1998, Travis McGriff set Florida and Southeastern Conference records with 1,357 receiving yards. He finished the season with 70 catches, second-most by a Gators player in a single season, and 10 touchdown receptions.

the Florida–Florida State game in 1993 and tried to be impartial. I couldn't do it. I was rooting for the Gators all the way, so I knew where I was going to college. The allegiances were just too powerful.

I was a redshirt my first season in 1994 and played some on the 1995 team that played for the national championship [the Gators lost to Nebraska 62–24 in the Fiesta Bowl]. In 1996 I was really starting to get in the mix, backing up Ike Hilliard. I started feeling like I was coming on and Coach [Steve] Spurrier was starting to feel more confident in me. But then I tore the anterior cruciate ligament [ACL] in my knee. That was really hard because we won the national championship [Florida finished 12–1 and beat Florida State 52–20 in the Sugar Bowl to win the school's first national title in football], and I missed the second half of the season.

The funny thing was that during that run I think we kind of took it for granted. We thought, "This is just how good we are, killing everybody." Seeing what happened after that, when we didn't go to the SEC Championship Games, you realized how special that time was. They tell you it takes six months to recover from a torn ACL, but it takes longer than that. You have to physically heal, and then there is the mental part of it. You have to stop thinking about it. It kind of stole the first half of my junior season in 1997. But in the second half of the year, I started feeling more confident. We finished strong with a win over No. 2 FSU in the Swamp [the Gators upset the Seminoles 32–29 on November 22, 1997] and then a [21–6] win over Penn State in the Citrus Bowl, so I was feeling good heading into my senior year. I was older, more experienced, and I finally was healed.

Looking back, I can see things clearer. There were so many great players at Florida, it was hard to emerge. It was the best group of receivers in the country when I was there. I really felt I could have done what I did my senior year all of those years, but there were so many good players around you who could do wonderful things. But with maturity, I'm thankful that it was as good as it was for one year.

My senior year, Jacquez Green had left early for the NFL, and the balls just kept finding me. We lost a tough game at Tennessee when we had seven turnovers [in a 20–17 overtime loss], but we got on a roll after that and got back into the top five. I had a great relationship with the quarterbacks—Doug Johnson and Jesse Palmer—and the highlight was Senior Day against South Carolina [a 33–14 victory]. They played a lot of zone and when they went to man they couldn't match up with us. So our plan was to throw it a

209

lot. In the second quarter, I caught a touchdown pass, and the defender kind of rolled my ankle. I was wondering if I should come out of the game because we had FSU the next week. My ankle had been beaten up for weeks. But I was having too much fun, so there was no way I was coming out of this game. I ended up with 13 catches for 222 yards. On the last catch, Doug called a fade, and the defensive back was playing bump coverage and stepped with his inside foot, which allowed me to make a move to get by him with my good ankle. I couldn't have scripted it any better. Doug made a perfect throw, and my last catch in the Swamp was a touchdown.

Now, my dad had been a big Carlos Alvarez fan, and at lunch that week he told me about Carlos's last game at Florida Field, how he had scored a touchdown and threw the ball in the stands because of all the frustration that had built up in him. Dad said I might want to think about doing that if it was late in the game and I was not going back in. So I did. It was a good throw. I got penalized, and Coach Spurrier wanted to know why I did what I did. I told him, and he said, "All right, my man, I was probably going to tell you to do that anyway."

It was a great way to finish up in the Swamp. I caught a long touchdown the next week against FSU and I thought we were going to kill them. But they came back and beat us 23–12 and played for the national championship against Tennessee. So the only two teams that beat us during my senior season in 1998 played for the national title. We finished with a big [31–10] win over Syracuse and Donovan McNabb in the Orange Bowl. That 1998 team was a great team. We just came up a little short of our goals.

The University of Florida is as much a part of me as anything I am. I'm not a silly fan with flags on my car. I don't need someone to recognize me. It's more internal now. There is forever a bond with anybody I connected with at school. You appreciate all of the people who were a special part of your life at a special time. I'm a Gator. It's what I am and what I did.

Travis McGriff, a native of Gainesville, Florida, followed in the footsteps of his father, Lee McGriff, when he played wide receiver for the Gators from 1995 to 1998. As a senior in 1998, McGriff set Florida and Southeastern Conference records with 1,357 receiving yards. He finished the season with 70 catches, second-most by a Gators player in a single season, and 10 touchdown receptions. In a 33–14 win over South Carolina on November 14, 1998, McGriff caught 13 passes for 222 yards, the second-highest reception and yardage totals by a Florida player in a game. After graduation, McGriff was selected in the third round by the Denver Broncos in the 1999 NFL Draft and played parts of three seasons before trying the Arena Football League. In Orlando, he was the AFL Rookie of the Year. He also served as the body double for Mark Wahlberg in the Hollywood film, *Invincible*. McGriff and his family settled in Gainesville, Florida, where he owns a restoration company, Puroclean, and runs a wide receiver camp during the summers.

The
NEW
MILLENNIUM

JEFF CHANDLER

KICKER

1998–2001

I'M A JACKSONVILLE GUY, born and raised in the town. In fact, my parents still live in the house they brought me home to all those years ago. I jumped right into sports in part because my brother Donnie, who was three years older than me, was so good at everything. I wanted to be like him.

So there I was tagging along with Donnie when I was three years old, and he is playing at the halftime of a Jacksonville Tea Men game. The Tea Men were part of the North American Soccer League and at the half these six-year-olds were going to play a game. But they were short one player. My brother told them I could play. I was three year olds, so I didn't do anything more than stand around at the middle of the field. I didn't move around very much. I just stood there in front of this huge crowd at the Gator Bowl. But it kind of gave me a taste of what playing sports was all about.

I started playing soccer, baseball, and tennis. When I was five, I was playing in the under-six league, traveling around all over the Southeast. I settled on soccer as my sport and I turned out to be pretty good. It kept me busy in the summer, which my parents liked, and it was a way to hang out with my friends. Really, it was a blast.

I didn't think about football until late in my junior year of high school. Craig Howard, who coached Tim Tebow at Nease High and is now at Lake City High, became our coach at Mandarin High. He had this big mass meeting and said that anyone who wants to should come out for the team. I really went to that meeting as a way of getting out of class, but I really bought in to what he was telling me. All of my friends on the team were telling me that they needed a kicker because one had gone to Alabama and the other to Central Florida. So I figured I'd give it a try. I went out there and kicked and I kind of had a knack for it. So I figured I'd keep doing it as long as I liked it.

I went through all of the summer workouts and two-a-days, but I was getting bored with just kicking a football, so I started playing some wide receiver. The truth is that we didn't kick a lot of field goals that year, but I did catch 30 or 40 passes and three touchdowns. I also threw a touchdown on a fake field goal.

I had some soccer scholarships coming my way, but they were partials at small schools that were no bigger than my high school. I wanted to go to Florida, and my parents, even though they are Bulldogs, were fine with it because it was in-state tuition. Florida has signed a great recruiting class that year, and one of the players they signed was this All-American kicker named T.J. Tucker. I remember one day I was at the track at our high school, and Coach Howard came out and told me that Tucker had just been selected high in the Major League Baseball Draft. That was good for me.

My first year at Florida, 1997, I was just trying to get comfortable. Collins Cooper was the kicker, and I did try one extra point. Later, we had to appeal to the NCAA to let that first year count as a redshirt year, which it did.

The next year the competition was pretty much opened up between Collins and me. We went into the season alternating. But in overtime against Tennessee, he missed a field goal that gave Tennessee the win [20–17], and it was my job from then on. I kicked well the rest of that season and went into the summer of 1999 knowing I'd be the guy. But I put so much pressure on myself during two-a-days because I knew we had one scholarship available. Finally, on the last day of two-a-days, Coach Spurrier brought everybody together and said, "We've got a scholarship available and we're giving it to Jeff Chandler."

That was one of those special moments you never forget. Unfortunately, 1999 also had my lowest moment when I missed an extra point in overtime against Alabama [40–39]. I got a lot of letters after that miss. I remember walking home hoping nobody would recognize me. But we still played well enough during the season to play for the SEC championship in Atlanta [the Gators lost to Alabama 34–7].

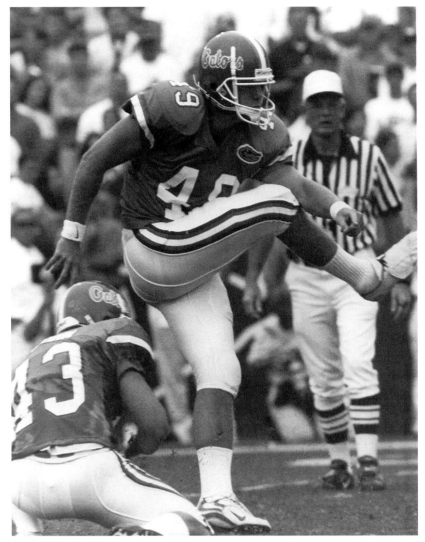

Jeff Chandler finished his career as Florida's all-time leading scorer with 368 points. He attempted (180) and made (167) more extra points in his career than any other Florida player.

The next season, in 2000, was a special one for me. I came to Florida with this amazing class of guys like Alex Brown, Andra Davis, and Marquand Manuel. I figured I'd walk out with four rings. But we had just missed each year. In 2000 we finally got it done, and I had the most memorable kick of my career. We were playing Georgia in an amazing game. They were up

17–9 and driving when Lito Sheppard made this incredible interception and return. Jesse Palmer dove us in and got the two-point conversion to tie the game. And then in the second half, I nailed a 54-yard field goal to give us a lead we'd never relinquish. I remember Quincy Carter, the Georgia quarterback, coming up to me after the game to tell me that was an unbelievable kick. To do it in front of my friends and family in Jacksonville, that really meant a lot to me.

We went to the SEC Championship Game at the end of the season and beat Auburn 28–6. It still means a lot to me that we won a championship. I get my ring out sometimes and look at it and think about it. I really enjoyed that season.

My friends would always tell me how it was so great that I got to play for the Florida Gators. Once you get away from it, you come to realize how awesome the whole experience was. Now that I'm far away from it, I see it, and I get far more nervous before games than I did as a player. But I did start realizing how big it was, how special it was to be a Gator when I was playing. It's funny because in the pros the only guys who really care about their college are the guys who went to school in Florida. I appreciate how fortunate I was to be in the atmosphere I played in every week and to play for the coach I played for and in front of the best fans in the world. The only way to explain it is that it was the best five years of my life.

217

It's crazy because when I was in San Francisco, there was a Gator Club, and when I was in Cleveland there was a Gator Club. You start to realize how far-reaching the Gator Nation is. People really love their university.

Jeff Chandler, a native of Jacksonville, Florida, was the Gators' starting kicker from 1998 to 2001. Chandler finished his career as Florida's all-time leading scorer with 368 points. He attempted (180) and made (167) more extra points in his career than any other Florida player, and his 67 field goals and 80 field-goal attempts are also the most in school history. As a junior, Chandler helped lead the Gators to a 10–3 record and SEC championship. Chandler made a 54-yard field goal in Florida's 34–23 win over Georgia on October 28, 2000, which ranks as the third-longest field goal in school history. He was a first-team All-SEC selection by the Associated Press as a senior in 2001. After graduation, Chandler played for three NFL teams, making 19-of-27 field goals before returning to Jacksonville. He currently works in sales and marketing for Football Fanatics.

JARVIS MOSS
DEFENSIVE END
2004–2006

I GREW UP IN TEXAS and attended Ryan High School in Denton. We won back-to-back state championships during my junior and senior seasons. Texas, Florida State, Florida, and Miami were recruiting me hard, and I visited all of those schools. I was kind of in a position where I wanted to get away from home, and Florida kind of sold itself. Ron Zook really recruited me hard and was just really personable.

During my senior season at Ryan High School, I developed a staph infection. I missed seven games that season, and it was really bad. It was a situation where nobody knew what was going on. I just went to sleep one night and woke up one morning and it was a totally different world for me during the next couple of years. I had severe pain in my lower abdomen. It was rock hard, and I didn't know what was wrong. The doctors couldn't diagnose what was wrong with me. I lost a bunch of weight, but I was just a young kid coming out of high school and was starting to develop. I never really had a chance to put on the weight or add strength like I was supposed to do. I never had a chance to develop into my frame.

I went to Florida in 2003 and was still having problems. They thought I had a sports hernia, at least that's what the doctors thought it might be. They were still trying to figure out what the problem was. I played in one game against Eastern Michigan as a redshirt freshman in 2004. I was still having problems adding weight and couldn't get on the field. I was still a young guy, so it wasn't as discouraging as it was a couple of years ago. It hurt not to be playing, but not nearly as bad as it did when I was a sophomore. By my third year at Florida, when I was still hurt and still wasn't playing, that's when it got really discouraging. I was having a hard time with it, just like anyone else would.

I actually considered quitting playing football a couple of times. I met with my trainers and coaches, and we discussed me just going to school and trying to get my degree and just giving football up. The mystery still wasn't solved. We didn't know what was going on. Fortunately, they figured out what was wrong with me. I still had a chance to resurrect my football career. Coach Zook was fired midway through the 2004 season, and it was strange for everyone who went through it. Coach Zook was the coach who recruited me to Florida and convinced me to move away from home. It was shocking to everyone involved with the change. I think all of the guys who came in under Zook did a pretty good job with the coaching change.

We had a lot of talented players at Florida, and I think Coach Meyer brought a lot of discipline to the Florida program. I think we needed some discipline. He brought in Coach Mickey Marotti, the strength coach, who really showed us how to work hard. There was a lot more discipline and demands than we had grown used to.

219

After Coach Meyer was hired as Florida's coach before the 2005 season, they really started testing me to find out what was wrong. They found out I had a staph infection. For seven weeks, I was hooked up to a fanny pack that had IVs connected to it. I had a line hooked up to my arm, and it was like magic. Whatever was pumping in that bag did the trick.

I gained a bunch of weight and went from 218 pounds to 240 without even trying. I slowly became the player everyone thought I'd be. I started making strides and getting the feel back for my body and my legs. It was an amazing feeling to be healthy again. I started to really develop into my own once I got healthy. Greg Mattison, the defensive coordinator and defensive line coach, really took me under his wing and helped me develop as a pass rusher. He showed me everything I needed to know.

During the 2005 season, I was mostly a third-down pass rusher. I got significant playing time and played quite a bit that season. I wasn't in the starting lineup, but I led the team in sacks and played a big role on defense. Jeremy Mincey and Ray McDonald were the starting defensive ends, but I played a lot behind them. I kind of had my coming-out party against LSU in 2005. I had three sacks in the game [a 21–17 loss to the Tigers in Baton Rouge] and it was a big game for me. I had a good day on the football field, that's for sure. I think it kind of quieted a lot of my critics and gave me confidence. I played pretty solid throughout the rest of the season. I played pretty consistently and worked hard. We finished 9–3 in Coach Meyer's first season and beat Iowa 31–24 in the Outback Bowl. It was a pretty good first season.

We opened the 2006 season and had pretty high expectations. We won our first six games, beating LSU 23–10 in Gainesville to move to 6–0. Both teams were ranked in the top 10, and it was a huge game. Tim Tebow came onto the scene in that game, throwing that little jump pass at the goal line. We lost at Auburn 27–17 the next week. We made too many mistakes in that game and should have won. We came back and beat Georgia 21–14 in Jacksonville and beat Vanderbilt 25–19 in the Swamp. We played South Carolina in Gainesville the following week, which was a huge game because Steve Spurrier was coming back to Florida. I blocked a couple of kicks in that game, including a long field-goal try at the end. It wasn't until after the game, when I was just standing on the field, that I realized what I'd really done. I had a lot of family at the game, including my brother, and I was looking up in the stands at thousands of people. I knew my brother was watching me and was proud of me. I think everybody knew at that point that we were right there in the national title hunt. We weren't sure what was going to happen with the national title, but our goal was to win the SEC. That's your goal every season.

We beat Florida State 21–14 two weeks later in Gainesville and put ourselves in contention to play for the BCS title. We had to play Arkansas in the SEC Championship Game in the Georgia Dome. It was a great feeling after being at Florida for three years and finally getting a chance to play for the SEC title. Florida is supposed to play for the SEC title every year, but we weren't able to get it done before then. It was just a great feeling for everybody who went through the coaching change and stuck with Coach Meyer. We beat Arkansas 38–28, and the next day they announced we were going to play Ohio State for the national championship. There was a lot of controversy about whether Florida or Michigan should play Ohio State, but Michigan had just lost to Ohio State during the regular season. We were SEC champions and felt we were the most deserving team.

Not a lot of people gave us a chance to beat Ohio State in the BCS title game. I don't think Coach Meyer and Coach Mattison had to tell us we could

Jarvis Moss became an impact player on the defensive line in the 2005 season. He led the Gators and was fifth in the Southeastern Conference with 7½ sacks as a sophomore, helping Florida finish with a 9–3 record in Coach Urban Meyer's first season.

beat Ohio State. We were such a tight team and had our own identity. We knew who we were and what Ohio State was. Our coaches didn't have to convince us we could beat Ohio State. I think everybody on our team knew we were better than Ohio State and faster than them before we even played the game. Our defensive game plan was just to get after quarterback Troy Smith, who won the Heisman Trophy. We felt like if we took Smith out of the ballgame, then we would see what Ohio State really was. Smith didn't play well, and they couldn't do anything on offense. We won the game 41–14, and it was a pretty convincing rout.

It was amazing to stand on that field in Arizona and know that we were national champions. It just meant the world to me and it's something I'll never forget. It's something I'll take with me to my grave. It's probably the biggest accomplishment in my life to this point. It's something not many people get a chance to do or accomplish during their lives.

I left Florida after my junior season and was drafted in the first round by the Denver Broncos. It was really gratifying after going through so much at Florida. My grandfather always used to tell me success is so much more satisfying when you go through adversity. I went through the hard times and I'd do it all over again if I knew I'd have the same opportunities I have now. It was all worth it.

Jarvis Moss, a native of Denton, Texas, was a Parade All-American when he signed with Florida before the 2003 season. During his first two seasons with the Gators, Moss was hampered by an undiagnosed staph infection, which hampered his ability to get stronger and bigger. Doctors finally solved his health problems before the 2005 season, and Moss became an impact player on the defensive line. He led the Gators and was fifth in the Southeastern Conference with 7½ sacks as a sophomore, helping Florida finish with a 9–3 record in Coach Urban Meyer's first season. As a junior, Moss started all 13 games during the 2006 season, helping the Gators finish 12–1 and win SEC and national championships. In a 41–14 victory over Ohio State in the BCS Championship Game, Moss sacked quarterback Troy Smith twice. One of his sacks resulted in a fumble that teammate Derrick Harvey returned for a touchdown. After leaving Florida after his junior season, Moss was a first-round selection of the Denver Broncos in the 2007 NFL Draft.

TIM TEBOW

QUARTERBACK

2006–2008

I KNEW FLORIDA WOULD BE A PROGRAM where the head coach was really passionate. I knew Florida was a program that had a chance to be very, very good, like it had been in the past. There were a lot of great athletes at Florida, and with the coaches that had come in and had one year here, Florida had a chance to be very good. The main draw for me was playing for Coach Meyer. He was a coach who is as passionate about the game of football as me and loved it. He was dedicated to it and worked really hard.

That was really the biggest factor for me. I decided to come to Florida early and got to Gainesville in January 2005. I think it helped a lot to come in early as a freshman. It helped me earn a lot of respect from my teammates with your play in spring ball and your work and dedication during the off-season conditioning program. Hopefully, that showed them I was an accountable guy and a guy who was going to work hard. They saw that all through the off-season, so I think that gave me an opportunity to be able to do what I did as a freshman. I was able to come in and be a support-type starter behind Chris Leak.

Chris had been the starting quarterback for a couple of years. Being able to get along with him was very important. Chris did a good job of handling everything, and I tried to go in and do the best I could and help the team out. I contributed as much as I could during that championship season. I think it was good for the team and everybody to see us working together.

There are a lot of great memories about that national championship season. The LSU game [a 23–10 win in Gainesville] was a big game. South Carolina [a 17–16 victory in Gainesville] was a huge game. They had a chance to win, and we blocked a field goal at the end. It was my first experience with everything. I think my first big opportunity, which was so surreal, was the fourth-and-two against Tennessee in the SEC opener. To get the first down, which allowed us to score the go-ahead touchdown [in a 21–20 win in Knoxville], was really big. To do that in Neyland Stadium was a big experience for me. All the experiences I was able to have in big games really helped me get ready for big-time college football and get ready for it.

We won our first six games during the 2006 season, then lost to Auburn [by a 27–17 score]. We came back and won the rest of our games going into the SEC Championship Game in Atlanta. We beat Arkansas 38–28, but still wasn't sure if we'd get a chance to play Ohio State for the national championship. We didn't really know what was going to happen. We heard at halftime that UCLA upset USC [which knocked the Trojans out of the BCS title game] and got excited about that. But we really didn't know if we'd get to play Ohio State.

The next day, the final BCS standings came out, and Ohio State was ranked No. 1 and we were No. 2. That was exciting. Gainesville was rocking that night. Everyone was excited about playing for the national championship. Nobody really gave us a chance to beat Ohio State in the BCS Championship Game. For six or seven weeks, Coach Meyer was building up Ohio State. He didn't really have to do too much to build up Ohio State because everyone else was doing enough of it. I think it's going to draw a team closer when everything is against you like that. You see it all the time: an underdog who has no chance, in college basketball and every sport, plays all out because they have nothing to lose and have no fear. I think that's kind of what happened against Ohio State that night.

We'd had a few great weeks of practices before we played Ohio State in Glendale, Arizona. Our defensive game plan was great and awesome. We held Ohio State to 82 yards. We just prepared so hard for them. The way the coaches prepared us on offense and defense was really how it was out on the field against them. A lot of things we planned on them doing, they did. The coaches, both on offense and defense, did a great job of putting together a game plan that was far superior to Ohio State's plan.

I took over as the starting quarterback as a sophomore, after Chris graduated. It was a big difference for me, but I think the experience I got as a

Tim Tebow became the first sophomore to win the Heisman Trophy in 2007. In his first season as Florida's starting quarterback, Tebow broke school and SEC records for rushing touchdowns (23) and total touchdowns (55).

freshman really helped me out. I was able to play in a lot of big situations as a freshman. In almost every game in 2006, I played in a big situation at some point in the game. If you're ready to play in a fourth-down situation as a freshman, playing in first-and-10 and second-and-10 is a lot easier. You're still ready for those big situations and then you just have to manage everything else. I had to be more of a leader because it was my team. I think it was a little bit easier for me because that's just the role I've had my entire life.

We started the 2007 really strong and beat Tennessee 59–20 in the Swamp in our third game. It looked like we were right back to where we were the year before, but then we suffered some injuries and we had a really young team. It was a great learning experience, but at the same time it got frustrating losing some games we had an opportunity to win. We lost some games [Florida finished with a 9–4 record in 2007, which was Tebow's first season as the team's starting quarterback] we felt we could have won and should have won. I think they were all learning experiences for a very, very young team. We knew if we played a little better offensively, defensively, or on special teams, we could have won those games. It just goes to show you how much those little things count in a game. In every one of those games, just one little play here or one little play there, and we would have won the game. If we'd have won a couple of those games, we would have been back playing for the SEC championship and maybe a national championship.

To win the Heisman Trophy as a sophomore was completely unexpected. It was a dream come true. It was a very unbelievable experience. Coming into the year, that certainly wasn't my goal. My goal was just to lead the team to an SEC championship. But when it happened, I was excited about it. Anytime you get honored, you really have to thank the people who got you there, like your teammates and your coaches. I learned very early that anytime you get an individual award, it's a reflection of your team. That's something that really helped me handle winning those individual awards. When I accepted those trophies, it was me accepting those awards for everyone at Florida.

Going to New York for the Heisman Trophy ceremony was really a neat experience. I'd watched it on TV, and it was exactly like I pictured it. It was a great experience and something I'll cherish for the rest of my life. Standing next to Danny Wuerffel [who won the Heisman Trophy in 1996 as Florida's starting quarterback] was something I'll never forget. He was definitely one of my role models growing up and was the reason I ended up being a huge Gators fan growing up. We're not very similar on the field, but we're very similar with how we handle ourselves off the field. That's why I really respected him, watching how he handled himself off the field with his humility and character. That's what really made him my role model.

Playing at Florida is a dream come true for me. Playing for Coach Meyer has been an unbelievable experience, and it's everything I thought it would be. Hopefully, the first two seasons were just the beginning of great things. It's been a whirlwind ever since I got to Florida. It's gone by very fast, but it's been a very enjoyable time. I've been able to see and do so much, and I've had a lot of fun experiences. Obviously, it's a dream come true to win a national championship in your first season and win the Heisman Trophy in the second. I've been able to do a lot of great things, and hopefully we'll win another championship.

Tim Tebow, a native of Jacksonville, Florida, became the first sophomore to win the Heisman Trophy in 2007. In his first season as Florida's starting quarterback, Tebow broke school and SEC records for rushing touchdowns (23) and total touchdowns (55). Tebow also won the Davey O'Brien Award as college football's best quarterback, the Maxwell Award as the country's best player, and the James E. Sullivan Award as the nation's most outstanding amateur athlete. As a freshman in 2006, Tebow helped the Gators win the national championship by throwing for five touchdowns and running for eight scores. Tebow was born in the Philippines, where his parents served as Christian missionaries, and he was home-schooled by his mother. Tebow remains involved with his father's orphanage and mission in the Philippines and also works in prison ministries in the Gainesville area.

G DICKEY · JIMMY DUNN · LARRY LIBERTORE · BRUCE CULPEPP

IS · TOM ABDELNOUR · CARLOS ALVAREZ · JOHN REAVES · JOH

ANDERSON · KERWIN BELL · KIRK KIRKPATRICK · TRACE ARMS

· CHRIS DOERING · JUDD DAVIS · JASON ODOM · BEN HANKS

CHANDLER · JARVIS MOSS · TIM TEBOW · DOUG DICKEY · JIMM

MELL · BILL CARR · LARRY SMITH · GUY DENNIS · TOM ABDELN

AWLESS · NAT MOORE · DON GAFFNEY · NEAL ANDERSON · KE

E MATTHEWS · TERRY DEAN · SHAYNE EDGE · CHRIS DOERING

ERRY JACKSON · TRAVIS MCGRIFF · JEFF CHANDLER · JARVIS M

E CULPEPPER · LINDY INFANTE · ALLEN TRAMMELL · BILL CARR

REAVES · JOHN JAMES · LEE MCGRIFF · BURTON LAWLESS · NAT

CK · TRACE ARMSTRONG · BRAD CULPEPPER · SHANE MATTHEW

M · BEN HANKS · JAMES BATES · DANNY WUERFFEL · TERRY JACK

G DICKEY · JIMMY DUNN · LARRY LIBERTORE · BRUCE CULPEPPE

IS · TOM ABDELNOUR · CARLOS ALVAREZ · JOHN REAVES · JOHN

ANDERSON · KERWIN BELL · KIRK KIRKPATRICK · TRACE ARMST

· CHRIS DOERING · JUDD DAVIS · JASON ODOM · BEN HANKS

HANDLER · JARVIS MOSS · TIM TEBOW · DOUG DICKEY · JIMMY

MELL · BILL CARR · LARRY SMITH · GUY DENNIS · TOM ABDELN